In this study book, a wise man shows how the grace of God in Christ, and the holy joy of Christian living, go beyond what many think. Would you appreciate a fully biblical and Reformed demonstration of how the love-words and love-works of our triune God transform life? Then you should read and digest *Holiness by Grace.*

—J. I. PACKER
Professor of Theology, Regent College

It should not be thought of as extraordinary that a book on the subject of holiness puts its focus on the word "delight." The very crowning of God's creation was the placing of his holy creatures, Adam and Eve, in the garden named Eden, which simply means "delight." Dr. Chapell makes it clear that the soul's delight will be realized only by godliness in the Christian life—and that, of course, is what the gift of grace is all about. A scholarly and practical study of "the beauty of holiness."

—D. JAMES KENNEDY
Senior Minister, Coral Ridge Presbyterian Church

What a great book! What a necessary book! What a life-changing book! A lack of God's clear desire for holiness in His people doesn't come from making the Gospel too good . . . it comes from not making it good enough. This is the book for which I have long prayed, and I enthusiastically commend it to you. If you miss it, you'll be sorry.

—STEVE BROWN
Professor of Preaching, Reformed Theological Seminary

Grace. We have an entire vocabulary of adjectives to describe it when we sing about it. And yet—if the truth be told—we Christians either have a stubborn tendency to refuse really to believe it, or we stumble over its implications. In *Holiness by Grace* Bryan Chapell comes to help us. Here is biblical teaching carefully presented, popularly written, and practically applied. At times what Dr. Chapell rightly says about the gospel of grace may not be easy to swallow. It chokes legalism and it burns the throat of license. But digest it and it will transform your life.

—SINCLAIR B. FERGUSON
Senior Minister, St. George's-Tron Church, Glasgow

Holiness by Grace addresses the tension between human responsibility and divine provision in the process of our sanctification. Dr. Bryan Chapell guides us through these tensions by assuring us again and again of God's mercy and grace that not only secures our ways to him, but also provides our daily motivation and enablement to serve him. The questions at the end are designed to delve more deeply into these truths leading us in our service to God with the acknowledgment that God must provide what we need to please him. We can never hear enough about God's grace. This book is a fresh reminder.

—ROSE MARIE MILLER
Author, *From Fear to Freedom*

This is a delightful book, full of sane, practical theology and application. It is not the sort of book that will satisfy armchair theologians pondering exactly how the Mosaic covenant relates to the new covenant; rather, it is the sort of book that teaches Christians how to live—aiming for holiness and delighting in it, responding to grace and being thankful for it, avoiding the countless pitfalls, and learning to please God.

—D. A. CARSON
Research Professor of New Testament,
Trinity Evangelical Divinity School

The classic Puritan pastor Richard Sibbes was called "the heavenly Doctor Sibbes" due in part to his God-given ability to make sovereign grace clear to the spiritually sick and weak and wounded. In that same way, Dr. Chapell is a "heavenly physical therapist" for in these pages he carefully instructs a church wounded and weak by theological error of the restorative and healing truth of Reformed sanctification. This volume helps the weary walk more holy.

—JOE NOVENSON
Pastor, Lookout Mountain Presbyterian Church

The historic Protestant doctrine is that we are not only *justified* by faith rather than our works, but we are also *sanctified* by faith rather than our works. Yet, though we give this teaching lip service, very few ministers and Christians know how grace-based sanctification really works. Bryan Chapell has produced a popular, practical, yet theologically sensitive book on this very issue—how God's gracious acceptance is the dynamic and guide for growth into holy character. This is a great book—an extremely timely book.

—TIMOTHY J. KELLER
Senior Pastor, Redeemer Presbyterian Church, New York

Holiness by Grace is a biblical and doctrinal introduction to grace-based godliness—a guide for recovering Pharisees. Bryan Chapell has a special ability to teach the Bible in a way that refreshes the heart. This book will help you see yourself the way God sees you, so that you can serve him the way he wants to be served.

—PHILIP GRAHAM RYKEN
Senior Minister, Tenth Presbyterian Church, Philadelphia

Holiness by Grace is a wonderfully clear, biblically nuanced presentation of what it means to truly grow in the grace of God. Chapell is Christ-centered without allowing modern grace movements to become reactions to older legalism. The church needs this book both to correct errors and to guide people more faithfully into the proven paths of the past.

—JOHN H. ARMSTRONG
Director, Reformation and Revival Ministries

Dr. Bryan Chapell has done a masterful job of demonstrating that a rigorous proclamation of the gospel of God's grace is not only consistent with a call to holy living, it is the only effective way to enable Christian believers to live out that call. I was personally enriched by his careful use of Scripture as the foundation for the teaching of each chapter. I pray that his influence will give us a generation of preachers who know how to preach grace.

—STEVE SMALLMAN
Pastor, Presbyterian Church in America

The role of God's grace in Christian sanctification is so little understood among believers today. Bryan Chapell deftly brings the light of Scripture to bear on this troublesome question through careful exposition and compelling illustrations. I highly recommend this book.

—JERRY BRIDGES
Former Vice President of Corporate Affairs, Navigators

HOLINESS

by

GRACE

Delighting in the Joy That Is Our Strength

BRYAN CHAPELL

WHEATON, ILLINOIS

Holiness by Grace

Copyright © 2001 by Bryan Chapell

Published by Crossway
            1300 Crescent Street
            Wheaton, Illinois 60187

Cover design: Studio Gearbox

Cover image: Veer Inc.

First printing 2001

First trade paperback edition 2003

Reprinted with new cover 2011

Printed in the United States of America

Trade Paperback ISBN: 978-1-4335-2442-4

Library of Congress Cataloging-in-Publication Data
Chapell, Bryan.
   Holiness by grace : delighting in the joy that is our strength /
Bryan Chapell.
      p.   cm.
   Includes bibliographical references and indexes.
   ISBN 1-58134-465-1 (alk. paper)
   1. Holiness—Christianity. 2. Grace. I. Title.
BT767.C47   2001
234'.8—dc21   2001000897

Crossway is a publishing ministry of Good News Publishers.

VP		21	20	19	18	17	16	15	14				
15	14	13	12	11	10	9	8	7	6	5	4	3	

Contents

My Soul's Delight

"God says, 'Be holy, for I am holy.'" The young preacher quoted the words of Leviticus with such fervor that I had little doubt he really expected us to live up to this command for untarnished righteousness. Yet, as my eyes scanned those seated between the pulpit and my pew, I wondered if he recognized the true challenge in his words:

- On the front row were two sisters, both divorced in the past year. One had recently confided to friends that her loneliness since her marriage had driven her into sinful relationships with other men. The second sister had found more frequent solace in alcohol that trapped her in a horrid cycle of depression that made her treat her kids cruelly, making her feel guilty, and causing her to drink again to escape her guilt.

- Behind the sisters was a successful businessman and long-term elder who had engineered the ouster of the previous pastor with a combination of biblical proof-texting and political intrigue. The elder's wife, seated next to him, had conducted a skillful phone campaign that created enough questions about the pastor's credibility to disarm any defense he tried to make.

- In that same pew was a young mother trying to manage two out-of-control preschoolers. Simultaneously she was ignoring disgusted glances from the nearby elder while glaring daggers at her own husband to motivate him to discipline the children.

- Directly in front of me a teenager sat at the opposite end of the pew from his parents as a geographical statement of what he felt about his relationship with them since he had been grounded for ignoring curfew the previous night.

- Ultimately my attention rested on me, the seminary professor who had been moody with his family for days because of a letter from a stranger that had criticized his work.

My eyes and my heart testified there was not a sinless person among us. Yet the preacher seemed oblivious to our obvious faults. He said it again, "Be holy, for God is holy" (see Lev. 11:44, 45; 19:2; 20:26; 1 Pet. 1:16).

Does God really expect us to be holy as he is? He is infinitely pure. I am an imperfect person. So is everyone about me (see Ps. 14:1-3; Eccles. 7:20). His standard seems either to ignore human frailty or to impose certain failure. We must make sense of this command for perfect righteousness lest our hearts harden into a shrugged, "Get real," or break into a sobbed, "I can't do it."

VISIONS OF HOLINESS

How does God enable us to meet his requirement of holiness? An answer lies along the path of John Bunyan's famous travelers in the children's version of *Pilgrim's Progress* that our family has read after dinners (which have had their own share of imperfect behavior).

Late on their journey, Bunyan's pilgrims discover a wonderful mirror. There is nothing unusual about the front of the glass. However, on the back of the mirror appears an image of the crucified Lord Jesus. Everyone who looks in the mirror's face sees an ordinary reflection that includes the blemishes and scars that always accompany our humanity. Yet anyone who observes these same persons from the reverse side of the mirror sees only the glory of the Son of God.

This amazing glass from *Pilgrim's Progress* pictures the answer to how we can be holy in this life. Our holiness is not so much a matter of what we achieve as it is the grace our God provides. Grace is God's willingness to look at us from the perspective that sees his holy Son in our place.[1]

God can certainly see the faults and frailties reflected in the mirrors of our lives. Still, he chooses to look at those who trust in his mercy through the lens that features the holiness of his own child in our place. As a consequence he loves and treasures us as much as if we had never sinned.

Many years ago, the preacher Phillips Brooks explained G-R-A-C-E as *God's Riches At Christ's Expense.* The acrostic beautifully expresses how the blessings of God, which Jesus alone deserves, are mercifully passed to us as a consequence of his suffering and dying for our sin. When we trust that Christ's work, rather than our own achievements, is the basis of our righteousness, then God mercifully grants us the riches of his love that only Jesus deserves. God looks at us as though we were as holy as his own Son, and treats us as lovingly despite our many imperfections.

Most Christians cherish the beauty of the truth that God viewed us through the lens of Jesus' goodness when we claimed him as our Savior. We trusted that Christ's death paid the penalty for our sins, and that we were made right with God—justified—not by our own holiness but by trusting in the holiness he provided. Just as objects look red when viewed through a red lens and green when viewed through a green lens, we believed that when God looked at us through Jesus he viewed us as his own child.

Belief in this provision of grace, whereby God chose to view us as his beloved through no good of our own, became the greatest joy of our souls. What robs many believers of this joy, however, is a misunderstanding of how God continues to view us after we have received the grace that justifies us.

After initially trusting in Christ to make them right with God, many Christians embark on an endless pursuit of trying to satisfy God with good works that will keep him loving them. Such Christians believe that they are saved by God's grace but are kept in his care by their own goodness. This belief, whether articulated or buried deep in a psyche developed by the way we were treated by parents, spouses, or others, makes the Christian life a perpetual race on a performance treadmill to keep winning God's affection.

While the Christian life can be characterized as a race (see Gal. 5:7; 2 Tim. 4:7; Heb. 12:1), we persevere on the course God marks out for us not by straining to gain his affection but by the assurance that he never stops viewing us from the perspective of his grace. God continually offers us unconditional love and the encouragement that our status as his children does not vary even though our efforts do.

When I see my son's energy flag in his cross-country meets, I shout encouragement to revive his resolve and keep him going. I know intuitively that threats or expressions of frustration would sap his strength for the long race ahead (and the many races to come) even if my pressure were to spur him on for the moment.

God is a better father than I, and his encouragement rings more powerfully, wisely, lovingly, and continually in his children's souls. We race in the confidence that his grace does not cease just because we have faltered. Grace becomes not only the means by which God once justified us, it is also the means by which we are continually encouraged and enabled to serve him with undiminished delight.

Since grace is the means by which we find the joy that gives us strength, it is vital that we refine our vision of how God views us. Whether our lives will be typified by joy or by despondency depends largely on the perspective from which we view ourselves. Will earth's or heaven's perspective dominate our vision?

The first purpose of this book is to make heaven's view so clear to us that we will never stop seeing ourselves as God sees us. For if we cannot lift our eyes from an earthly perspective, then we will so focus on our weaknesses and stumbles that the race to please God will be misery. But if we remember that God is the lifter of our heads (Ps. 3:3), then we will raise our eyes to see the affection in his own. When we see that his regard for us does not waver, then his grace will quicken our steps, strengthen our hearts, and delight our souls to carry on.

———— VIEWS OF GRACE ————

Another concern must be addressed, however, in a book that seeks to stimulate greater holiness by grace. We must confess that talking about God's unconditional love in order to promote godliness is counterintuitive. If all we do is keep assuring people that God loves them, then what is to keep them from taking advantage of grace and doing whatever they want?

In recent decades a number of wonderful movements of grace have begun to sweep across the evangelical world. These groups include the Sonship, World Harvest Mission, and New Life ministries that have flourished from the seminal influence of the late Jack Miller; Redeemer churches associated with Tim Keller; New City Fellowship churches and ministries in various cities; and the L'Abri fellowships spawned by the teachings of Francis Schaeffer. To these early and deep fountains of grace could be added a great number of ministers, churches, and institutions in evangelical circles that have recently made grace a chief focus of their ministries. Contributors are as diverse as John Armstrong, Charles Swindoll, Joyce Meyers, R. C. Sproul, Steve Brown, Michael Scott Horton, Jerry Bridges, and Phil Yancey.

Without a doubt a grace awakening is occurring, but the new emphasis does not come without varying accents, challenges, and concerns. Concerns that the new emphasis on grace will result in antinomianism (i.e., disregard for the law of God) have become quite numerous and acute. The history of the evangelical church in North America can partially explain the reasons for these concerns.

Much of the evangelical church finds its cultural roots in the modernist/fundamentalist controversy of the early twentieth century. Not only did those who stood for historic Christianity against modern skepticism fight against disregard for biblical truth, they also warred against the lifestyle changes being adopted by those who discredited the right of Scripture to govern their lives.

Concern about lifestyle issues is necessary for biblical Christianity. Early leaders among the North American evangelicals rightly insisted that the Bible has commands that God's people must obey in order to honor him. Problems came, however, when patterns of personal conduct became almost as much an emphasis in evangelical preaching and teaching as the message of God's grace. As a consequence, people began to think of their conduct as a qualification for God's acceptance.

The result of the strong emphasis on lifestyle issues was the creation of codes of conduct that supposedly distinguished real Christians from the secular world and nominal believers. Strict adherence to the codes became the mark of serious Christianity in many churches, even when the particulars could not be biblically proven. In fact, many of the standards of the evangelical code (e.g., do not play card games, drink alcoholic beverages, smoke, or go to movies) became so much a part of the culture of most conservative churches that few people in them even thought to question whether the Bible actually taught all that the churches expected.

Part of the concern about a renewed emphasis on grace is simply a fear of the loss of evangelical identity as interest wanes in adherence to the codes that have distinguished Bible-believing Christians over the past century. The fear has some merit. The codes have, in fact, kept many Christians from dallying with cultural practices and adopting societal patterns wherein lie great spiritual danger. Those who become strong advocates of a grace emphasis must acknowledge the legitimacy of this concern and show how their teaching will provide protection from secular dangers when the codes of conduct are undermined.

Admittedly, strong advocates of the new grace emphasis may not feel that it is their responsibility to deal with the behavior issues that concern advocates of the codes. Preachers of grace typically see the old evangelical codes as destructive forms of legalism that need to be dismantled. Many of us have been personally wounded by legalistic attitudes in the church and resonate with the need to fight their spiritually corrosive influences.

Still, it is not enough for the advocates of grace simply to react against legalism. We must also respond to the license that always tempts Christians when preachers say, "God will love you no matter what." Legalism makes believers think that God accepts them on the basis of what they do. Licentiousness makes believers think that God does not care what they do. Both errors have terrible spiritual consequences.

Jesus said, "If you love me, you will obey what I command" (John 14:15). Grace should not make obedience optional. When God removes good works as a condition for his acceptance, he does not remove righteousness as a requirement for life. The standards of Scripture glorify God and protect his people from spiritual harm. We cannot undermine the legitimate standards of the Bible without grave consequences.

God does not love us because we obey him, but we cannot know the blessings of his love without obedience. Thus, a grace focus that undermines Christ's own demand for obedience denies us knowledge of and intimacy with him. This is not grace.

Grace that bears fruit is biblical. Grace that goes to seed uses God's unconditional love as an excuse for selfish indulgence. Such egocentric living ultimately burdens us with the guilt and consequences of sin that God has designed his grace to remove.

Resting on God's grace does not relieve us of our holy obligations; rather it should enable us to fulfill them (see Eph. 4:7-13). As the assurance of God's love allows us to cease striving to please him for our own benefit, our good works will begin reflecting more of the selfless righteousness that is truly holy.

Through such other-oriented obedience our lives become more Christlike. God's glory and the good of others increasingly replaces self-centered motivations. And, as our obedience becomes a gratitude response to God's grace rather than an attempt to bribe God for blessings, holiness more and more characterizes our actions (Titus 2:11-14). We increasingly and forever serve God in the holiness he grants by his grace, making the pursuit of his holiness our delight (2 Tim. 2:1).

Discovering the gracious source of this delight, and employing it to avoid the dangers of both legalism and licentiousness, is the purpose of this book. In *Holiness by Grace,* we will journey through key biblical texts that explain how our union with Christ rather than any merit of our own is the basis of our sanctification as well as our justification. This exploration removes our performance as a means of establishing or maintaining our salvation, but it confirms the biblical emphasis on obedience as a gratitude response to God's mercy.

We will explore both the natural and the supernatural effects of grace on the human heart to show how grace leads from guilt to godliness. We will see how a grasp of biblical grace both releases from legalism and rescues from license.

In technical terms, my intention is to explain the role of grace in sanctification. This progressive process by which God makes us more and more like Jesus cannot function if we think that our works earn God's affection, or if we think that our works do not matter. Grace corrects both errors and in doing so grants us the unqualified joy that is our strength for obedience (Neh. 8:10).

Grace overwhelms us with God's love, and as a result our heart resonates with the desires of God. His purposes become our own. Our soul delights in his service as love for him and thanksgiving for his mercy make us long to honor him. True grace produces joy and promotes godliness.

Part One

PRINCIPLES
of
GRACE

The Power of Joy

"Mom on Strike." The words appeared on a sign planted in the front yard of a home near us. A young mother tired of the whining, back talk, and lack of cooperation from her family declared herself "On Strike!" She put the sign declaring her resistance in her front yard and moved out of the house . . . into a tree house in the backyard. From there she vowed not to come down until things had changed.

A local television station got wind of the story and interviewed the family. While the young mother's comments interested me, what I really wanted to hear was her husband's explanation. Garnering the sympathy of husbands everywhere, he shrugged toward the television camera and said, "I have the kids doing their chores again. And I've told them to cool it with the sarcasm. We are trying to make amends and do whatever we can to get her to come down." His comments, though tinged with some humor, revealed an assumption that is the cause of much spiritual pain— the assumption that our words and actions can atone for our wrongs.

On a human level, the husband's remarks make perfect sense. When we have had a problem with people, have failed to meet their expectations, or have caused them pain, we typically resolve to make amends. Wayward children, spouses, employees, students, and politicians all vow to make atonement for their sins with the hope that their actions will compensate for their wrongdoing.

This perfectly reasonable human response gets us into trouble, however, when we try to approach God in the same way to compensate for our wrong. When we know we have failed or frustrated him, we long to make amends. We search the Scriptures for some spiritual discipline or sacrifice that will make us right with God because we do not want him to be "on strike." We long for God to come down from whatever "tree house" he occupies and reenter our lives with his transforming power and compassionate blessing. But how can we make God "come down," when his standards are so high?

—— WHAT DOES GOD REQUIRE? ——

To get a view of how high God's standards are, we have only to glance at Jesus' reiteration of them at the beginning of Luke 17. First, Jesus tells his disciples that they must _cause no sin_ (see vv. 1-3a). Their actions must be so blameless that not only do they not personally transgress God's law, but also they avoid causing naive and innocent children to stumble spiritually. Next, Jesus says the disciples must _confront others' sin_ (see v. 3b). For the sake of steering others from the spiritual harm of their own actions and to defend the testimony of the church, the disciples must risk personal discomfort and damage by rebuking others who sin. Finally, Jesus says that the disciples must be willing to _forgive any sin_ (see vv. 3c-4). Even if someone sins against them seven times in a day and comes back to repent, Jesus says that his disciples must forgive the offender. These really are high standards.

The disciples immediately recognize that the standards Jesus has outlined are beyond human reach. In response they plead, "Increase our faith" (v. 5). The disciples recognize that the Savior must grant them spiritual capacities beyond their own making in order to meet his standards. Their request for an increase of faith is a sanctified way of saying, "You are going to have to help us out here, Lord, if these really are your expectations."

Jesus responds to the disciples by indicating that they are correct in assuming that the supernatural power required to serve him is a matter of faith. He says, "If you have faith as small as a mustard seed, you can say to this mulberry tree, 'Be uprooted and planted in the sea,' and it will obey you" (v. 6). Yes, the power of God does come down as a result of faith. But in what should we place our faith? Should we trust that God will bless us when we get good enough? Are we to believe that, when we achieve a mental state absent of doubt, he will overlook our failures and do what we want? Neither of these solutions, both of which depend on us reaching deep into ourselves for an extra measure of holiness, is the answer. The parable and account that follow tell us that what will move God to act in our behalf is not the excellence of our actions or of our thoughts, but rather total reliance on mercy that we do not deserve and cannot earn.

———— WHAT WILL MOVE GOD? ————

What will move God to express his power in behalf of his people? Jesus explains by annulling common misconceptions that still exist today. He tells the parable of an ungrateful landowner to teach us that God does not open his heart and extend his power to his people simply because they have done their duty:

LUKE 17:7-10

[7]"Suppose one of you had a servant plowing or looking after the sheep. Would he say to the servant when he comes in from the field, 'Come along now and sit down to eat'? [8]Would he not rather say, 'Prepare my supper, get yourself ready and wait on me while I eat and drink; after that you may eat and drink'? [9]Would he thank the servant because he did what he was told to do? [10]So you also, when you have done everything you were told to do, should say, 'We are unworthy servants; we have only done our duty.'"

GOD IS NOT MOVED BY THE DEEDS WE DO

This parable troubles us. The character Jesus uses to represent the divine perspective seems so unsympathetic. Not only does the master not invite the hardworking servant to his table, Jesus also says the master *owes* the servant no thanks. In fact Jesus says that, from the way this fictional master treated his servant, we should learn that even when we have done all we were told to do, we should still say, "'We are unworthy servants; we have only done our duty'" (v. 10).

When we do our duty

Perhaps these harsh-seeming words will make more sense when we transfer the parable to a more modern setting. For instance, we could imagine taking our family to a restaurant to be served by a waitress who had been working hard all day. Even if we were to acknowledge that she was doing a good job and had a right to be weary, we would still be surprised if, along with the meal that we had ordered, the waitress were to bring an extra plate and chair to our table. We would be further amazed if she then sat down to dine with us. Her doing all that we had asked her to do would not be reason enough for her to think she had earned a place at our table. We would reason, "She was simply doing her job, her duty, and that does not suddenly give her the right to join our family."

This modern comparison is actually not quite as striking as the point that Jesus is making in the context of his culture. At that time, being invited to a nobleman's table was a high honor—tantamount to being a part of the master's own household. A more accurate modern analogy to Jesus' parable would be a realtor who, after helping us purchase a home, tried to move in. Imagine our consternation if, after our movers had left, suddenly another moving van pulled into the driveway. If our realtor were in the second van, we would ask, "What are you doing?" Were her response, "Well, I helped you buy this home, so now I'm moving in," we would not hesitate to say, "Now, wait a minute! You were just doing your duty, and that does not earn you the right to our house!" Jesus is saying something very similar. Dutiful obedience alone does not give us a right to the household of heaven.

Though these modern analogies may help us make more sense of his words, Jesus does not intend to give any less offense to his listeners in his parable. We should remember that Jesus is not speaking to Pharisees but to his own disciples. No doubt they were sputtering in frustration at his words and whispering, "But, Lord, we left our homes, abandoned our livelihoods, and have sacrificed acceptance in our religious communities to follow you. Surely you do not mean that God owes us nothing for having done our duty!" Still, Jesus' words turn even his disciples from ever considering their obedience, however great its measure or duration, as qualifying them for heaven's household or making them worthy of divine acceptance. The same message applies to us. Our efforts before God will never earn us entry into his kingdom, or obligate him to love us.

When we trophy our good works

However much we may want—or feel the need—to trophy our good works before God in order to merit his acceptance, our accomplishments remain insufficient to obligate him to care for us as members of his family. I considered how foreign such ideas are to our natural thought when I visited a friend who had various large game trophies from Africa displayed around his home. A zebra skin hung on the wall, antelope hides covered chairs, and the foot of a great elephant had been turned into an enormous sitting stool.

Other guests and I asked my friend to tell the background of the trophies. He began to explain where each animal was taken, but then, even as my friend was speaking, it became obvious that he also was sensing the hidden questions on his guests' minds. We were thinking, "Aren't these endangered species? Though these are impressive large game trophies, did you really shoot Bambi?" Sensing our questions (which he had probably answered for many previous guests), my friend began to offer qualifications for each of his trophies. He said, "These animals were shot before they were rare, before there were restrictions on such hunting. And I personally didn't shoot them. My father-in-law did." In effect, my friend had to apologize for his trophies.

Jesus' parable forces us to do the same. Though we may want to display the trophies of our good works, obedience, and spiritual accomplishment, we must recognize that there is not sufficient goodness in anything we do to require God to move in our behalf. When we display our trophies of good deeds, God does not disregard the good in them. But if we try to force our way into his heart by such deeds, he must respond, "Do not forget that what I actually require is that you cause no sin, confront others' sin, and forgive any sin. And, even if you had met these standards perfectly (though you have not), you would have only done your basic duty and I owe you no special blessing for that."

Initially, the discovery of our need to apologize for our "spiritual trophies" is not pleasant. We want to gain honor from God by comparing our goodness to the shortcomings of others. Thinking we have accomplished more good, instinctively we consider ourselves more deserving of divine love. Thus, when we find that our good works do not leverage God and that we cannot trophy our good works before him, we become frustrated.[1]

When we put our works on the scales

The realization that our good works will not move God to love us runs counter to our natural reasoning. Most people justify their qualification for heaven in terms of balancing scales. They readily admit, "Nobody's perfect," but they believe that God will receive them because their good works outweigh their bad. What such people fail to face is the biblical assessment that even our best works end up on the wrong side of the scale in terms of qualifying us for acceptance by God.

For such reasons we can identify well with sixteenth-century German Reformer Martin Luther's feeling that, sweet songs to the contrary, God's determination to love us through our faith in his grace alone is initially "an exceedingly bitter thing." Luther wrote,

> [I]t will be exceedingly difficult to get into another habit of thinking in which we clearly separate faith and [works of] love. . . . [E]ven though we are now in faith . . . the heart is always ready to boast of itself before God and say: After all, I have preached so long and lived so well and done so much, surely he will take this into account. . . . But it cannot be done. With men you may boast. . . . But when you come before God, leave all that boasting at home and remember to appeal from justice to grace.
>
> [But] let anybody try this and he will see and experience how exceedingly hard and bitter it is for a man, who all his life has been mired in his work righteousness, to pull himself out of it and with all his heart rise up through faith in this one Mediator. I myself have been preaching and cultivating it [the message of grace] . . . for almost twenty years and still I feel the old clinging dirt of wanting to deal so with God that I may contribute something, so that he will have to give me his grace in exchange for my holiness. And still I cannot get it into my head that I should surrender myself completely to sheer grace; yet [I know that] this is what I should and must do.[2]

The message that our gracious God loves us fully despite our sin necessarily implies that he does not account our good works as the reason that he must show us his affection. This truth provides comfort to those whose failures afflict their consciences, but it also robs all of us of any cause for pride in self and of all personal resources for brokering God's gifts into personal rewards. Long-term Christian workers may find these truths particularly distasteful. It is easy to *feel*, even if we would theologically dispute the claim, that God owes us his favor for faithful service.

An old tale speaks of a man who died and faced the angel Gabriel at heaven's gates. Said the angel to the man, "Here's how this works. You need a hundred points to make it into heaven. You tell me all the good things that you have done, and I will give you a certain number of points for each of them. The more good there is in the work that you cite, the more points you will get for it. When you get to a hundred points, you get in."

"Okay," the man said, "I was married to the same woman for fifty years and never cheated on her, even in my heart."

"That's wonderful," said Gabriel, "that's worth three points."

"Three points?" said the man incredulously. "Well, I attended church all my life and supported its ministry with my money and service."

"Terrific!" said Gabriel, "that's certainly worth a point."

"One point?" said the man with his eyes beginning to show a bit of panic. "Well, how about this: I opened a shelter for the homeless in my city, and fed needy people by the hundreds during the holidays."

"Fantastic, that's good for two more points," said the angel.

"TWO POINTS!!" cried the man in desperation. "At this rate the only way that I will get into heaven is by the grace of God."

"Come on in," said Gabriel.

Because of "the great disproportion" between our best works and God's true holiness,[3] we are unable to trade our righteousness for God's favor. Our bargaining chips of good works have no currency with God. God will bless according to his purposes good works done in obedience to him, but we cannot bind him to our definition or preferred degree of his blessing.[4] God's blessings, for instance, may come in the form of difficulties that bring us closer to understanding his heart by allowing us to share in Christ's sufferings (Phil. 3:10).

If the reason we obey God is to bribe him with our goodness, we need to be reminded that God will be no one's debtor (Job 41:11; Rom. 11:35). We cannot bank on having a great academic career because we vow to study hard. We cannot secure an absence of family difficulties because our dinner devotions are consistent. We cannot guarantee financial success in our business because we operate with integrity. Our attempts to barter for God's kindness with our goodness, great efforts, and long-standing resolutions will not move him.

As we discover that the works we thought would justify us before God cannot do so, we ultimately realize that the old gospel song "Rock of Ages" really got it right:

> Not the labors of my hands can fulfill thy law's demands;
> could my zeal no respite know, could my tears forever flow,
> all for sin could not atone; thou must save, and thou alone.

> Nothing in my hand I bring, simply to thy cross I cling;
> naked, come to thee for dress; helpless, look to thee for grace;
> foul, I to the Fountain fly; wash me, Savior, or I die.[5]

Many of us regularly sing these words with the thought of our initial salvation in mind. We rejoice that God made us right with him (or "justified" us, as the theologians say) apart from any goodness in us. But health and vigor will be added to our spiritual service as we understand that this song applies to us at every stage of our Christian lives. To grasp fully the grace that daily restores our confidence in his love, we must keep our hands empty of any claim that God must bless us on the basis of our goodness. For if he loves us because of what is in our hands, then the days will come when we will believe that his affection has diminished because our works are small, or that his care has vanished because our deeds are wrong.

When we seek his blessing by our merit

Despite the teaching of Scripture, I am at times no less troubled than Christ's disciples were with God's determination to resist human efforts to purchase his love. I want to believe that God must be good to the organizations I serve, to the family I love, and to the career in which I strive because I have tried to be good. Such reasoning abandons me, however, when I honestly compare my righteousness to Christ's standards and ask, "Have I really caused no sin, confronted others' sin, and forgiven any sin?"

When I face the reality of the inadequacy of my works to merit God's favor, then I recognize that I must depend on his goodness and not on mine. At times this dependence is scary because it lifts control from me, but there is no other choice when I recognize the true character of my good works. According to Scripture even my best works are only "filthy rags" (Isa. 64:6). There is too much of human imperfection and mixed motives in my best deeds to have them obligate God to do as I wish. Capturing the essence and implications of our limitations, John Calvin wrote,

> To man we may assign only this: that he pollutes and contaminates by his impurity those very things which are good. For nothing proceeds from a man, however perfect he be, that is not defiled by some spot. Let the Lord then call to judgment the best of human works: he will indeed recognize in them his own righteousness by man's dishonor and shame.[6]

Such words should not cause us to think that God never desires or blesses our goodness. Walking in God's ways is itself a blessing (Ps. 1; Matt. 5:3-10). For example, being faithful to one's spouse brings integrity to a marriage that is a blessing. Speaking honestly can enhance one's reputation and help secure faltering relationships. Honoring one's parents typically develops good character and protects from harm. Still, no degree of human goodness will lock God into a path of blessing according to our choosing, as though we had become his master through our merit.

God promises to bless obedience by using it for his purposes. The blessings that result, however, should be seen less as credit for our goodness and more as evidence of his faithfulness to his purposes. Ordinarily those purposes involve God's displaying before the world the kindness that he showers upon those who trust in him rather than in their own works. Family unity, personal well-being, financial stability, and community regard are examples of the blessings that regularly flow from honoring God's standards. However, God does not limit his blessings to earthly dimensions (Matt. 5:11-12).

God's ultimate purpose is to make us more and more like Jesus in faith and character (Rom. 8:28-29). Our ultimate need to trust in things eternal and not earthly is served as we experience undeserved earthly blessing. But this need is also refined in the difficulties we face that lead us (and those who observe our faith) to greater dependence on, and satisfaction in, God alone (Ps. 73:26; 2 Cor. 4:17; 1 Pet. 1:7). In such trials God still truly blesses our faithfulness to him, but these blessings can as well involve the mercy of removing us from the grasp of this world's pleasures as rewarding us with worldly delights (Heb. 12:11; James 1:2-4).

Whether God chooses the ordinary path of rewarding our goodness with observable blessing, or the extraordinary path of blessing our obedience with trials that will strengthen our character and stretch our faith, his love is never lacking (Heb. 12:6-11). Were it not for his mercy, which receives our best works with a divine delight that they would not warrant on their own, such imperfect works would justly receive the treatment of "filthy rags."[7]

Divine blessing flows from God's mercy rather than from our merit. Thus, we cannot guarantee that his care will flow according to our plans simply because we conform in some degree to biblical standards. Our works do not obligate God to care for us in the way that *we* think is best. We cannot put God on a leash through our goodness, nor obligate him to our wishes by our deeds. God blesses according to the wisdom of his eternal mercy rather than in proportion to our works of earned merit.

GOD IS MOVED BY THE DESPERATION WE OWN

But if our works in themselves will not move God to care for us, what will? The Bible answers, in the account that immediately follows, the troubling truths of the parable of the unthankful master:

LUKE 17:11-19

11Now on his way to Jerusalem, Jesus traveled along the border between Samaria and Galilee. 12As he was going into a village, ten men who had leprosy met him. They stood at a distance 13and called out in a loud voice, "Jesus, Master, have pity on us!"

14When he saw them, he said, "Go, show yourselves to the priests." And as they went, they were cleansed.

15One of them, when he saw he was healed, came back, praising God in a loud voice. 16He threw himself at Jesus' feet and thanked him—and he was a Samaritan.

17Jesus asked, "Were not all ten cleansed? Where are the other nine? 18Was no one found to return and give praise to God except this foreigner?" 19Then he said to him, "Rise and go; your faith has made you well."

A group of lepers begin to call out to Jesus "in a loud voice" (vv. 11-13). They raised their voices as a consequence of the custom of that day that required a leper to keep his distance from all others. Such a person had to go outside the walls of the city. He could no longer know the warmth of his own family's touch. He could not even enter a place of worship to seek comfort for his soul and to petition God for help.

Lepers had to leave home, livelihood, and religious community. And, lest anyone get close enough to contract their contagion, they had to call out, "Unclean, unclean!" The phrase communicated not only the condition of their physical health but the presumption of that culture that some spiritual impurity had caused the awful illness. In this desperate condition ten lepers loudly cry out, "Jesus, Master, have pity on us!" (v. 13).

And what does Jesus do when these desperate people plead with him for mercy? He does show them mercy. Jesus shows pity to those who have nothing to claim but desperation. He is moved by a desperate cry for help. What is the message to us? Our God is not moved by the deeds that we trophy, but by the desperation that we acknowledge as our own.

Melting hearts

Our own relationships reveal how powerfully moving a call of desperation can be. My wife and I have friends whose son in his middle teens has rebelled against them and against God. For four years there have been uncountable protests of innocence for unacceptable conduct, and innumerable promises to "straighten up." But each justification, though it may initially have made sense, has turned out to be a righteous veil for actual wrongdoing. Each promise, though it may have been briefly honored, has been broken.

So much pain, embarrassment, and discouragement have been inflicted on these parents that the wife confided to us that she did not know if she loved her son anymore. Her heart had grown hard against her own child. What melted it again was a cry of desperation.

After an escapade followed by more protests of innocence from the son, and more hasty promises to do better, the mother turned her back on her son. Not able to listen again to his excuses and rationalizations, she left the room. As the young man then sat alone on the sofa in the family room, he began to leaf through a family photo album that sat on a coffee table. The pictures of better and happier days past filled him with increasing emotion. One picture struck him with greater poignancy than the rest, and he called his mother back into the room to look at it.

The photograph showed the son as a young child under the approving smile of his mother. The teen now pointed to the photo and said, "Mom, when I see this picture, I understand why you don't know if you can love me anymore. In the picture, hope fills your eyes as you look down at your little boy. But I have dashed all your hopes, Mom. Please forgive me that I have dashed all your hopes."

And what did the mother do? Her hardness broke and she embraced him, with a heart renewed in love for him. She did not delude herself that there would be no more troubles. What moved her were neither protests of innocence nor fresh promises to do better. Rather, she was moved by his statement of absolute desperation. The Bible tells us that this is what moves God also.

God's heart is moved, not when we protest our innocence by pointing to our (inadequate) good works, nor when we promise that we will do better in the future. Though there is no reason for God to love us, yet he does. This is the nature of grace that we must treasure to know the joy that God wants for our lives. Until we recognize that there is no reason God will be moved to love us other than the spiritual need we acknowledge, we have no good news to tell others or ourselves. How could it be good news that God waits to love us until we reach an unattainable standard of righteousness, or that he makes "filthy rags" meritorious? Biblical faith is most evident not when we demand that God honor our flawed deeds, but when we trust that he will mercifully respond when we humbly and helplessly cry out, "Jesus, Master, have pity on us!"

Owning desperation

Those who cry out in desperation have more hope of moving God's heart than any who would trophy their own righteousness before him. Those who face the hopelessness of their spiritual condition apart from God's mercy are nearer to experiencing his grace than those who pride themselves on their goodness. Not beyond God's mercy is the homosexual dying of AIDS, who in a broken spirit says, "People may condemn me for a life they do not approve but, to tell you the truth, I would have loved anything that loved me back." In fact, such a man may be nearer to expressing what melts the heart of heaven than I am on the days that my preaching, my position, and my righteousness swell my pride in my personal deserving of God's blessing.

To experience God's grace, I must readily and repeatedly confess my own hopeless condition. What makes me willing to do this is the knowledge that it is my desperation that inclines God's heart toward my own. The awareness that he does not turn away from my desperation will actually draw me to honest confession and deep repentance.

The assumption that God only loves the righteous will tempt me to hide from him (and myself) the flaws under the public veneer of my character and my fears of deeper failures. However, when I know that God will not turn away from me when I unabashedly cry out for his pity, then I am more willing to acknowledge the monsters of sin in my own heart. Unafraid of God's rejection, I can confront the wicked face of my avarice, my anger, my ambition, my lust, my lack of forgiveness, my doubt, and say, "You, Monster, are mine. Though I hate the spiritual disease your presence indicates, I acknowledge the symptoms of my infection. You, Monster, are why I am so desperate for my Savior's mercy." Such honesty moves God to pity us in our desperation, even as the knowledge of this grace makes us willing to cry out for his pardon.

Our Lord's response to the lepers' cry for mercy should compel us to confess our sin to him no matter its degree or persistence. We need not wait until we have corrected the wrong in our lives to ask him to forgive us. We should not attempt to compensate for our sin before we ask him to love us. Remember that Jesus cleansed all ten lepers when they cried out for his mercy, even though in his divine nature he could have known that only one

would return to thank him. Neither past failing nor future weakness will
dissuade our Savior from showing mercy to us when we honestly acknowledge our desperate need for his grace.

———— WHAT SHOULD MOVE US? ————

By showing us what moves God, the Bible also shows what should motivate our goodness. Jesus commends the one leper who returns to give
him thanks. The commendation teaches us not only the importance of
honoring God but also that such honor should not spring primarily from
a desire for personal gain but rather from the delight of selfless gratitude.

TURNING FROM A DESIRE FOR GAIN

The thankful leper displays his lack of preoccupation with his own gain
by returning to Jesus. Because of our familiarity with this account we may
fail to observe the potentially great dangers the leper hazards by his return
to Jesus. He willingly risks both a change in his health and a change in the
Physician's demeanor.

Not for self-promotion

The leper risks a health change, because he offers thanks for his healing
before he has it certified by the priests. One aspect of the miraculous nature
of this healing is its swiftness. Jesus commands the lepers to go to the
priests, who will declare them cleansed of their disease (v. 14a). The lepers are healed while they are on their way to the priests (v. 14b). Then, the
one leper turns back to thank Jesus, before even getting the priests' official
declaration that he has been cured (v. 15). The risk in doing this, of course,
is that what has changed so quickly could change back just as quickly.

We should consider what the leper risks by placing a higher priority on
thanking Jesus than on first securing his certificate of health. The diseased
man has not known family, affection, or worship for months or even years.
He has been denied the warmth of his family's arms, the security of his
home, and the comfort of his church. Now, all he has to do is see a priest
who will declare him clean, and the former leper can return to his home,
neighbor, and faith fellowship. He has only to go a few more steps to stand
before a temple official who has the authority to restore all that is precious

in the leper's life, yet he does not. The man whose healing is so recent as to be suspect, returns to thank the One who made him well (v. 16a).

Something more powerful than pursuit of his own gain motivates this former leper. *Self-promotion* cannot be his motive, for he risks a return of his leprosy by returning to Jesus before going to the priests. But a change in health is not all that the healed man risks.

Not for self-protection

The leper also risks a change in Christ's demeanor. Initially this *Jewish* holy man, named Jesus, addressed and healed the lepers as a group. But the one who returns to offer thanks is not Jewish (see v. 16b). He is a Samaritan, a race that traditionally hates the Jews and is hated by them. In returning alone to Jesus, the Samaritan can now be singled out. Jesus could now say, "Oh, there was an infidel among those I healed," and then undo the miracle for this foreigner. But *self-protection* is absent from the Samaritan's motivations. There is no apparent maneuvering for personal gain in his return to Jesus. The losses the thankful leper risks indicate that neither self-promotion nor self-protection drives him.

The message implicit in the account of the lepers coordinates with the one already made clear in the preceding parable: what we do for God cannot make God our debtor, and should never be done primarily for our gain. For if we are serving God primarily for our personal gain, then whom are we really serving? Only self. Too many Christians fail to realize this. They serve God in order either to get favors from him (in which case their real motive is self-promotion) or to keep "the ogre in the sky" off their backs (in which case their real motive is self-protection). In each of these cases the motive behind the service is nothing more than sanctified selfishness and, thus, the efforts do not actually honor God. What such people think is gaining them "brownie points" with God is actually to their demerit in heaven's accounting, which considers the motives of the heart as well as deeds of service.

Dealing with God according to his grace is hard to conceptualize for Christians used to thinking that they must broker God's affection with their deeds. However, we can understand how such self-seeking offends God when we consider relationships beyond the spiritual sphere. For instance, I occasionally desire to honor my wife by giving her flowers. If she were to say to me, "Thank you, Sweetheart. Why did you give me these flowers?"

and I were to answer, "Mostly because I want some favors or forgiveness from you in return," then I would not be surprised if her smile vanished.

While there may be wonderful benefits for me and for our marriage in honoring my wife, if my primary motive for giving her flowers is my own gain, then she will recognize the selfishness of my actions even if I do not. God is no less astute than my wife. He knows whether the primary motivation of my obedience is his honor or my gain. Thus, I should understand why he would not find delight in what I might offer him to buy favor for myself rather than to honor his love. This does not mean that I cannot desire to be blessed by my service to God. In fact, God promises to bless our obedience according to his loving purposes, and in some measure he uses these blessings to encourage us to honor his standards. The point is not that his blessings should never motivate us at all, but they cannot be the driving force of our service. His blessings are the oil that helps the machinery of obedience operate, but love for God and desire for his glory are the pistons and wheels.[8]

The biblical hierarchy of motivations indicates that we must love and serve God first, others second, and ourselves last (Matt. 22:37-39; Phil. 2:3-4). This does not mean that we should have no concern for ourselves (were that even possible), for it is fitting and proper to love what God has redeemed with the blood of his own Son (Ex. 19:5; Titus 2:14; 1 Pet. 2:9-11). Since God treasures us as he does his own child, then we should not disdain our own value as do some who mistake self-hatred for holiness (Luke 12:7; 1 Cor. 6:19-20).[9] There is an appropriate and healthy Christian love of self that should cause us to delight in God's blessings, but this self-love is not the primary motivation for Christian service.

TURNING TO A DELIGHT IN GRATITUDE

But now a dilemma seems to fall upon us. If our deeds neither move God to love us nor should be pursued primarily for our own gain, then why should we do them? The historic *Heidelberg Catechism* with rather amazing theological candor asks the question for us: "[Since] we have been delivered from our misery by God's grace alone . . . , why then must we still do good?" Or, to put the question more colloquially: "Since God's love depends on grace, why bother to be good?" The answer: " . . . [S]o that in all our living we may show that we are thankful to God for what he has done for us, and so that he may be praised through us."[10]

This is precisely the motivation evident in the leper. He turns away from the self-absorbed course of the others in his group because of his compelling desire to express his gratitude to Jesus. By the healed leper's actions and Christ's commendation, the Bible teaches us that what should move us to serve God is our delight in expressing thanksgiving to him for his grace.[11]

Compelling love

If the primary reason that we honor God is our profit, then we will discover there are many occasions where honoring him offers us no apparent benefit. In those moments we will turn from his ways unless what motivates us is a desire to honor God for his grace rather than a seeking after our own benefit. What ultimately keeps our motives biblically prioritized and holy before God is the profound conviction that obeying God will merit us nothing. This is why Jesus tells us that, when we have done all that we should do, we are still unprofitable servants.

Jesus does not nullify the value of duty in order to dissuade us from serving God, but to keep us from depending on duty to gain God's acceptance. When we understand that our works in themselves earn us no merit with God, then the only reason to do those works is love for him. Thus we learn to serve God not for personal gain but for his glory—not for love of self but for love of the Savior.

Duty compelled by love may sound like an undemanding religion until we recall that there is no more powerful force to motivate the human heart than love. Fear is not more powerful. Guilt is not more powerful. "There is nothing more powerful than love," writes the seventeenth-century English minister Samuel Bolton. "Things impossible to others are easy to them that love. Love knows no difficulties. . . . Love is an affection that refuses to be put off by duties or difficulties which come between it and the person loved."[12]

What compels the mother back into the burning building for her child is love. And what most powerfully and persistently compels us to obey God when there is no apparent earthly gain is love inspired by the mercy of God in Christ (Luke 1:68-75; Rom. 8:15; 2 Cor. 5:14; 1 John 4:18). When we grasp how great is God's love for us, most fully revealed at the cross, then our hearts long to please him with works that fulfill his loving purposes—even when those purposes may be obscure to human eyes. Love for God expressed in thankful praise and service is the ultimate and highest motivation of all Christian worship, obedience, and mission. We do not expect that our efforts will earn our Savior's love or repay his sacrifice, but rather in thankful devotion we desire to do whatever brings him delight in heaven and glory throughout the earth.[13]

The Scriptures highlight the power of a thankful response to Christ's mercy by recording that the leper risked what he had gained to return to Jesus praising God in a loud voice (Luke 17:15). Just as he had previously called out for mercy in a loud voice, he now praises God with similar volume. The degree of his appreciation reflects his previous degree of desperation (cf. v. 13). His example reminds us that to the degree we recognize our need, to that degree our praise of God will find appropriate expression. As the great twentieth-century theologian B. B. Warfield writes,

> We are sinners, and we know ourselves to be sinners lost and helpless in ourselves, but we are saved sinners, and it is our salvation which gives tone to our life—a tone of joy which swells in exact proportion to the sense we have of our ill-desert. For it is he to whom much is forgiven who loves much and, who loving, rejoices much.[14]

If we do not perceive our need great, then we will not rightly give ourselves to the praise of our Savior (Luke 7:47).

Because awareness of our deep spiritual need causes proportionally great praise, we have further reason to acknowledge that our best works are not worthy of God's favor. Scripture's denial that our best works are sufficient in themselves to please God or to compensate for our weaknesses makes our spiritual desperation more acute and, thus, our appreciation of grace becomes more emphatic. Overwhelming gratitude for the spiritual deliverance our Savior alone provides will engender a humble and glad willingness to dedicate the strength of our lives to our Savior's glory.

Childlike willingness

A pastor tells of the time that a daughter brought home a chocolate teddy bear from a gift exchange at her school.[15] The next day the girl's mother opened the door of her daughter's bedroom only to discover her three-year-old son was there. He had been caught red-handed, chomping down his sister's chocolate teddy bear. The boy backed against the wall like a cornered criminal, knowing that there was no hiding his guilt (or his chocolate-smeared hands and cheeks). He immediately began to sob his confession. The mother told him that, despite his tears, he would still have to tell his sister what he had done when she got home from school.

The afternoon was torture for the little boy, as each passing minute seemed like an hour of wondering how his sister would react to his crime. When his sister finally came home, the boy ran to the door. The anxiety that had been building all day behind the dam of his guilt burst from him in a torrent of tears and confession. He cried, "Sally, I'm so sorry, I ate your teddy bear." He was a sorry sight, standing there sobbing in his guilt. Blessedly, the one to whom he confessed was the kind of big sister who was always looking for a chance to love up her little brother. So she took him in her arms, kissed him, and said, "It's okay, Johnny, I will love you anyway and always."

Though he was still crying, the little boy began to giggle. Tears were still running down his cheeks for his shame, yet at the same time he was laughing for joy. With a vigor made more strong by the joy the tears made deep, he hugged his sister with all his strength.

This is a wonderful picture of every Christian who rightly perceives the nature of God's grace. When we face the reality and seriousness of our sin, we are rightly broken to the point of tears. This degree of desperation only makes our joy more deep, however, when we recognize that our God is still willing to say, "Do not despair, Child; I will still love you anyway and always." The love and gratitude that such a gracious pardon generates then becomes the motive for embracing our Lord and his purposes with all the strength of our being. Like the healed leper who fell down at Jesus' feet with a zeal made strong by gratitude, our thanksgiving for spiritual deliverance powerfully moves us to honor Christ with our lives. Thus, the joy that beacons through the tears of repentance moves us to new and more empowered obedience. In such renewed service we discover the truth of the biblical principle that "the joy of the Lord is our strength" (Neh 8:10).

The beautifully worded *Westminster Confession of Faith* captures the power and motivation that follow our awareness of release from the bondage of spiritual guilt through God's mercy alone:

> The liberty which Christ hath purchased for believers under the Gospel consists in their freedom from the guilt of sin, the condemning wrath of God, the curse of the moral law; and, in their being delivered from . . . [the] dominion of sin; . . . as also, in their free access to God, and their yielding obedience unto Him, *not out of a slavish fear, but a child-like love and willing mind* [emphasis mine].[16]

This is a different kind of religion from that of the guilty oppressiveness that motivates so many Christians and mires them in an unrelenting slavery to fear of God's disapproval. Because God accepts us on the basis of his unmerited pardon, rather than on the basis of our earning his affection or compensating for our guilt, we are enabled to serve him with an unrestrained childlike love that is a joyful response to his care. The power of this joy to strengthen and heal our lives makes God's mercy the primary message we must share in our churches, counseling rooms, classes, homes, and workplaces.

Teaching God's merciful grace does not undermine Christian obedience. Grace is by definition an unconditional release from the judgment we deserve, and accompanying undeserved blessing based on God's mercy alone. Knowledge that God has provided such loving care motivates us more powerfully than any other force to honor him as the Bible directs. Thus, if our teaching of grace causes us to make light of sin, or to slight the requirements of the Savior, then we have not really understood either the monstrosity of our sin or the greatness of the heart that forgives it. When we truly perceive how great is the heart that pardons us, then our hearts begin to beat in harmony with that heart. Honoring our Lord becomes the joy of our lives, and love for him becomes the power that fuels that joy.

Gospel zeal

If we have become bogged down in a guilty depression, have begun to equate religious piety with endless despondency over our shame, or have identified holiness with unrelenting sadness, then we have not grasped the grace that marks the gospel. Grace distinguishes its possessors by their joy. The good news proclaimed in the Bible neither slights the seriousness of sin nor shades the wonders of the pardon and power God provides his people. This full gospel message must also characterize the attitudes of God's people, because those with whom we share Christ's living water will be affected by the springs from which we drink. If we are guilt-driven, then so will be our spouses, children, and coworkers. If we pretend to be guiltless, then we will encourage shameless behavior. However, if we exhibit joyful gratitude for the grace of God that pardons our guilt, then we will reproduce grateful spouses, children, and fellow believers who are zealous for God's purposes.

The tears of confession *and* the joy of pardon are required to produce the gratitude that empowers the Christian life. Biblical grace neither minimizes the guilt of our sin nor grants liberty for its expression. We know grace in its fullness when we are broken to the point of tears over the shame of our sin. We, in fact, strive to see our wrongdoing in all its horror and betrayal of our Savior; for when we do, the marvel of our God's grace becomes all the more profound and mobilizing. We delight in the actions that please our Lord and bring him praise precisely because we find strength to embrace him and his purposes in the joy made more real and more deep by our tears of shame. Such actions gain us nothing. Apart from his work, we are still unworthy servants; apart from his cleansing, we are still unsanctified lepers; apart from his blessing, we are still Samaritans trying to be religious.

Such understanding denies us candy-coated perceptions of our lives. We really are the temptable and tempted, the vulnerable and frail, the weak and wretched sinners that the Bible portrays us to be. But we recognize at the same time that such honesty is neither helpful nor healthy if tears of remorse do not at the same time turn us in gratitude toward the One who has delivered us from our guilt. In this soul-deep thanksgiving is the power of new obedience for Christ's sake. We can claim the biblically-balanced, empowering joy our Savior offers when we understand that God is not moved by our deeds but rather pours his mercy on those who confess their desperation and delight in his praise.

The pouring out of mercy and power is evident in this leper's miraculous healing, but we need carefully to consider its source. Jesus said to the Samaritan, "Your faith has made you well" (Luke 17:19).[17] To what faith does Jesus refer? The Samaritan does not repeat any Creed or proclaim the deity of Christ. All he does is fall at Jesus' feet and, in essence, say, "Everything that is now right about me, you did." The leper makes no claim of his ability, and points to no deserving on his part as the reason that Christ has made him well. He simply throws himself at Jesus' feet and says, "Thank you" (v. 16).

"Ah," we may be tempted to say, "that's not very much faith. Why, that's practically a 'mustard seed' of faith compared to the kind of mountainous faith we expect to see in the Bible." But Jesus said in this very passage that if we were to have faith "as small as a mustard seed," then we would see the power of God come down (v. 6). As we will see in future chapters, this belief in God's unmerited grace will transform our lives by unleashing us from the performance treadmill of trying to gain God's affections by our deeds or despondency. When the confession of our hearts is, "Everything

<u>that is right about me, Jesus did,"</u> then the <u>power of heaven's joy comes</u> to earth for us.

—— RUNNING THE RACE OF JOY ——

Some time ago I had the privilege of visiting a senior board member of Covenant Seminary in the hospital. Jim Orders was dying of cancer and knew it. When the cancer was first discovered Jim said to me with a smile, "I always wondered how the Father would take me home." He had an absolute trust in the goodness of his God no matter what the difficulty. Still, Jim's dealing with the cancer was never a matter of resignation. Far from it, he was in a race.

Jim raced to finish a book on the history of his family and family business that recounted the grace of God in his life. He didn't write because he believed that his writing would make God love him more, but because he was so filled with a loving zeal for the Savior. Jim entitled his book *Nothing Happened by Accident.* He deeply believed that the caring character of God revealed in the sacrifice of Jesus Christ was operative in every stage of life.

I have never met a man more zealous for the honor of his Savior, nor more certain of the cause of his zeal. Jim believed that his best works merited him nothing, and that God had saved him from his sin solely for mercy's sake. Out of thanksgiving for God's grace, Jim served on the boards of numerous Christian organizations, dedicated his business to God's glory, witnessed to fellow businessmen one-on-one for years in personal discipleship programs and, finally, raced against the clock to record the mighty acts of God in his life.

Jim Orders did not believe any of these deeds would gain him one more ounce of God's love—that is not why he so zealously gave his life to God's service. Jim threw himself into homage of the Savior with such energy and joy because he so loved the God who saved him through faith in a great mercy not of human origin. Gratitude compelled Jim to serve his God, and the resultant joy that radiated from his heart made it obvious to all that, though he was dying, this was one of the most "well" persons you could hope to meet. Faith in God's mercy brought joy through the tears. It always does. May each of us learn to embrace this faith that is the health of our souls, the joy of our hearts, and the truest source of Christian obedience.

United for Life

"[M]ay God bless my discovery of the powerful means of holiness so far, as to save some . . . from killing themselves." Pastor Walter Marshall was grieving as he wrote these words. People in his church were despairing that they would ever obtain the spiritual maturity and victory for which they longed. Despite their continual striving for holiness, they felt themselves unable to escape sinful habits and patterns of thought. Their despair was becoming more acute as they realized that years of battling, praying, and grieving over sin did not seem to break their bondage. Sin had not become less troublesome in their lives nor less burdensome to their hearts.

Those for whom Marshall was concerned believed themselves forever bound to passions and habits that marked them as spiritually destitute. No religious formula or personal discipline had brought the victory over sin that these desperate souls craved. Persistent failure to be what Scripture requires and their own hearts desired had become spiritual torture almost too painful to bear. Were there no answers? Was holiness a mystery without resolution? With deep love for his people, this seventeenth-century pastor answered with *The Gospel Mystery of Sanctification*. In this classic book, Marshall articulated why he had to write about holiness, and what benefits he hoped would follow when God's people truly understood the means the Bible provides to help them grow in faithfulness:

> Some of the more ignorant zealots [for personal holiness] do inhumanely macerate [torment] their bodies with fasting and other austerities to kill their lusts; and, when they see their lusts are still too hard for them, they fall into despair, and are driven, by horror of conscience, to make away with themselves. . . . [M]ay God bless my dis-

covery of the powerful means of holiness so far, as to save some one or other from killing themselves. . . . [And, instead, I pray that] God will enlarge the hearts of many by it, to run with great cheerfulness, joy, and thanksgiving in the way of his commandments.[1]

Marshall was concerned for those who were so despairing of their spiritual bondage that they were mutilating their flesh and even considering ending their lives to separate themselves from sin. He himself had known this kind of struggle. For years he, like many of us, believed he had to accumulate sufficient good works before he could seek God's blessing. With his own righteousness Marshall had tried to find peace with God, but the reality of inescapable personal imperfection had led to torment instead.

CAUSES OF DESPAIR

Many of us know this torment. When we belong to churches that faithfully teach God's standards, we yearn for holy living but we also become deeply aware of our failure to live as God or we ourselves desire. Consistent teaching on holiness and even the godly examples of others that are intended to encourage us, instead function as mirrors of condemnation. They reflect ever more vividly our bondage to sin, reminding us that our religious performance yet falls short of the maturity for which we long. As a result, godly instruction can lead to despair.

How do we encourage striving after godliness without depriving ourselves of the holy joy of which Marshall writes and for which our hearts long? Marshall answers by echoing truths the apostle Paul provides in the book of Galatians. There Paul confronts those who are saying that what we do in and to our flesh is the basis of our standing before God. Religious extremists in the Galatian church had apparently persuaded both immature and mature believers (including the apostle Peter for a time) that what we do—our level of holy performance and sacrifice—is what establishes our acceptance with God. Paul reminds everyone of the gospel they had originally embraced with joy.

CAUSE FOR HOPE

Paul argues passionately that, while our personal well-being and our God require righteous conduct, God alone can provide our right standing with him. And he does this only through what Christ accomplished for us. Biblical standards meant for our good do not establish our relationship with

God any more than a parent's rules establish his relationship with a child. Rules are an expression of love, but they do not establish love.

We are united to God not on the basis of our good deeds but on the basis of faith in what he has done for us in Christ. Even this faith is not a work of merit but is a gift of God's grace, so that we can be assured that our relationship with God does not lie in our human performance or resolve (cf. Eph. 2:8-9). Thus, to find release from the bondage and burden of sin, and to access the joy that is the strength of the Christian life, we must believe that we can rely entirely on our union with Christ to make us right with God.

But what is the nature of this union, and how does it enable us to grow in godliness? Paul shows in Galatians how we are united to Christ in his death, in his life, and by our faith, in order to demonstrate how God enables us to live more and more as he intends, and to escape the entanglements of our sin. This process of becoming more Christlike in heart and conduct theologians call sanctification. Sanctification is the work of God's grace in us that allows us to receive the benefits and power of Jesus, which in turn enable us to overcome the evil that can so burden our hearts.[2]

WE ARE UNITED TO CHRIST'S DEATH

Using himself as an example for all believers, Paul says, "I have been crucified with Christ" (Gal. 2:20). His meaning flows from the earlier statement, "For through the law I died to the law so that I might live for God" (v. 19). Paul refers to all of the standards for moral righteousness that God gave in the Old Testament as "the law." Though the requirements of the Law were good, no one could perfectly fulfill them. As a result, says Paul, we cannot make our way to a holy God through human performance. The Law is a dead end in terms of uniting us to God. And thus, says Paul, he died to the Law; he lost all hope that it could provide spiritual life for him.

Paul had to turn to God for another path of spiritual life. He explains the nature and reason for that new path:

> "We who are Jews by birth and not 'Gentile sinners' [i.e., we who know the Law and its requirements, as opposed to the pagan nations without the Law] know that a man is not justified by observing the law, but

by faith in Jesus Christ. So we, too, have put our faith in Jesus Christ that we may be justified by faith in Christ and not by observing the law, because by observing the law no one will be justified (vv. 15-16).

This is a remarkable theological revelation from a Jew whose ancestors had attempted to follow the Law of Moses for two thousand years. Paul says that, by revealing the holiness required for union with God, the Law also revealed the futility of trying to find God through finite human effort. Thus, by its very standards of perfection, the Law showed its inability to be a lifeline for fallen humanity and pointed us to the need for another means of life. That means, says Paul, is <u>faith in Christ.</u>

With these few words about the Law, Paul is dipping into a cool well of biblical history to provide refreshing waters of truth for the Galatian Christians whose lips are parched from pleading with God to love them for their own works. Paul is showing, as he will later say more explicitly, that the Law was given by Moses "to lead us to Christ" (see 3:24). We were always supposed to understand that we are made right with God by faith in what Christ has done rather than in what we do.

THE DEATH OF SELF

To modern Christians, these are familiar truths, but Paul uses them in ways that may yet seem novel to drive us to a deeper level of understanding regarding the basis of our status with God. For example, if the Law is dead to me—unable to establish any relationship with God—then anything that my performance of the Law would establish is also dead. My expense of energy and effort, my achievements, and all of what my best being in itself can accomplish counts for nothing in terms of providing my spiritual life. Whether I believed that my efforts were working to my merit or to my demerit is irrelevant. All of what characterized me on the basis of my doing and my being is dead. The implications are astounding and not a little alarming. <u>If all of my doing and being count for nothing, then I am as good as dead. And that's just the point!</u>

We might compare the spiritual status of someone depending on their goodness for spiritual life with one of those campy (and biblically inaccurate) movies about people who have been in an accident and do not yet realize that they are dead. These people move about, talk, and wave to other people to get their attention. But despite their words and actions those in the accident go unnoticed. Ultimately they recognize that all they do is without consequence. Suddenly the realization hits them that, if all of their activity has no effect, then they are dead.

As startling as it is to perceive the deadly consequences of trusting in our works to establish our spiritual life, Paul's analogy is even more striking. The apostle says that we should perceive ourselves as crucified (Gal. 2:20). Though we move about and strive to achieve certain levels of significance and sanctity by our energies, we should understand that we are united with Christ in his death. Paul means even more than that we should lovingly draw near in heart to the One who died in our behalf.

Our union with Christ in his crucifixion means that we are with him on the cross. He took our identity, including all our sin, in himself on the cross. I, too, hang with him there. Looking through his eyes, the soldiers gather beneath me to gamble for my clothes, my nakedness is exposed, the travelers on the road mock my name, my mother weeps for me, my disciples flee, the last gasps of agony are from my lips, my blood pools on the ground, and the life that ebbs away is mine.[3] I am dead, crucified with Christ. So are all who trust in his work rather than their own to reconcile them to God.

As horrible as is the image of our own crucifixion, we must recognize that it is the necessary antidote both to spiritual pride and to spiritual despair.

THE DEATH OF PRIDE

Spiritual pride dies when we realize that all of our comparisons with others based on relative levels of apparent goodness count for nothing in terms of gaining us standing with God. What we may want God to account to our credit has no currency with him, because the economy of good works is dead. Being better than the next guy, being a more astute observer of his sin, or being more insightful about scriptural truth does nothing to earn me status with God. Paul presses this point with the Galatian church because some of them were saying that greater adherence to the Law ensured their relationship with God (3:26-28). Paul wants them (and us) to know that trying to establish one's spiritual identity by righteous conduct or religious performance is futile because we do not, and God does not, much value the actions of dead people.

Party spirit, gossip, spiritual stratification, and social cliques die in the church when spiritual pride dies. It dies as a natural consequence among us who are crucified with Christ when we realize that our works in themselves count no more toward gaining us spiritual status than do the deeds of the dead. Of course, if no one's performance gains him upper-class identity, then no one is second-class in God's family. When we treasure our mutual value, the tensions drain from among us because we no longer need to highlight the failings of others to prove our own worth to God.

When the fresh breezes of grace began to waft across our seminary campus some years ago, students began to comment that one of the differences they perceived in us was the lack of contention among faculty. Professors complimented rather than critiqued one another in their classes. In their exit interviews, graduating seniors said that this was one of the most noticeable differences between their seminary and college experiences. They were so accustomed to professorial one-upmanship in their previous academic settings that its absence was almost startling in their graduate studies.

Our campus harmony, of course, should not itself be seen as a source of pride, but rather as the evidence that we strive to remember that no one is better than any other. We are only a faculty of fellow sinners whose status before God is solely a consequence of his mercy rather than of our merit. Whatever are our human accomplishments, they cannot be held up before God or against others when our righteousness depends entirely on Christ. Spiritual pride must die when we are united to Christ in his death.

THE DEATH OF DESPAIR

Spiritual despair also dies when we recognize that God is not holding against us our failures to measure up. Because the legal performance standard is dead, then all measuring of my worth by it also dies. My guilt no longer condemns me (see also Rom. 8:1). After all, you cannot accuse a dead person of anything. All of the accusations of my heart, all the judgments of others, all the failures to be what I desire and God requires, all the sin of habit and pattern—while it is real—is dead in terms of its ability to form or foil my relationship with my Lord (Col. 2:13-14).

The "dead" status of our failings enables us to acknowledge wrong without fearing that we will destroy God's love for us by doing so. Confident of our union with Christ in his death, each of us should be able to affirm statements such as these:

- I was not honest in my schoolwork. Dishonesty characterizes me, but that identity is dead . . . the record of my wrong is nailed to the cross.

and you who were dead in your trespasses and the uncirc. of your flesh, God made alive together c Him, having forgiven us all our trespasses, by canceling the record of debt that stood against us c its legal demands. This He set aside, nailing it to the cros

- I have not been fair to my spouse. I have said and done things that I deeply regret, but what was true of me is nailed with me to the cross.

- Moral failure that my own heart hates has been in my life. That sin is nailed to the cross.

- Because finances were tight and my fears were great, I acted without wisdom or integrity. While I understand that there may be earthly consequences to this failure, I rejoice that it cannot block my access to my God. He has taken the spiritual debt for all my sin and nailed it to the cross.

- I am not as far along in my Christian walk, knowledge, or maturity as others that I know. I fear that I will never catch up to the spiritual maturity they seem to express so readily. My background will never compare to theirs, my reputation will not match theirs. Yet, any record that could be held against me, my Lord has nailed to the cross and I bear it no more.

God does not determine his relationship with me on the basis of what is dead according to his diagnosis. This truth is a glorious antidote to despair over sin in our past, or to present failure to meet all of God's standards. Samuel Bolton writes,

> Even though the believer falls into sin, yet the law cannot pronounce the curse on him because, as he is not under the law, he is freed from the curse of the law. A man is never afraid of that obligation which is rendered void, the seals torn off, the writing defaced, nay, not only crossed out and cancelled but torn in pieces. It is thus that God has dealt with the law in the case of believers, as touching its power to curse them, to sentence them and condemn.[4]

All the negatives that are true of me based on my personal performance are dead because I am crucified with Christ. I can look at incidents in my life that bring me shame and not despair that God will not or does not value me because of them.

One of the events from my past that I most regret occurred when I was returning with my young family from a holiday visit with relatives. A snowstorm enveloped us as we were driving home in our aging car with bad tires. As other drivers fought the blizzard, traffic slowed and the trip that should have taken only a few hours stretched into the night. Time and again my wife urged me to pull off the road and get a hotel room for the sake of our baby's safety. But we were living on so little money at the time that I could not bear the idea of paying for a night's lodging. So I kept driving. Only when the roads became impassable did I pull off the road. My wife had been right all along, but my pique at having to pay for the lodging turned into rage against her for the embarrassment I felt at having been proven wrong.

I look back on the events of that night in virtual disbelief of my own immaturity. How could I have been so willing to put my family at such great risk for a few dollars' savings? How could I have let temporal worry about money consume me when I believed in a God who had secured my eternity? How could I have vented so vehemently and unfairly at the wisdom of my precious wife, when I was the one who had been wrong? My actions fill me with shame even as I recount them these many years later. I would have trouble facing them even now were it not for my assurance that heaven has already put my guilt on Christ's cross. Horatio Spafford's famous hymn well reflects the joy that I know because I am united with Christ in his death:

> My sin—O the bliss of this glorious thought!—
> my sin, not in part, but the whole,
> is nailed to the cross and I bear it no more;
> praise the Lord, praise the Lord, O my soul![5]

WE ARE UNITED TO CHRIST'S LIFE

If the spiritual identity that we have based on our achievement is dead, then who are we? This is an especially important question in an age where people often identify themselves by what they do, or achieve, or earn. If the record of our religious performance does not establish who we are (because that identity established by the Law is dead—crucified with Christ), then what is our identity?

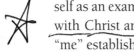

Paul answers by proposing an amazing substitution. Again using himself as an example to represent all believers, he says, "I have been crucified with Christ and I no longer live, but Christ lives in me" (Gal. 2:20). The "me" established by my religious performance has no life. Still, I move and walk and talk. How does this occur? Paul says, "I no longer live (that is, the identity established by my religious performance no longer exists) but rather Christ lives in me."

LIFE IN CHRIST

Most people barely touch the tip of the vast significance of Paul's statement that "Christ lives in me." The words are of much greater and far deeper import than a sweet endearment akin to "I have Jesus deep in my heart." Nor is Paul simply saying that Jesus is the energizing force of our lives. The statement that Christ lives in us appears in the immediate context of Paul's proof of the death of self based on religious performance. The life of Christ exists where my identity established by my efforts has been extinguished. Thus, Paul declares that we have being—status and stature and standing before God—on the basis of Christ's life. His life substitutes for my life on an ongoing, daily basis.[6]

This means that, even as I realize that the identity I tried to establish by obedience to the Law is dead, the life *Jesus* lived to fulfill the Law is mine. His life is in me. Thus, I am united with him. I gain the benefits of his being, his reputation, his standing with God, and the credit for his righteousness.[7] Because Christ lives in me, I, who was dead apart from him, live. His life is mine. I do not (and should not) claim to be God, but he grants me the privilege of his Son's status by virtue of my union with Christ.

This spiritual reality of my new identity permits me once again to look through the eyes of Jesus at the events of Scripture. I can see a crowd gathered on another mountainside prior to Calvary. Though Jesus preaches to them of the righteousness of God and his kingdom, the wisdom of this Sermon on the Mount is mine. Another time, a man approaches Christ with torment of spirit and body. Jesus commands a legion of devils to come out of him, but the victory is mine. As the Savior approaches a small town, a widow comes toward him in a funeral procession. The coffin bears the body of her only son. Christ touches the coffin despite its ceremonial uncleanness, and her son rises. The compassion and power of that act are mine. In a wilderness, Satan approaches and tempts God's Son with allurements that would satiate pleasure, power, and pride. Jesus resists him with the Word of God, and the righteousness of that resistance is mine.

All of the credit for Christ's sermons, miracles, resistance to evil, and suffering for good is mine. How can this be, since I certainly am not personally responsible for any of these activities, nor am I deserving of any of the credit?

His righteousness is mine because Christ's life is in me. He supplies my identity because God has made him my life (see 1 Cor. 1:30; 2 Cor. 5:21).[8]

HOLY IN CHRIST

We can scarcely take in this notion of what the theologians call our definitive, or positional, sanctification. The terms seek to capture the way that God has accounted to each Christian the righteousness Jesus fulfilled. Without our earning it, God declares us holy (sanctified) by virtue of our union with Christ (Rom. 12:1).[9] Though our lives are far from perfect, God has taken away all the pollution of our sin and replaced it with the righteousness of Christ. This does *not* mean that I never do any more wrong, nor that God will not discipline me for sin. It means that God relates to me with the love and status with which he relates to his own Son.

I am treasured as God's holy child because Jesus lives in me, and I live through him. I can say with Paul, "For to me, to live is Christ" (Phil. 1:21); and, Christ is my life (Col. 3:4). I have this position and status, not because I have kept God's standards, but because he who lives in me has kept them. While I still need to grow in holiness (progressive sanctification) in order to honor God and experience his blessings, heaven already credits to me Christ's righteousness as the basis of God's love for me. Anthony Hoekema writes,

> Sanctification, therefore, must be understood as being both definitive and progressive. In its definitive sense, it means that work of the Spirit whereby He causes us to die to sin, to be raised with Christ, and to be made new creatures. In its progressive sense, it must be understood as that work of the Spirit whereby He continually renews and transforms us into the likeness of Christ, enabling us to keep on growing in grace and to keep on perfecting our holiness.[10]

Because of definitive sanctification, I get credit for what I did not, do not, and cannot earn; this blessing comes through my union with the life of the One who fulfilled all God's righteous standards in my behalf. Even now he allows me to share his identity.

The nature and benefits of sharing Christ's identity could be seen in a comparison to the modern gas stations that allow us to use our credit cards at the pump. I have learned to appreciate these pumps not simply because I no longer have to hike into the office of the station to pay, but because I don't have to go to the station at all. If my son needs the car, I can give him my credit card to use in the pump. At his current economy he usually doesn't have the means to get what he needs. So he uses the card with my name on it. With my permission and according to my desire, he assumes my identity. Though he cannot fulfill the conditions required for payment, my son has all of my credit available to him. He meets the qualifications required to use that pump because the machine gives him the credit that really is mine. My son, though he could not provide it himself, acts with my identity and, thus, has all the credit that I have earned.

BELOVED OF GOD

Because we operate with Christ's identity, though we could provide no righteousness of our own we receive the credit of his righteousness. We are accounted as having his status and identity. Knowledge of our union with Christ's life makes sense of some of the most beautiful statements of Scripture:

- We are clothed with Christ (Gal. 3:27).

- We are already seated *with him* in heavenly places (Eph. 2:6).

- Each of us is God's treasured possession (Eph. 1:14).

- We are fellow citizens with God's people—members of his household (Eph. 2:19).

- Each Christian is God's dearly loved child (Eph. 5:1).

These statements make no sense if we base our identity only on our human abilities and accomplishments, but when we understand that God in his grace has chosen to grant us the identity of his Son, then we understand how the qualities Paul describes apply to us now.

Our union with Christ addresses our greatest concerns about our failures to meet God's standards. At one level, each of us must confess, "I am not all that I should be." Still, such failure does not alter the status God gave us when he determined not to assess who we are in relationship to him by what our lives produce but rather by our identity with the life of his Son. The difference this makes in our lives becomes apparent when we assess ourselves from God's perspective. Though our sin is still real to us and must be confessed daily, we recognize that sin does not create our identity. Our lives are hid in Christ (Col. 3:3); we are characterized by his righteousness (Phil. 3:9). The joy that God intends for us comes when we consider that while we see our sin, God chooses to gaze upon his Son in us.

If we are as spiritually sensitive as the parishioners for whom Pastor Walter Marshall was concerned, then the impact of our union is immediate and immense. We still see our dishonesty, hypocrisy, insensitivity to family, openness to lust, willful criticism of others, and resistance to change what we know displeases God. Exposure to biblical truth in our church experience may even polish the mirror of self-reflection to make our failures more apparent and painful. Still, what shines more brightly to the eyes of faith is the image of Christ in us that God has chosen to see and to love. Because we have the identity of the Son, we have the favor of the Father.

STRENGTHENED BY GRACE

Our heavenly Father's love should create a proper regard for self, despite shame for our wrongdoing, that curbs self-destructive attitudes and actions.[11] Seeing the reality of Christ in us grants us the ability to claim the hope and help that God offers to each treasured child. The challenge to have people see themselves as God does, however, never goes away whether we are dealing with Walter Marshall's days or our own.

A pastor recently said to me, "Bryan, when I was in seminary, I had no idea how messed up most people's lives were. But the greatest problem I have is not providing answers to problems, but convincing people that their sins have not caused God to write them off. So many of the people I deal with believe that they are worthless to God and, as a result, they are helpless."

We must listen carefully to the wisdom in these words: "[They] believe that they are worthless and, as a result, they are helpless." Some Christians fear that teaching about the security of our union with Christ will cause people to be less concerned about the wrong in their lives. These concerned Christians reason that confidence in our relationship with God apart from our actions will encourage people to do as they wish. It is true that those who have no real love for the Savior can seek to take advantage of the grace that they presume exists for them. However, those who are truly in union with Christ increasingly have the desires of the Author of that union, since his heart beats within them. More importantly, when any of us lose sight of our privileged position as a result of our union with Christ, we lose our ability to resist sin.

Without confidence in our relationship with Christ, we become like my children, who at a young age would not stand to walk across a rope suspension bridge. The anchors and ropes that held the bridge were perfectly secure, but without confidence in their security my children could not progress a step standing up. In great anguish they crawled out on the bridge even as other people confidently walked past them. The image can represent those Christians who are not confident of their security in Christ. They crawl forward in their pursuit of holiness, helpless to stand against the winds of difficulty and temptation, rather than confidently venturing forth to serve the Lord on the strength of the union he grants them with himself.

As this suspension bridge also illustrates, our holy position or status (i.e., our definitive or positional sanctification) that results from our union with Christ is not the end of God's purpose in our lives. While it is great to know that my spiritual value is not determined by my legal performance, still I want to progress in my spiritual life. All sincere Christians delight to know that positional sanctification is ours, but we still desire progressive sanctification. How do I make progress in godliness as I live out what God intends for me with my new identity? The point being made by the pastor who connected helplessness to worthlessness—and by Paul in Galatians—is that faith in our union with Christ is the key to overcoming sin in our lives.

——— WE ARE EMPOWERED BY FAITH ———

How do we take the knowledge of our eternal status in Christ and convert it into living a godly life today? The plain answer is that we access the power of our union with Christ by faith. Paul says that the life that he *now* lives (through Christ in him),[12] he lives "by faith in the Son of God, who loved me and gave himself for me" (Gal. 2:20).

At one level—of past significance—this is a marvelous statement of how Christ's sacrifice was first applied to us by faith when we became Christians. Because we had faith that Christ paid the penalty for our sin by his death on the cross, we received the benefit of his righteous fulfillment of the Law applied to us. God accounted us as just and righteous in his sight through Christ's work and not our own. This message of our past justification by faith alone in Christ alone is clearly spelled out here and elsewhere (e.g., Rom. 4:23-25; Eph. 2:8-9; Gal. 3:13-14; 1 Pet. 2:24).

Still, there is another level—a present, daily one—at which this union by faith operates. We have entry into a justified relationship with God through faith in Christ's work, but Paul does not perceive the atoning work of Jesus as exhausting its benefits when we were justified. The resultant union we have with Christ by faith also enables us to continue to live as God desires now.[13]

THE POWER OF FAITH

Paul's emphasis on the present, continuing implications of our union with Christ is quite striking and is emphasized by the term "now" that appears in the Greek text of Galatians 2:20. Literally the text reads, "The life I am living now in the body, I am living by faith in the Son of God." Similar phrases, emphasizing the continuing power of justifying faith to enable godly living, occur throughout Paul's writings. For example, the verse that sparked Luther's Reformation, "The just (or righteous) shall live by faith" (Rom. 1:17; Gal. 3:10), though traditionally and correctly applied to how we are justified once and for all by God, also has a strong continuing application to Christian living.

By faith we have been made right with God, but we also presently live for God "by faith." In the book of Romans the apostle explicitly states the power of faith to both justify us and enable us to continue to stand for God. Paul writes, "Since we have been justified through faith, we have peace with God through our Lord Jesus Christ, through whom we have gained access by faith into this grace in which we now stand" (Rom. 5:1-2).

We enter the Christian life by faith, but God also provides for us to continue living by faith in what he has done, not in what we do. Paul strongly and directly corrects the Galatian Christians, who have begun to look to their own works not only for making them right with God but also for keeping them right with God:

GALATIANS 2:21–3:3

[21]*"I do not set aside the grace of God, for if righteousness could be gained through the law, Christ died for nothing!"* [1]*You foolish Galatians! Who has bewitched you? Before your very eyes Jesus Christ was clearly portrayed as crucified.* [2]*I would like to learn just one thing from you: Did you receive the Spirit by observing the law, or by believing what you*

heard? ³Are you so foolish? After beginning with the Spirit, are you now trying to attain your goal by human effort?

Our union with Christ provides resources for continuance in the Christian life, which is also to be lived by faith. What is this life of faith in which those who have union with Christ now live? It is the experience of godly living that is built upon (or springs from) the union with Christ that faith grasps. This is a vital concept to understand if we are to grow in holiness as God intends. Most Christians instinctively try to validate, or ground, our justification in our sanctification (i.e., we instinctively try to keep our justification in effect by our good behavior). Richard Lovelace well characterizes this mind-set in his classic *Dynamics of Spiritual Life:*

> Only a fraction of the present body of professing Christians are solidly appropriating the justifying work of Christ in their lives. Many have so light an apprehension of God's holiness and of the extent and guilt of their sin that consciously they see little need for justification, although below the surface of their lives they are deeply guilt-ridden and insecure. Many others have a theoretical commitment to this doctrine, but in their day-to-day existence they rely on their sanctification for justification . . . drawing their assurance of acceptance with God from their sincerity, their past experience of conversion, their recent religious performance or the relative infrequency of their conscious, willful disobedience. Few know enough to start each day with a thoroughgoing stand upon Luther's platform: *you are accepted,* looking outward in faith and claiming the wholly alien righteousness of Christ as the only ground for acceptance, relaxing in that quality of trust which will produce increasing sanctification as faith is active in love and gratitude.¹⁴

There are two consequences of basing our justification on how sanctified we have made our lives. First, we jeopardize our faith in our justification—since our lives are never as truly holy as God requires. Second, we unplug our sanctification from its power source, which is faith in our union with Christ rather than confidence in our works.

THE POWER OF TWO CONFIDENCES

The mind naturally reasons, "God may have justified me by faith, but to stay in this estate of grace I've got to live at a high level of sanctified goodness." The problem is that our goodness is always marred, and thus we are left having either to ignore our sin or doubt our salvation. Thus, Paul reverses our natural reasoning by telling us that our sanctification is to be grounded in confidence in our justification. We are enabled to grow in godliness by the resources of our union with Christ—our sanctification springs from the justification that is by faith. How does this work? How does faith in my justification lead to my sanctification; i.e., how does faith in my union with Christ promote godliness? The answer is that our union with Christ allows us to have two confidences that are the empowering mechanisms for godliness in the Christian life: 1) confidence that our status does *not* change; and, 2) confidence that our ability *does* change.

Confidence that our status does not change

Paul says that he has faith in the Son of God who, "loved me and gave himself for me" (Gal. 2:20). These words first express Christ's attitude toward Paul and, then, describe an action that springs from it. Jesus loved Paul, a sinner guilty of murder and persecution of the church, *and* Jesus gave himself out of that love for the sinner. Both the love and the sacrifice are expressed in the Greek as aorist participles, indicating completed action. Thus Paul makes it clear not only that Christ loves us apart from our personally qualifying for his affection, but also that Christ's love for us is complete and that his atoning work in our behalf is complete. His regard for us and the way that this regard is secured are both fixed.[15] The beauty of this lies in understanding that my performance does not affect Christ's love for me. While God is not pleased with my sin and may discipline me in order to turn me from destructive paths and practices, his love for me does not diminish in any degree. He gave himself for my sins in their entirety, so that I might have his love in its entirety.

In the life that I now have by faith in Christ's justifying work in my behalf, my status of being loved does not change. My sins past, present, and future are covered by the One who has loved me and has given himself for me (Rom. 6:10; Heb. 9:28; 10:10; 1 Pet. 3:18). By being in union with him, I have the same regard from my heavenly Father as God has for his Son (Gal. 3:26-27; Eph. 2:18-22; 5:1-2). Accepting this reality of God's unchanging regard is necessary for us to make progress in the Christian life.[16]

Just as it was our tendency before we were believers to judge our status by our past sin, it remains our tendency as believers to judge our status by our present wrongdoing. But since Christ's love and atoning sacrifice never cease to operate in my behalf, Christ continues to be my identity and the "me" characterized by my performance continues to be dead (Rom. 6:8-11). The identity established by my works is already dead, and my identity created by Christ's righteousness will always live. If I cease to be conscious of this already-dead and always-alive reality, then I cut myself off from the promises of God that enable me to continue serving him without despairing over my failure to achieve holiness on my own.

Who I am in Christ can be compared to an ear of corn plucked from its stalk. Thinking of my life as that ear of corn, my first impression is that I am only a husk, because that is all I see when looking at the unprocessed ear. This husk represents my works. My tendency is to look at what I have done that is wrong and is obvious to my human sight, and to say, "Look at what a terrible person I am. That cheating shows who I really am, as does that lustful glance and that mean-spirited comment. That unholy person is who I am." But this characterization based on our misdeeds is not true for us who are in union with Christ.

Through the perspective of Scripture and the eyes of faith I must learn that the husk, though real, does *not* truly characterize who I am. In fact, the husk is dead. Depending on how recently it was picked and how dry are its surroundings, the husk—like my sinful nature—still has vestiges of life in it in varying degrees. But the fact is, that husk is dead. It has been cut off from its life source and has no chance of continued life. The only thing that still has life in it to reproduce is the corn inside. Paul says that life inside me is Christ himself—and he is the only real life in me. Significant influences of my old sin nature still cling to me, but they are dead and the only thing that has life is Christ. The fact that more—or less—husk still clings to me does not change the fact that the only thing living in me is Christ, who is my identity.

Because Christ is the only life in me, what I do in the flesh does not change my status with God. By my striving to do what God requires, and by God's disciplining me, more of my old, dead "husk" identity is being stripped away and more of the living Christ in me is being revealed (the old me is decreasing that he might increase). Still, because Jesus loved me and gave himself for me that he might be my identity, God already loves me completely. That privileged status does not change, even though my progressive sanctification will not be complete until I am with him in glory.

Since God has secured his love for me completely through my union with Jesus, my own attitude should change about my performance of the duties God requires. I should recognize that doing my duty cannot secure any more of the love that he offers, since that love and the means of securing it are complete in Christ's work. This awareness takes the energy-sapping, heart-mutilating striving for God's affection from my life. The paths of obedience lead me to where I may understand that love more fully, but they provide no more of God's love. If my striving were what made God love me more, then when the Holy Spirit eventually showed me that my best works are filthy rags, I would be forced forever to doubt that I had much of God's love. As a result, I would always question his care. Yet, because of my union with Christ, I need never doubt that I am fully loved, even as the husks of my sin cling to me.

The difference that the knowledge of our unchanging status makes in our lives can be demonstrated through the way many Christians regularly practice the means of grace (i.e., *prayer;* reading, hearing, and meditating on *Scripture;* and seeking God in the *communion* of believers through fellowship, worship, seeking godly counsel, and participation in the sacraments).[17] Many people feel that these means of grace are the instruments by which we secure God's love even on a daily basis. In our humanity it is natural to think in terms of such a barter system of love, but such thinking creates the impression that these Christian disciplines are not means *of* grace but means *to* grace. We reason, as a consequence, that practicing more of the means of grace will cause God to love us more and, thus, the more we do them the more of his love we will get. Conversely we reason that we will have less love by not adequately pursuing these practices. For instance, I have heard Christians say, "I knew that I would have a bad day because I shortened my quiet time of Scripture reading this morning."

We damage ourselves and our spiritual walk with God by reasoning that practices even as noble as the means of grace will gain us more of God's affection. We will inevitably be forced to ask, "How much more must I do to earn his love?" The answer will not be pleasant. For when will we ever be able to exercise the spiritual disciplines to warrant a holy God's affection? The magnitude of his holiness compared to the puny efforts of our most strenuous disciplines will drive us to obsession with our works and/or despair of his satisfaction with them. Prayers and readings that may seem initially to be good buckets to extract love from the well of God's heart, ultimately will be recognized as mere thimbles being lowered into a bottomless pit of divine expectation that keeps his care remote.

But what if God's love were not seen as a well, remote and accessed only by endless striving, but rather as the very air around us? Then we would not perceive the means of grace as measures we take to produce God's love for us, but simply as means for using more fully the provision that already surrounds us. We would then see the Christian disciplines as means of opening our mouths to breathe in all the loving resources God has already provided. Opening my mouth in prayer and praise does not manufacture more of God's love for me, any more than opening my mouth makes more air. The means of grace simply allow me to experience the fullness of the love that God has already fully and completely provided.

Seen in this "airy" way, Christ's love is never conditional upon my actions; rather it is always available for my needs. Now, knowing that I function much better with lots of divine "oxygen" encourages me consistently to use all the means of grace to take in the benefits of God's loving provision. Still, the status I have as one surrounded by loving "air" does not change from day to day just because I have not breathed in enough of its benefits. Faith that Christ's love surrounds each Christian enables us to live the life of godliness we desire. We interpret all events, whether delightful or difficult, as part of this loving air. Thus, we are able to cease striving for affection and instead live partaking of the joy that is our strength, being daily renewed by the means of grace God provides to energize us and bring us joy.

Our family discovered the freedom and power of one means of grace after hearing Edith Schaeffer answer a question about maintaining family devotions. Typical of her convictions and priorities, Edith extolled the value of family devotions such as reading Scripture around the dinner table. Then she said, "But we must be careful not to make our devotions a payment we make to God for his goodness, as though he will hate us—or will love us less—because we forget one night or must rush off to a meeting or, honestly, just want to watch a special TV show that starts in two minutes. Having devotions as a family is very important, but it is not more important than being a family and communicating to our children that we don't secure God's love by our disciplines. If we have to have family devotions to keep God loving us, then our children will learn not to love such an inhospitable God."[18]

Edith's words were fresh air to my family. We had tried so long to be consistent in our devotions but were constantly discouraged, even angry with one another, because of the seemingly unavoidable gaps in what we wanted to be habitual. Our dogged insistence on "doing the devotional" did not simply reflect a desire to nurture our family in the Lord; rather, it had come to reflect a need to prove to ourselves and to others that we were a "good" Christian family. However, our consistent "failures" constantly reminded us that we were not as good as we wanted to be. The resultant guilt that drove us made devotions a constant pressure for the parents and a source of dread for our children, especially as they entered adolescence. We managed to surround family devotions with so much tension and guilt that "forgetting" them made life easier for everyone.

When we considered Edith's words, however, we realized that missing devotions did not make us a bad family, any more than doing them made us a good family. What the Bible we were reading was telling us (when we would really listen) was that our status with God did not change just because we did not measure up to an arbitrary standard of devotional discipline.

We still need to nurture our family with God's Word, and having devotions is an excellent way to accomplish that. But we also need to be confident that God will not love us less because we sometimes choose other ways to nurture our family at mealtimes. We still do devotions; but we don't beat ourselves up when we miss and we try not to applaud ourselves when we manage to be consistent. Sometimes I still question if we have let ourselves "off the hook" and have not been as disciplined as we should have been. But while more discipline could always have been exercised, the worn-out Bibles and dog-eared storybooks piled beside our dining table attest to years of family time around God's Word—time that we have managed to accumulate without condemning one another for being human. Confidence in our unchanging status before God has kept us encouraged and energized in our pursuit of family holiness.

Confidence that our ability does change

Awareness that we can be energized and strengthened by our union with Christ takes us to the second aspect of the confidence we find in the life of faith. Not only does faith in Christ give us confidence that our status does not change, it also gives us confidence that our ability does change. Paul says that he "lives by faith" in the Son of God who loved him and gave himself for him (Gal. 2:20). These statements assure us of Christ's continuing influence in our lives. We not only have Christ's righteousness by virtue of our union with him, but we also have his power. This point is emphasized by Paul's saying that though we are dead, Christ lives in us. His life substitutes for ours in supplying our ability to please God, as well as supplying the righteousness that God accepts.

FAITH IN OUR NEW NATURE —— By our union with Christ, our God makes us fundamentally new creatures (2 Cor. 5:17; Gal. 6:15). Once, we were dead in our transgressions and sins (Eph. 2:1); we were "not able not to sin" (*non posse non pecarre* is the classic theological language). But now with the living presence of the God of Creation in us, though we are still in the same bodies we are fundamentally different creatures (1 Pet. 1:23).[19] *Born again*

God has regenerated us by his Spirit so that we now have Christ's presence and power in us. With this new nature we have new desires, new goals, new priorities, and new abilities (Rom. 8:5-11). In fact, through our union with Christ we are able *not* to do the wrong that the Holy Spirit has revealed to our consciences (*posse non pecarre*).[20] This does not mean that we become sinless in this life. As Anthony Hoekema writes of those united to Christ, "We are genuinely new, though not totally new."[21] The limitations of our humanity and the resistance of our wills to the Spirit's influence remain until we are perfected in heaven's glory. Still, our new nature enables us increasingly to discern and defeat the forces of evil in our lives. As our sanctification progresses, there is an ever-widening swath of the Spirit's influence in our lives.

As new creatures in Christ, the condemnation and dominion of sin are removed from our lives. We are no longer slaves to sin, but progressively have the power to resist the wrong that the Spirit reveals to us. Richard Lovelace beautifully describes the difference that faith in this reality can make:

> God's gracious provision for our needs includes God's grace for sanctification as well as for justification. It is not enough to tell believers, "*You are accepted* through your faith in Christ." We must tell them also, "*You are delivered* from the bondages of sin through the power of the indwelling Christ. . . ."
>
> In order to combat this sense of helplessness before the binding power of indwelling sin, believers should first be assured that sanctification, like justification, is grounded in union with Christ. The power of sin to rule their lives has been *destroyed* in the cross

of Christ; we have died with Christ, and have been raised up together with him in newness of life. Therefore, we are not to set the estimates of our power to conquer sin according to past experiences of our will power, but are to fix our attention on Christ and the power of his risen life in which we participate: for we have died and our life is now hidden with Christ in God. . . . This power is accessible in our experience through *faith*, not through simple striving of the will.[22]

Faith in our union with Christ provides the "double cure," ridding us of sin's "guilt and power."[23] Because God has regenerated us as new creatures, we can actually breathe the air that God provides to enable us to run the race of holiness in this life. Faith in our ability to do so is what allows us to run with confidence, perseverance, and power (cf. Heb. 12:1-2).

We should not mistake faith in our new ability to overcome ungodly habits and patterns as an eraser of all sinful influences in our lives. We require faith for growth in godliness precisely because sin will continue to assault our souls. Jerry Bridges astutely prepares believers for battles ahead by writing, "Sin is like a defeated army in a civil war, that instead of surrendering and laying down its arms . . . continues to wage a guerrilla war. . . . Sin as a reigning power is defeated in the life of a believer, but it will never surrender. It will continue to harass us and seek to sabotage our Christian lives as long as we live."[24] We are prone to capitulate to these attacks if we are not convinced that the reign of sin is over. Our hearts have been released from its rule, and faith in the reality of our emancipation grants us power to repulse renewed campaigns of temptation and entrapment from our enemy.

FAITH IN THE HOLY SPIRIT. ——— Our power over sin by virtue of our union with Christ is not, however, mere self-convincing that we are able to resist it. While confidence that we really are different is part of winning the victory over sin, our power does not come from mere mental resolve. Through Christ a true supernatural force is at work in us that makes otherwise impossible changes occur. By faith we exercise this resource of God's grace also. We can discern this resource by observing that the phrase in Galatians that most closely and commonly parallels living "by faith" is living "by the Spirit" (e.g., 3:1-5). Christ's presence in us is manifested in the Spirit's power that gives us new passions (5:16-17) and new character (5:22).

While my status before God changes not at all, my ability to change for the good is fundamentally altered and improved by the indwelling Spirit of God. As a result, I am not bound to past or present sin. Tomorrow doesn't have to be like today. There is hope for change. James Buchanan describes the power and impact of the Holy Spirit:

> The consideration of the continued presence and constant operation of the Spirit of God in the soul of every true believer is fitted at once to encourage and animate him in the path of holy obedience, and to impress him with an awful sense of reverence and godly fear. It is a strong consolation, and a cheering ground of confidence and hope, that amidst all the corruptions with which he is called to contend, and the innumerable temptations by which he is assailed, he is not left to depend on his own wisdom and strength, but may ask, in believing prayer, the supplies of the Spirit of grace, and rest on the promise, "My grace is sufficient for thee; I will perfect my strength in weakness."[25]

Because I am a new creature in Christ Jesus, the Spirit of God indwells me and I have the means of grace available to me by which the Spirit teaches, trains, and "rewires" me so that I can mature in knowledge and righteousness.

The supernatural rewiring that the Spirit effects reminds me of the electric trains I played with as a child. When I wanted the train to reverse its course, I did not push it in a new direction with my hands. While such an effort would work for a while, I would not have the energy or the ability to keep the train traveling a different course. Instead, a switch in the wiring reversed the polarity of the train so that it naturally and continually traveled in the new direction. In a similar way, the Spirit changes our hearts in a way that our own efforts cannot achieve. When the Spirit supernaturally reorients our hearts to love and obey, we have the inclination and power to follow him. Thus, spiritual change is more than a matter of the practice of spiritual disciplines, or even of resolving to act on the reality of our union with Christ. We progress in sanctification as we humbly and prayerfully depend upon the Holy Spirit to mature our wills and transform our affections so that we stay on the course that he has designed.

Evidence of this "rewiring" that marks us as fundamentally new creatures in Christ exists not in the total absence of sin in our lives, but in our changed attitude toward it. While Christians sometimes still yield to temptation, they now hate their own susceptibility to the wrong. Once this godly hatred did not exist because the mind, untouched by the indwelling Spirit, loved the world and was hostile to God (Rom. 8:5-7; James 4:4-5; 1 John 2:15). The repulsion we feel for the sin in our lives is our internal witness of the new nature that God's Spirit has supernaturally created in us.

It is important to realize that the "rewiring" work of the Spirit, by which he changes us from the inside out, is a supernatural process that cannot be directly linked to the means of grace (such as prayer and Bible study) in a one-to-one ratio. While these disciplines are important tools for our spiritual maturity, we should not assume that their use automatically or proportionally makes the Holy Spirit work. Were the ratios exact, then legalistic uses of the disciplines of grace would be more pervasive than they already are. Instead, the Spirit seems more to respond to humble repentance and dependence on God alone for changing the heart, and then to use the regenerated heart's longing for change to create new pursuits and godly passions.

The new affections of a Spirit-changed heart combined with the nurturing instruction of the means of grace mature us in faith, but the processes vary greatly among individuals. Some grow quickly, while the progress of others seems undetectable over many years. Like physical growth in children, spiritual growth varies for each individual. While all should grow, we do so at different paces . . . sometimes spurting forward, other times plateauing. We grow according to God's plan and purposes, but there is not a linear math to prescribe our advances. "A believer deeply conscious of his or her shortcomings does not need to say, Because I am still a sinner, I cannot consider myself a new person. Rather, he or she should say, I am a new person, but I still have a lot of growing to do."[26]

No growing occurs, however, without the realization that we cannot progress in our faithfulness to God without the supernatural work of the Spirit. This acknowledgment keeps us from pride in our maturity, or from too hasty judgment of others' spiritual condition. For instance, I can be tempted to take pride in my parenting by virtue of my children's wonderful record of scholarship and conduct. However, I may learn upon my entry into heaven that the reason God so blessed me was that my faith was too weak to have persevered with the more troubled children of other Christian parents (whom I too frequently judge for their apparent failings).

The challenges of raising a child are as much for the sanctification of the parents as they are for the benefit of the child. Perhaps this is the reason that childbearing and rearing come so early in our adult life cycle.

Growing families are God's pressure cooker to mature many of us quickly for the spiritual trials that he knows are ahead. Only the Spirit knows what is best for the spiritual nurture of each individual, and he matures us by means natural and supernatural that will be fully revealed to us only in glory. Our cause for rejoicing now, however, is faith that our union with Christ makes available to us the work of the Spirit that enables us to change.[27]

The enabling union God provides in Christ is the ultimate antidote for the despair of believing that we must find within ourselves the resources to earn God's love. Pastor Walter Marshall quieted that despair of his parishioners when he wrote, concerning our union with Christ:

> It is not a privilege procured by our sincere obedience and holiness, as some may imagine, or a reward of good work, reserved for us in another world; but it is a privilege bestowed upon believers in their very first entrance into a holy state, on which all ability to do good works doth depend, and all sincere obedience to the law doth follow after it, as fruit produced by it.[28]

The gracious benefits of our union with Christ that Marshall describes have communicated hope to many hearts. In 1890, Charles Haddon Spurgeon, while conducting the funeral service of a beloved deacon, cited one of Marshall's favorite expressions of that hope: "Lord Jesus, we are one with Thee. We feel that we have a living, loving, lasting union with Thee." Then Spurgeon said, "Those three words have stuck by me; and ever since he [the departed deacon] has gone, I have found myself repeating them to myself involuntarily—'a living, loving, lasting union.' He owed everything to that."[29] So do all who would know the joy of constancy and progress in the Christian life.

══ REJOICING IN FAITH ══

Faith in our unchanging status and in our changed ability are the powerful resources for spiritual change made available to us by our union with Christ. These resources do not remove our need to seek godliness with vigor and dedication. Progress in sanctification requires work from us, but we are made willing and able to work because of our sure relationship with the Lord who gave himself for us, rose from the dead, and now indwells us with that life-changing power. By virtue of our union with Christ our sinful identity is dead and his righteous identity is ours.

With our status as God's beloved we *enter* the Christian life, but Christ's identity *remains* ours through our continuing union with him. By faith, the resources of this union become the means by which we live the life our God and our regenerated hearts desire. Pastor Marshall beautifully summarizes:

> Your way to a holy practice is first to conquer and expel . . . unbelieving thoughts by trusting confidently on Christ, and persuading yourselves by faith that his righteousness, Spirit, glory and all His spiritual benefits are yours, and that He dwells in you, and you in him. In the might of this confidence, you shall go forth in the performance of the law; and you will be strong against sin and Satan, and able to do all things through Christ who strengthens you.[30]

Confidence in our unchanging status and in the ability God provides for us to change makes real spiritual progress available. The assurance of God's Word that this progress is not impossible rescues us from despair and enables us to claim the blessings and joys of a godly life.

When my wife taught in high school, a special learning consultant came to instruct teachers about learning disabilities. While at the school, the consultant also tested some of the children who were struggling academically. She discovered that one, whom I will call Bill, had a malfunctioning connection between what his brain knew and what he could actually transfer to his hand to write on a test. Once she discovered this disconnect between the status of knowledge in Bill's mind and his tangible expression of it, the consultant was able to suggest forms of oral testing that enabled Bill to show what he really knew.

There was still much learning and catching up for Bill to do. But once he knew that his status was not that of an academic washout and that he had the ability to improve, his despair and resignation about his schoolwork disappeared. His transformation was evident when the consultant asked Bill to talk in front of his teachers about what he had discovered about himself.

The consultant asked, "Bill, what did you think about yourself before we found how you could show your progress?"

Bill replied simply, "I thought I was stupid."

Then the consultant asked, "What do you think now?"

Again, Bill replied simply but with tears rolling down his face, "Now I know that I am not stupid."

"That's right," said the consultant, "and though there are still things for us to work on, I want you never to forget your real abilities."

Bill had never been stupid; he just did not know his real status, nor his real power to improve. It was a very special gift for the consultant to share with Bill the knowledge of both.

God has done something even more precious for us. Some of us—because of our sin, lack of progress, or comparison with others—have determined ourselves to be spiritually stupid, or even hated by God. Thus, in the Bible God tells us our true status and ability. Because of our union with Christ, we are not hated. Weakness, wrongdoing, and failings cling to us, yes. But they do not establish who we are. We are the beloved of God. Though sin still exists in our lives, we have the status of the One who gave his life for us and to us—God's own Son. And because of the love of that Child who now indwells us, we have the ability to change and progress in our Christian walk. Yes, there is still work to do, but as we seek to obey *Rom. 6* our God we must remember that we _can obey_ him because of who we are. *- Roms. 8* We are God's beloved children for whom he gave his Son, and to whom he has given his Spirit. As the Bible says, "How great is the love the Father has lavished on us, that we should be called children of God! And that is what we are!" (1 John 3:1).

Part Two

PRACTICES
of
FAITH

Repentance That Sings

Imagine a junior league coach instructing his young pitchers as they watch game films of some historic major-leaguers: "Now, men, watch Luis Tiant closely. He's a very fine pitcher. When he starts his windup, he pivots on one foot and then, to gather momentum, he actually turns his back on the batter before spinning around to deliver the pitch. See how he turns his back to the batter? Don't do that!"

"Now," says the coach during the next film clip, "I want you to see the windup of Fernando Valenzuela. He faces the batter as an all-star pitcher should. Watch him. Watch how, when he is right at the apex of his windup, he looks up in the air and rolls his eyes back in his head before delivering the ball. See how he takes his eyes off the plate? Don't do that!"

Finally, as the last clip rolls, the coach says, "The pitcher I really want you to watch is Dwight Gooden. This is a straight-ahead, eyes-on-the mitt, great pitcher. The mechanics are great. The form is great. His windup is picture perfect. See how he tries to be perfect with each pitch? Don't do that either. It will eat a hole in your soul, as Dwight Gooden learned through much heartache in his life."

This imaginary pitching coach speaks with real wisdom not only about the mechanics of pitching but also about the nature of the human spirit. His words echo what Jesus also teaches about how the pursuit of self-perfection can assault the soul. We are not accustomed to thinking this way. We understand how sin can become a harsh taskmaster and place us under bondage by its allurements and compulsions. However, we do not usually consider how vigorously striving after holiness apart from the provisions of our union with Christ can be just as enslaving.

If we fail to understand how we rely on God's grace alone to make us right with him, our Christian walk necessarily becomes a showy parade of pride in spiritual gifts and achievements, permeated with envy of others' accomplishments. Such pride and envy will also create an insatiable appetite for spiritual experiences that will prove we have met, or can gain, God's approval. Jesus wants to liberate us from the unappeasable demands of personal merit. Thus, he must turn us away from the mistaken belief that the perfection of our performance will gain his favor. To do so he introduces us to a rich young man who wants to use his "major league" religious performance to gain God's favor:

MARK 10:17-22

17As Jesus started on his way, a man ran up to him and fell on his knees before him. "Good teacher," he asked, "what must I do to inherit eternal life?"

18"Why do you call me good?" Jesus answered. "No one is good— except God alone. 19You know the commandments: 'Do not murder, do not commit adultery, do not steal, do not give false testimony, do not defraud, honor your father and mother.'"

20"Teacher," he declared, "all these I have kept since I was a boy."

21Jesus looked at him and loved him. "One thing you lack," he said. "Go, sell everything you have and give to the poor, and you will have treasure in heaven. Then come, follow me."

22At this the man's face fell. He went away sad, because he had great wealth.

This account of the rich young man may seem a strange place to learn the nature of repentance. We typically think of this young man as one who refuses to repent. Yet by this inverse image we are able to distinguish what true repentance must be and, perhaps, may see enough of ourselves mirrored to seek a new path toward God. Acting virtually as the "coach" of our repentance, Jesus uses this encounter to say to us, "See? See how this young man strives to make himself right before God? See how he uses his words and his actions to convince himself that he deserves what God grants? Don't do that! You need to repent of all confidence in your accomplishments—as well as all fault in your failures—to know God's grace."

Repentance that rests on grace alone is not easily reconciled with our instinctive patterns of thought, so Jesus arrests our attention with the surprising way that he responds to the young man's request. Jesus' words trouble us because they initially seem to affirm the young man's suspicion that we earn God's favor with our good deeds. However, Jesus uses the desires and claims of the young man to reveal to him—and to us—the anemia of human goodness even when it engages in religious exercise. Against the background of the cross, and with the example of the young man, Jesus tells us that though the outward form of our spiritual observances may be great, and the mechanics of our religious performance seemingly perfect, they still lack what is needed for spiritual health.

This lesson is particularly apt for those whose religious exercises are conscientious and disciplined. Especially in church settings where we consistently teach the importance of obedience to God, there can be a strong inclination to see what we do so meticulously, strenuously, seriously, and sacrificially as what secures our standing with God. It will not. While God requires and blesses our obedience, we do not secure our eternal relationship with him by our actions. Even words of repentance will not heal when they become only a religious ritual we repeat to make ourselves right with God. Why? What keeps well-intended religiosity from qualifying as biblical repentance? We learn the answer by identifying what is missing from this religious young man's heart even as he bows before Jesus and calls him "good teacher."

A LOATHING OF SIN'S EVIL

Jesus works in behalf of this rich man by causing a number of powerful spiritual truths to converge that should make the man perceive the depth of his spiritual poverty. Jesus points first to the uniqueness of God's holiness.

THE HOLINESS OF OUR GOD

The young man runs up to Jesus and addresses him as "Good teacher" (v. 17). To this courteous greeting Christ offers a troubling but instructive rebuke: "Why do you call me good? . . . No one is good—except God" (v. 18). True repentance always begins by understanding the astonishing truth of this simple statement: only God is good. There is none like him. No one is comparable. No one measures up. Between his perfection and our performance there is a gulf unbridgeable by human means. As high as the heavens are above the earth, so far is God's goodness above our own.

Jesus' words echo the experience of the prophet Isaiah, who saw a vision of God on his throne above the earth (Isa. 6:1-8). Though Isaiah's world was falling apart due to the corruption of the people of Israel, God remained undiminished, even untouched by the deterioration of human affairs. The essence of our God's holiness is that he is wholly other. He is separate from anything that would sully his glory or diminish his perfection. He is majestic, elevated, high and lifted up. He is not entangled by his creatures' failures. He is not tainted by earth's stain. He is pure. The radiance from that purity is so brilliant that even the heavenly hosts cover their eyes and themselves in his presence. They want neither to see nor to be seen in the intensity of the blinding and burning illumination of God's holy glory. Nothing created, either in heaven or on earth, appears as virtuous in the presence of this glorious holiness. Only God is truly good.

Before the purity of God's nature, all human righteousness withers into inadequacy. Many sensed this anew at the national clergy conference hosted by the Promise Keepers movement in February 1996. Forty-five thousand church leaders gathered in the Georgia Dome in Atlanta. During one of their meetings a conference leader led the clergy in an antiphonal recitation of the angelic chant of Isaiah 6: "Holy, holy, holy is the Lord Almighty; the whole earth is full of his glory." As the forty-five thousand voices filled the stadium with the resounding proclamation of the holiness of God, some got out of their seats and knelt on the ground. Others fell face-downward in recognition and honor of the majesty of God's holiness.

These church leaders' worship demonstrated why <u>true repentance starts with recognition of the holiness of our God.</u> We cannot rightly perceive the greatness of his goodness without apprehending the puniness of our own. Such a realization causes us to fall down in humility before God as did psalmist and apostle when apprehension of God's unique goodness tore from their hearts this assessment of humanity: "There is no one that does good, not even one" (Rom. 3:12; cf. Ps. 14:3). Only God is good.

THE REALITY OF OUR SIN

Jesus knows that the young man will not apprehend the significance of God alone being good, so he engineers an exchange that should clarify the truth. To the young man's question, "What must I do to inherit eternal life?" Jesus replies, in essence, "Keep the commandments" (Mark 10:18-19).

Jesus' response startles us. It sounds as though he is telling the young man that good works really do forge the path of salvation. Before we go further, we have to ask, did Jesus really believe that our deeds would save us?

The answer lies within the passage. The account begins with the words, "As Jesus started on his way . . ." (v. 17), and by its end we learn where he was going. "We are going up to Jerusalem," he [Jesus] said, "and the Son of Man will be betrayed to the chief priests and teachers of the law. They will condemn him to death and will hand him over to the Gentiles, who will mock him and spit on him, flog him and kill him. Three days later he will rise" (vv. 33-34). Christ's plan makes it clear that he did not believe that our works would save us. He knew that he had to die for that. Jesus' instructions to the rich young man do not reflect a plan of salvation, but underscore the Lord's plan of revelation—to help the man see himself.

The young man asks, "What must I do to inherit eternal life?" The question itself reveals a certain amount of hubris. We cannot *do* anything to *inherit* something. What we inherit comes to us by virtue of our birth and what someone else has done (which is a vital spiritual truth for those who believe that we inherit heaven as a result of our rebirth and what Christ has done). But Jesus plays along with the pretentious question by offering a preposterous answer.

Jesus says, "If you want to get eternal life from a holy God on the basis of what *you* do, then keep all of his commandments." That is to say, "If you really think that it's all up to you, then the way that you gain eternal life is plain: be perfect!" Samuel Bolton explains the rationale of Christ's strategy:

> When men will be saviors of themselves, when they look for righteousness by the law, Christ bids them go and keep the commandments . . . and this He does to humble them and bring them to Himself. But if men are humble and broken by a sight of their sins, then, without mention of the law at all, He comforts them with the free promises of grace, saying: "Come unto Me, all ye that labor and are heavy laden, and I will ease you. . . ."[1]

The young man's proposal to justify himself before God is plain to Jesus, and clarifies why Jesus must speak to him in such an abrupt manner.

Even more preposterous is what the young man says next. To Jesus' proposal that he should keep all the commandments, the young man replies, "Teacher, . . . all these I have kept since I was a boy" (v. 20). We must consider these words in the light of those preceding. Jesus has just said, "Only God is good." Now, what does the young man reply only seconds later? "I am, too"!

With his claim to have kept *all* the commandments, the man elevates himself to the stature of God. In doing so, he has committed the worst sin possible for a Jew: he has broken the first commandment against having other gods. Yet because he does not perceive how preposterous is his claim to have achieved the holiness that God requires and alone possesses, the man remains unaware of the horror of his wrong. The words of the book of Revelation well apply to this man:

> "You say, 'I am rich; I have acquired wealth and do not need a thing.' But you do not realize that you are wretched, pitiful, poor, blind and naked" (Rev. 3:17).

The rich young man's words and actions remind us that, <u>without apprehension of God's holiness, we cannot see the reality of our sin</u>. True repentance must include awareness of the magnitude of our spiritual destitution; therefore real repentance must begin with recognition of God's incomparable and unachievable holiness.

When we do not apprehend the true nature of our wrongdoing, we do not hate it sufficiently to seek its expulsion. True repentance requires grief and remorse that cries out, "How could I have done such a thing? Please, God, take the guilt and presence of this evil from my life!"

Without such a loathing of the sin that has been magnified by God's holiness, not only will we fail to repent, we will not even see our wrong. Steve Brown, the wonderful radio preacher of grace, recently reported the reaction of a man to a sermon in which Steve confessed to being "a sinner as much in need of God's pardoning grace as anyone else." Said the man afterwards, "All my life, I've heard pastors and missionaries say what awful sinners they are, but you are the first one I believe . . . because you seem to believe it."[2] Confession of such need of grace will not come until we begin viewing our lives from heaven's holy perspective.

Few of us will believe that we are in dire need of repentance if we base our understanding of our own need on comparisons to the obvious failings of others. It is the comparison to God's holiness that makes what is minor in the world's eyes wrenching to the Christian heart. That is why Paul would say, late in his ministry, "Christ Jesus came into the world to save sinners—of whom I am the worst" (1 Tim. 1:15). As Paul grew in Christ, he became increasingly aware of his sinfulness before a holy God.[3] The more our understanding of God matures, the more we recognize our need of repentance.

I too must recognize that true repentance will not come until I believe that I am the worst of sinners. This does not mean that I have committed the most heinous of crimes. Rather, I must acknowledge that with the privileges, position, background, and knowledge God has given me, my sin is a greater betrayal of my Savior than the actions of those who act in ignorance and disadvantage. None of us can truly repent nor become spiritually mature until this realization and humility grips us.

THE EVIL OF OUR RIGHTEOUSNESS

To make us realize how great is our need of repentance, Jesus gives us a special perspective in this passage. To expose this young ruler to the depth of his sin Jesus, who knows that the young man will not face his sin, confronts him with "the evil of our righteousness." The early American evangelist George Whitefield first used this phrase, to confront the self-righteous with the inadequacy of their own goodness to qualify them for heaven.

I rediscovered the arresting power of Whitefield's phrase when recently talking with another pastor in an airport restaurant about the nature of true repentance. When I said, "George Whitefield taught that we need to sense not only the evil of our sin but the evil of our righteousness," a woman listening nearby turned to us. "Oh no!" she said. "Do you mean that I have to feel guilty for good, too?" I smiled and said, "No, that is not really the point, but God wants us to know that our good works are not good enough to make him love us. That is why we need Jesus no matter how good we think we are." The goodness in our good works can be truly good and a blessing to others. There is a danger in making people think that there is nothing they can do that will please God or help others. Still, there is never sufficient goodness in our best works to make them truly holy by God's ultimate standard.[4] That is why our best works still fall short of qualifying us for heaven.

A problem of wealth?

Jesus must make plain to the rich young man the inadequacy of our best works for building a ladder to heaven. When the man says that he has kept all the commandments, Jesus probably at least raises a mental eyebrow and observes the situation. Here is a man who has just blasphemed God by claiming to be as holy as he; yet this blasphemer thinks he is good enough for God! So if he really thinks that he has fulfilled all of God's law, what can

Jesus require that will make the man realize that our goodness, even remark-able goodness, falls short of all the holiness God requires?

Jesus indicates that the man only lacks "one thing" to gain what he desires. Then Jesus indicates the magnitude of that one thing. Jesus says that the young man must, "go sell everything you have and give to the poor. . . . Then come, follow me" (Mark 10:21). By his appearance and responses the young man has made it plain that he is living for himself. When Jesus identifies this "one thing" lacking, the man readily recognizes what Jesus requires. He requires everything.

We should not interpret Jesus' words as meaning that all wealthy people must give away all their money in order to gain heaven. While Jesus makes it clear that wealth can be a stumbling block to our trusting in him (v. 25), God also grants wealth for his purposes (e.g., 1 Chron. 29:12-14; Prov. 22:4; Luke 8:3; Acts 16:14-15). Before we give all our wealth away (for in comparison to most of the world, virtually everyone in North America is "wealthy"), we should recognize the danger of inverting the message of this account. Were we to teach that any great act of human effort or charity qualifies us for heaven, then we would fall into the error of the rich young man's perspective.

Christ's message to this young man is that nothing we can do will give us standing before God; nothing we can do is enough. Even if the man were to sell all he has and give to the poor, he still must continue to "fol-low" Jesus. And if the rich young man were to follow Jesus, where would that road lead? It would lead to a cross in Jerusalem where Jesus will show that his resources alone can pay what God requires.

A rite of passage!

Even marvelous obedience does not contain sufficient goodness to merit God's acceptance. This understanding matures our repentance as we real-ize that, if even our best works fall short of God's holy requirements, then our faults are all the more despicable.

One of the things my father taught all his sons was how to use a cross-cut saw. His daddy and his daddy's daddy had taught their sons, and my father was not going to let this rite of passage for rural Southern manhood end with him. One brisk fall morning, we began sawing on a log that we did not know had a rotten core. When we had just sawed partially through the log, it split and fell off the sawing frame. The timber hit the ground so hard that a large piece was sheared off the rotten log. In my childhood imagination the unusual shape of the sheared piece looked like a horse head. It so captured my interest that I took it home with me after that day of sawing.

For my father's next birthday, I attached a length of two-by-four board to that log head, attached a rope tail, and stuck on some sticks to act as legs. Then I halfway hammered in a dozen or so nails down the two-by-four body of that "horse," wrapped the whole thing in butcher block paper, put a bow on it, and presented it to my father. When he took off the wrapping, he smiled and said, "Thank you, it's wonderful . . . what is it?"

"It's a tie rack, Dad," I said. "See, you can put your ties on those nails going down the side of the horse's body." My father smiled again and thanked me. Then he leaned the horse against his closet wall (because the stick legs could not keep it standing upright) and for years he used it as a tie rack.

Now when I first gave my father that rotten-log-horse-head tie rack, I really thought it was "good." In my childish mind this creation was a work of art ready for the Metropolitan Museum. But as I matured, I realized that my work was not nearly as good as I had once thought. In fact, I understood ultimately that my father had received and used my gift not because of its goodness but out of *his* goodness. In a similar way our heavenly Father receives our gifts, not so much because they deserve his love, but because he *is* love.

A new measure

The "great disproportion" between our good works and God's holiness never goes away in this life. Our works will never earn God's affection, just as they will never merit his pardon. Our best deeds will never be sufficiently free of the contamination of human motive and imperfection that they are acceptable to God on their own merit.[5] As the authors of the *Westminster Confession* wrote,

> . . . [A]s they are wrought by us, they [our good works] are defiled, and mixed with so much weakness and imperfection, that they cannot endure the severity of God's judgment.
>
> . . . [B]elievers being accepted through Christ, their good works also are accepted in Him; not as though they were in this life wholly unblameable and unreprovable in God's sight; but that He, looking upon them in His Son, is pleased to accept and reward that which

is sincere, although accompanied with many weaknesses and imperfections.[6]

Not only do our good works not pardon our sin; they are, in fact, so mixed with our sinfulness that, if God did not act in love, they would actually be subject to his judgment. This understanding of the "evil of our righteousness" gives us a new measuring rod for our sin, which we would not dare to use were we not certain of God's grace.

If even our good works are blameworthy, then what is the true character of our sin? The answer can only be that it is utterly abhorrent to God, and should be to us. We cannot repent until this reality has hit us. John Colquhoun, in his classic description of the means of spiritual growth, wrote that true repentance is characterized by "a sense not only of our evil doings, but of the evil of our doings; not only of our sin but of the exceeding sinfulness of our sin."[7]

The repentance that enables our progressive sanctification does not come without our learning to loathe the evil of our wrongdoing. This loathing becomes the true attitude of our hearts as we meditate on the holiness of our God, the reality of our sin, and even the evil of our righteousness. These are the graces of perception that God supplies in his Word to break us from our affection for the sin that so easily entangles us (Heb. 12:1).

God wants us to understand the true malignancy of our sin—the problem is too severe to be remedied by our goodness. Even if the extent of the disease is not readily apparent to human eyes, the Bible's analysis of the seriousness of our condition should cause us to examine all the arteries, vessels, and capillaries of the way we live. As we test all our relationships, patterns of speech, entertainments, habits, and even religious practices, we progressively discover the cancerous cells that threaten our spiritual health. These discoveries will create healthy dissatisfaction with our level of personal goodness even as they turn us toward the true means of our ultimate healing.

A new discernment

A friend told me recently of his pastor's response to a sharp criticism. The pastor's response to his critic was, "I will listen to every word that you have to say and take it to the Lord for examination. I want to be corrected if I am wrong." Remarkable to the man who reported this to me was his pastor's greater desire to discern the possible evil in his own heart than to dodge blame or reproof. This is the mark of a repentant heart: it recognizes the awfulness of sin (even hidden sin) and listens to the prompting of the Spirit and the counsel of others to see "if there is any offensive way in me" (Ps. 139:24). The unrepentant person cannot face sin, and therefore seeks to blame others, minimize the sin, or deny its presence. The repentant person sees sin as it truly is—an assault on the peace and purity of the soul—and thus is thankful for correction.

The benefits of repentance for the relationships of our lives were reflected in a recent letter from Ugandan missionary Rick Gray. He wrote of an event in his life that demonstrated the necessity of discerning the contaminating evil even in a work as noble as translating catechism lessons:

> . . . I need to be aware of my subtle tendency to make ministry an end in itself: whereby I do things so that I can feel good about myself. . . . [A]nother peril of ministry becoming too activity-focused is that it causes me to lose sight of Jesus, and to lose the sense of His Spirit's leading. While checking the 1st draft of the "Katekisimo" [catechism] I became intent on finishing a certain amount of pages per day. One afternoon as time was ticking away, and my dear Mubwisi co-translator struggled to come up with just the right Lubwisi word to express the English meaning, I grew impatient with him. I became harsh and unsympathetic to his inability to go faster. My penchant to get the job done blinded me to Christ's presence with us, and deafened me to the Spirit's conviction of my sin.
>
> Unless I maintain a Jesus-centeredness in the midst of ministry, I will be unable to love people well and bring glory to God. Only as I realize my self-worth is determined by how awesome is the Savior's love for me, and not by how productive is my work for Him, will I be free from my drivenness and need to accomplish tasks. When I gaze upon his nail-pierced hands and believe they are actually reaching out to embrace me, then I am empowered to reach out with similar compassion and care to those around me.[8]

The understanding that we should desire repentance because it removes contaminants from our relationship with God and with others helps distinguish false from true repentance. False repentance is less concerned with the spiritual contamination of sin than it is with the personal consequences of sin. True repentance is chiefly concerned with the wrong we have done to our Savior and to others. Repentance of the first kind is

self-preoccupied; true repentance is a selfless seeking of spiritual fellowship
and renewal. False repentance flees correction; true repentance seeks it.

———— A LONGING FOR SIN'S CURE ————

Because true repentance makes us sense the depth and awfulness of sin, it
naturally leads to the next element of repentance that is missing in the rich
young ruler's responses. If our sin is truly abhorrent to us, then we want to be
rid of it. We long for a cure to the disease of sin. At least two attitudes characterize this longing: a desire to offer confession, and a desire to receive grace.

A DESIRE TO OFFER CONFESSION

Again Jesus indicates what true repentance requires by making clear what
the rich young man will not offer. In his professing that he has kept all the
laws, the rich man displays not only his ignorance of the real requirements
of the Law but also his lack of desire to open his heart to God. When the
Spirit has truly touched our hearts regarding the presence and awfulness of
our sin, confession leaps to our lips. We see our sin for the spiritual poison
that it is, and we long to spit it out. This young man indicates no such
longing. He desires to receive reward rather than to offer confession (Mark
10:17). True repentance is not so much asking, "What honor do I get from
my faith?" but rather, "How may I give myself in humility to God?" The
heart that is most spiritually sensitive and committed is simultaneously
most aware of its need of grace.[9]

   During the Great Awakening, when the Spirit of God revived much of
our nation's early faith, Jonathan Edwards was presiding over a massive
prayer meeting. Eight hundred men prayed with him. Into that meeting a
woman sent a message asking the men to pray for her husband. The note
described a man who in spiritual pride had become unloving, prideful,
and difficult. Edwards read the message in private and then, thinking that
perhaps the man described was present, the great preacher made a bold
request. Edwards first read the note to the eight hundred men. Then he
asked if the man who had been described would raise his hand, so that the
whole assembly could pray for him.

   Three hundred men raised their hands. Each had been convicted by
the Spirit of their sin, and now they longed to confess. A repentant life is so

characterized. Rather than hiding sin, or minimizing it, or blaming others, the repentant heart longs to confess.

Humble acknowledgment of our wrong characterizes the prayer times of the repentant life. We do not hide from God matters large or small, obvious or obscure. We not only want to confess to God the sin we are aware of, we pray for his Holy Spirit to reveal the things hidden from our own consciences so that we might confess them as well (Ps. 19:12-14). True repentance is evident when we are as much concerned about deep and hidden sins as we are about the faults that others can observe. The repentant heart desires full confession. It is more concerned about relationship with God than about reputation among men (Ps. 51:4-6).

A DESIRE TO RECEIVE GRACE

If we know that our best works will not merit pardon for sin, and we long to confess wrong so that we may be rid of it, then what ultimately must we seek? We ultimately seek grace. Unlike the rich young man, who wants to "do" something so that he can broker his good works into spiritual blessing (Mark 10:17), the repentant heart senses its unworthiness and yearns for God to fix the damage to our souls that we cannot fix.

A Christian friend told me recently that he and his wife had discovered that their daughter had disobeyed them and handled the family car in a way that caused an accident. The daughter could not afford to pay for the repairs or the traffic ticket. So the parents paid for the repairs and the fine with the agreement that their daughter would pay them back over time. The parents did not need her money, but hoped that making her responsible would help teach her lessons needed for her own safety and maturity.

The payback system required some discipline and diligence from the daughter, and she struggled to keep the arrangements. The parents had to keep reminding her of her obligations, which frustrated the daughter as well as the parents. Finally, after one of the reminding sessions, the daughter exploded: "Daddy, don't you and Mom know that I realize what I did was wrong? I know I was irresponsible. I know it is my problem. I wish you all would just get off my case so that I could figure out a way to fix this." Replied her father, "Honey, what I really want you to figure out is that by yourself you can't fix this."

Our heavenly Father's words are quite similar. Because we too easily echo the words of the rich young man—"What must I do . . . ?"—God replies, "What I really want you to know is that what you 'do' will never be enough to fix your situation. Your sin is too great and your abilities are too limited for you to fix the mess of your life. You need my grace. You must turn away from all of your own resources and trust that only what I provide will fix your situation."

A willingness to rest

We can mentally assent to these truths about grace without applying them to the ways we actually deal with guilt. The failure of grace to affect our hearts may be evident in our very words of confession. What we consider "our repentance" may simply be a good work that we are trying to offer God as a way of brokering our pardon. We can find ourselves saying, in effect, "See, God, I feel real guilty. I got down on my knees, prayed the prayer for pardon, and tried to make things right. I said and did what you wanted. Now are you happy?"

There is nothing intrinsically wrong with any single component of such repentance, unless we are trusting that offering such a plea to God will make him forgive us. If we view repentance in this way, we make repentance itself a work. In effect, we offer God the bribe of our contrition for his forgiveness. While contrition is necessary, the degree and duration of our remorse is not what earns our pardon. We have already seen that no human activity is without stain before God's holiness. This means that even the "work" of repentance cannot merit forgiveness.

Repentance is not so much a doing as a depending. It is not so much a striving for pardon as a posture of humility. In true repentance we confess our total reliance on God's mercy. We acknowledge the inadequacy of anything we would offer God to gain his pardon. In true repentance we rest upon God's grace rather than trying to do anything to deserve it. We lean heavily on the words of Isaiah: "In repentance and rest is your salvation, in quietness and trust is your strength" (Isa. 30:15).[10]

Reliance on God alone for mercy is the essence of repentance. We can make a grave mistake by overemphasizing the human-action implications of "repentance" supposedly derived from the biblical term's historical origins. The Hebrew word we translate as repentance means "to turn."[11] If we are not careful, we may press this vocabulary insight to imply that repentance is primarily a turning from doing bad things to doing good things or, at least, saying the right things to God. Repentance is not a work of turning to new behaviors or to any conjured phrases or emotions in us. The songwriter reminds us, "Not what I feel or do can give me peace with God;

not all my prayers and sighs and tears can bear my awful load."[12] Such human efforts cannot be our basis for being made right with God.

Repentance is not a turning from one category of works to another; rather it is a turning from human works entirely to God. *The Westminster Shorter Catechism* says this beautifully in answering the question: "What is repentance unto life?" The answer:

> Repentance unto life is a saving grace, whereby a sinner, out of a true sense of his sin, and apprehension of the mercy of God in Christ, doth, with grief and hatred of his sin, turn from it unto God, with full purpose of, and endeavor after, new obedience.[13]

New obedience follows true repentance, but we put no hope for pardon in what we do. Repentance is not real if we have no intention of correcting our ways, but the correction is not a condition of our forgiveness.

In biblical repentance we turn to God alone—relying on his mercy and grace—not to anything in us or done by us in order to secure his mercy. These truths also indicate that, while Scripture commands us to identify our sin and sorrow for it, neither the accuracy of our identification of the sin nor the degree of our sorrow for it compels God to forgive us. There is great comfort in this for the conscientious believer who recognizes that we are always inaccurate (or incomplete) in our perception of sin and never adequate in our remorse for it.

We can confess whatever our heart knows to be our sin, with the confidence that God's heart is large enough to cover what we are unable fully to expose (Ps. 19:12-13). In so doing we even confess the inadequacy of our repentance, with the confidence that we can rest under the broad mantle of his grace. Like the man who cried to Jesus, "I believe, help my unbelief" (see Mark 9:24), we should be able to say to God, "I repent even of the inadequacy of my repentance, in order that I may rely solely on your mercy."

Remorse precedes true repentance. Changed behavior follows true repentance. But this necessary prelude and postlude of true repentance are *not* themselves the essence of repentance. True repentance is a denial that anything in us ever would or ever could satisfy God's holiness or compel his pardon. We humbly concede that we can offer him nothing for what he alone can give. Then we rest in his promise to forgive those who humbly seek him. Remorse for our sin makes us repentant; but it should also make us so aware of the inability of our hearts adequately to register what God requires, that we do not trust our sorrow to make us right with God. Similarly, while our gratitude for God's pardon should make us "endeavor after new obedience," the very source of our gratitude—awareness of the awful shortcoming of all our actions—keeps us from trusting in our obedience to make us deserving of God's forgiveness.

A desire for renewal

Repentance, therefore, is fundamentally a humble expression of a desire for a renewed relationship with God—a relationship that we confess can be secured only by his grace. We long for his pardon, presence, and Spirit to repair the damage our sin has caused to our relationship with him. Through this we learn another mark of false repentance: a primary concern with bartering away the consequences of sin. True repentance, though certainly not desiring to face those consequences, willingly accepts them if they move us closer to fellowship with and understanding of our God. This is so because biblical repentance is primarily concerned with the renewal of our fellowship with him.

True repentance that springs from a desire for renewed intimacy with God is never the fruit of fleeing the punitive God of our imaginations. Mindful of God's love, we approach him with humility but also with deep longing. Repentant hearts cry out to him as for a distant loved one, "Let me draw near to you, my Lord. My heart and my flesh cry out for the living God. How I yearn for the reality of your love afresh in my life. Please do not persist in anger for my sin, but let me know your unfailing love" (cf. Ps. 84 and 85). Only awareness of unfailing divine love can produce what the repentant heart seeks when it prays, "Create in me a pure heart, O God, and renew a steadfast spirit within me. Do not cast me from your presence or take your Holy Spirit from me. Restore to me the joy of your salvation and grant me a willing spirit, to sustain me" (Ps. 51:10-12).

Repentance confesses to God, "God, forgive me. The allure of this temptation was more real to me than the beauties of your promises and presence." Repentance implores God, "Please graciously restore the reality of your care into my heart and life, so that your love will be so precious that I cannot further exist with my betrayal of you. Help me to meditate more upon the character of your love revealed by Christ's sacrifice than upon the circumstances of my life that make me doubt you." Repentance petitions, "God, I want to seek you the way simple people do when they say that they know you are near by the way that your Word has become alive in their souls." None but the biblically repentant heart seeks after God with such unashamed love.

——— A LOVING OF THE SAVIOR ———

To love God as fervently as biblical repentance requires, we must know his character. So we are also led, in this account of the unrepentant rich man, to see deeply into the heart of our Savior. This revelation only makes more sad the preoccupation with self that keeps the rich young man from giving himself to the One who is Love.

True repentance (which the rich young man lacks) demands apprehension of the ugliness of sin, but it also requires seeing the beauty of the Savior. Even if our wrongdoing is abhorrent to us, we still will not turn to the One who can deal with it if he is no more attractive to us than our sin. This is why Paul reminds us that "God's kindness leads you toward repentance" (Rom. 2:4). If we perceive God only to be an ogre in the sky waiting to pounce on those who do not properly bow and scrape, then biblical repentance—requiring a love response to God—is impossible. Thus, to make true repentance not only possible but desirable, the Gospel of Mark lets us peek behind the curtain of the Savior's thoughts so that we will know his character and desire his fellowship.

Delight in His Vision

In view of the young man's blasphemous boasts, few verses are more precious in Scripture than the one that describes Jesus' attitude toward him. How does Jesus react to the rich man who has just refused to acknowledge his sin and has portrayed himself as being the equal of God? Allowing us to see behind the Savior's eyes, the Bible says, "Jesus looked at him and loved him" (Mark 10:21). This revelation of the undeterred heart of our Lord should serve as a magnet to our souls when we have wandered from his ways.

I remember the night in high school when I stayed out too late, well beyond my curfew. I had been having fun with my friends, and the time got away from me. I was wrong and no excuse would make my actions right. I did not want to go home, because I thought that I knew what was waiting for me there. An arms-crossed, toe-tapping, voice-raised, punishment-dispensing set of parents would be at the door. Knowing that each minute of further delay was digging me deeper into trouble, I still didn't rush to go home. I simply could not motivate myself to go and confront the anger that I was sure was waiting for me.

There was no incentive to turn from my wrong, when I believed that my return home would only commence my punishment. When I finally did go home, an upset mother and father met me as I expected, but their reactions were a surprise. Though they told me that we would have to deal with the wrong the next morning, they hugged me and told me how happy they were that I was safe. Though I had sinned against them, they said and showed that they loved me. I may have missed a curfew a few times after that, but never by so much. And never again did I fear going home.

Because I knew my parents' love even in their correction, I matured under their care. This is our heavenly Father's intention also. He encourages us to turn to him in repentance, not by promising that there will be no correction for our sin, but by showing us his heart through the ministry of Jesus. This account paints the rich young man's sin darkly so that the love of Jesus will shine more brightly. He is able to love even those who arrogantly resist his will. He can know the worst of our sin and still look at us and love us. Because God's character never changes, he looks at us in our sin and still loves us. His arms remain open, and his ears are still attentive to our cry. He may be angry at our rebellion, but he is never angry at our return (2 Chron. 30:9; Isa. 44:22; Jer. 3:14, 22; 4:1; Joel 2:12-13; Zech. 1:3). His kindness draws us back to him and away from our sin.

DELIGHT IN HIS PATH

The quality of the love in Christ's arms is revealed not only by the look in his eyes at this stage of his journey but also in his sacrifice at the journey's end. The beauty of our Savior shines in both the love he showed and in the life he shared. For our blasphemies and pride, for our rebellion and arrogance, he would surrender himself to die (Mark 10:33). The beauty of love displayed in our Lord's willingness to walk this path encourages us to walk with him just as he encouraged the rich young man to do.

My first "date" with my wife came when I was on an outing with her family. As the new, single minister of their little country church, I was invited to the family's picnic. We went to a restored Victorian-era village known as Elsah, Illinois, snuggled into the bluffs along the Mississippi River.

Though the October air was cool, the day was bright, and after our lunch the young woman I had just met offered to show me the village, which she had already visited many times. Against the brilliant hues of the fall leaves in the sunlight, this beautiful blonde with green eyes in a red sweater asked me, "Would you like to take a walk with me?" It was not a difficult question to answer. I said, "You bet!" Her beauty made me delight to follow her.

Jesus reveals a different kind of beauty about himself, of course, in this passage as he shows his love for the unlovable. Still, seeing our Lord's loveliness of heart, we know what the young man's response should be when Jesus says, "Follow me" (v. 21). The natural response to one who has seen the beauty of the Savior is to follow him.

We delight to walk with our Lord down the path of life because through our repentance we have understood how altogether lovely he is (Song 5:16). Our obedience is not the foundation or condition of God's receiving our repentance; it is the natural outflow of a heart that has experienced his grace. Our new willingness to follow Christ helps reassure us that we have experienced the transforming power of grace. Our delight in walking with him validates love for him in our hearts even amid remorse for sin against him. Thus, though there may be many stumbles and setbacks along the path, true repentance leads naturally to new obedience.

Though the Bible does not teach that obedience is a condition of God's pardon, it cautions against thinking that God will forgive where there is no real change of heart. God is not waiting for us to fix our lives before he forgives us, for then none would be forgiven; but he does not promise forgiveness where repentance is not sincere. While we should not delay repentance until we have corrected our sin, we also should not think that God will accept repentance from a heart still in rebellion against him. If repentance is only a tool to manipulate God into averting the consequences of our wrongdoing, without any real intention of changing our ways, then we should remember that God will not hear those who cherish sin in their heart (see Ps. 66:18; James 4:6).

Still, God is pleased to receive sincere confession "although accompanied by many weaknesses and imperfections."[14] He will forgive even though we remain susceptible to temptation and may repeatedly fail to do what he—and we ourselves—desire (cf. Gal. 5:17; Rom. 7:19-25). Through repentance God provides the spiritual nourishment we need to walk his path, even though we may need to partake of that sustenance many times. What will keep us returning to the table of repentance is delight in the fare that our Lord spreads for us there—his pardon, his grace, his tutelage, his love, and our joy.

DELIGHT IN HIM

The reason we should keep on the Savior's path despite the stumbles that distress us is evident in the mental state of the rich young man as the story ends. As he leaves without repentance, there is something else missing from his life: he has no joy. "He went away sad, because he had great wealth" (Mark 10:22).

We ought to ask, "Why did he go away sad? He still had all his money." The simple answer is that he did not have Jesus. By not being willing to leave his other god, wealth, the young man kept himself from fellowship with the Lord. He denied himself the blessings of walking with his Savior.

In terms that we wish the rich young man would understand, songwriter Lynn DeShazo describes the repentant heart's perception of Christ:

Lord, you are more precious than silver,
Lord, you are more costly than gold,
Lord, you are more beautiful than diamonds,
And nothing I desire compares with you.[15]

Repentance that renews precious fellowship with our incomparably wonderful God ultimately furthers our joy. Just as we cannot enter into true repentance without *sorrow* for our guilt, we cannot emerge from true repentance without *joy* for our release from shame.

Neither of these emotions merits forgiveness or makes repentance work, but repentance operates effectively only within the environment of a conscience filled with *both* of these natural responses to grace. This is why, after his sin with Bathsheba, David confesses to God, "Against you, you only have I sinned and done what is evil in your sight," and prays also, "Let me hear joy and gladness; let the bones you have crushed rejoice. . . . Restore to me the joy of your salvation. . . . O Lord, open my lips, and my mouth will declare your praise" (Ps. 51:4, 8, 12, 15). Thus, the repentant life is characterized by each of the following: an apprehension of the destitution of all our works; a confession of wrong with a willingness to turn from it; *and,* an appreciation for the pardoning grace of God, which results in joy.

REPENTANCE THAT SINGS

If we could see the dimensions of spiritual illness as plainly as we can the effects of physical disease, then perhaps the nature and effects of repentance would be more obvious to us. On November 8, 1995, Dan and Carol Walker welcomed to the world a newborn son, Joel Daniel. Just ten or fifteen minutes after the newborn had finished his first feeding, he turned completely blue and went limp in his mother's hands. Carol screamed, "What's wrong with my baby?"

A nurse took Joel Daniel from his mother's arms and ran with the newborn to the nursery to try to restore his breathing. Carol later wrote, "Dan, myself, and others in the room began praying earnestly that our boy would live. Each passing moment seemed like an eternity. We wanted the miracle of life for our son! The next minutes and hours we continued to cry out to God on behalf of our firstborn child. Finally, the nurse came in with the words, 'Your son is alive.'"

Due to a rare disorder that kept a valve at the base of the child's esophagus from operating properly, his life had been in greater danger than anyone had known. This one episode did not end the danger. After repeated crises, the parents desperately wanted the surgery that would provide a cure. Despite the difficulty such early surgery would be for them and their baby, Carol and Dan longed for it. When the day of the surgery came, friends gathered with the parents in the baby's hospital room to await the outcome. Again, prayers were earnestly offered for the health of the child. Finally, the doctor came to report that the surgery was over, and that Joel Daniel would be fine. The small crowd in the room cheered, and burst into spontaneous singing of the Doxology:

> Praise God from whom all blessings flow;
> praise him all creatures here below,
> praise him above, ye heavenly host:
> praise Father, Son, and Holy Ghost.[16]

When they perceived how great was the physical danger, these parents longed for a cure. Then, in recognition of their personal helplessness, they called for the one who could help. They put themselves entirely in the healing hands of another and, when help mercifully came, they were filled with joy.

When the attack of sin on our soul is as real to us as such a physical attack on our bodies, then how we are to seek God's help and respond to it will be clear. In the light of God's holiness, we will perceive how awful is the disease of our sin and how helpless we are against it. Then we will cry out to God for the help that he alone can give. And when his mercy has made us whole, recognizing how great is our rescue we will experience overwhelming joy.

Viewing the spiritual dynamics of repentance through the analogy of a physical healing corrects some common misconceptions of what God expects of us. No one doubts that God expects repentance, but what characterizes a repentant life? As most would expect, a repentant heart expresses an honest loathing of our spiritual disease, and a longing for God to heal our relationship with him. But surprising as it may seem, a life characterized by repentance also exhibits joy. When we have seen the malignancy of the sin in our soul, and have perceived how freely God's mercy flows to remove it from our lives, then we naturally exhibit joy.

The evidence of complete repentance is not the stereotypical gritted teeth and grinding resolve, or even groaning and groveling. The reverberations of repentance sound more like singing. Yes, God can lead us through a dark night of the soul to enable us to see and to grieve for sin. And as we wrestle against our pride and rebellion to find rest in the mercy of God, we may know great pain. But when we have understood, trusted, and received the freeing grace of repentance, rejoicing fills our hearts. Without this joy that is our strength, the new obedience that should be the fruit of true repentance is impossible. Like the rich young man we, too, go away sad and unwilling to follow Jesus. By contrast, biblical repentance renews in us thanksgiving and gratitude for God's mercy. Knowing his pardon, we delight to serve him with a childlike love and a willing mind. Repentance renews our joy.

Escape from Temptation

First-time father Michael Bryson was not about to let his wife's first real Mother's Day pass unnoticed. He wrapped up his six-month-old son, Jason, plunked him in a baby carrier, and went to the hospital where Miriam Bryson worked as a nurse. Then in front of patients and coworkers alike Michael surprised Miriam with flowers, candy, and balloons that said, "World's Greatest Mom." It was a special moment for all but, after all the laughing and crying and smooching was over, Miriam had to say good-bye. She went back to work, and the two men in her life returned to the car for the trip home.

Going home, of course, was not nearly as much fun as preparing for the surprise. And getting all that "stuff" back into the car wasn't as easy as getting it out. Michael snorted in preoccupied disgust as he balanced the baby carrier on the roof of the car while tossing the candy in the front seat, arranging the flowers on the floor, and wrestling the balloons out of the wind into the backseat. Finally, he got everything arranged and headed home.

Suddenly the trip became quite odd. Other drivers began to honk at Michael and flash their lights. He could not figure out what was happening until he hit about fifty-five miles per hour on the highway. That is when he heard a scraping sound move across the top of the car. Then Michael watched in horror through the rearview mirror as the baby carrier—still holding Jason—slid off the roof, bounced on the trunk, dropped to the road, and began to toboggan down the highway behind the car.

The driver in the car behind Michael's had spotted the baby carrier on the roof and was prepared. He screeched to a halt behind the carrier to shield it from the oncoming traffic. Michael, of course, also braked to a hard stop, ran back to Jason, and discovered the baby carrier had more than fulfilled its design function—the baby was safe! Then as the waves of fear, guilt, and relief hit him, the new father began to sob uncontrollably on the highway.

The tears, however, did not stop a passing policeman from writing Michael a citation, nor a local newspaper from publishing the story. The reporter even interviewed Jason's mother, who thankfully by that time had not been arrested for the manslaughter of her husband. Instead, Miriam demonstrated great restraint and care. With remarkable understanding she said, "This is so unlike Michael; he really is a good father."[1]

We understand, too. Sure, we all initially shake our heads and say, "How could he?" But when we remember all the dumb mistakes we have made— born of our own fluster, flurry, and distraction—then we recognize there is some of Michael Bryson in all of us. Common to our humanity are the flaws that make us all susceptible to such terrible and potentially tragic errors.

The apostle Paul also writes about this all-too-human nature we share, but he has no intention of minimizing its effects. Paul recognizes that our tendency to minimize our susceptibilities makes us less resistant to the power of temptation in our lives. So he reminds us that what is common in us cost the life of another child. Our errors required the blood of the Son of God.

Paul speaks plainly of the pervasiveness of our weaknesses, knowing that if we do not face them, our repentance (see preceding chapter) will have no eternal purpose. If we truly love God, we long to keep his Spirit from grieving for our wrong, and to make progress against the temptations that have required us to seek his mercy (Eph. 4:30-32). Our desire to be rid of the guilt of our sin creates a longing also to be free of its power. In one of the most precious passages of all Scripture, Paul reminds us not only how powerful and common is our temptation but also how to escape its clutches:

1 CORINTHIANS 10:13

No temptation has seized you except what is common to man. And God is faithful; he will not let you be tempted beyond what you can bear. But when you are tempted, he will also provide a way out so that you can stand up under it.

Paul writes to Christians who have fallen into the world's snares and proclaims, "There is a way out!" God promises to enable us to overcome our besetting sins and shaming weaknesses. We access God's grace by acknowledging what he tells us about the persuasiveness and power of the temptation we face, and then by resisting it through confidence in the resources he provides.

KNOWING TEMPTATION'S MEASURE: ―――― IT IS BIGGER THAN WE ARE ――――

Paul says that no temptation has seized us but such as is common to man (v. 13a). A temptation is not itself a sin. We sin when we yield to temptation. However, we are not prepared to resist any temptation if we have not properly assessed it. Thus, to help us prepare, Paul describes temptation in terms of its commonness and its horror.

THE COMMONNESS OF TEMPTATION

The Bible assures us that the temptations we face are common among humans. Even Jesus faced temptation (Matt. 4). How does saying that the temptations that we experience are common help us escape their clutches? The knowledge that others struggle as we do rescues us from the weakening despair of thinking that we are unique and strange when we feel tempted.

Rescue from Isolation

The power of realizing the commonness of temptation becomes plain to us when we consider honestly the struggles that supposedly mark us as peculiar or even freakish. We feel less strange, and less out of control, when we understand that we only struggle with what others also find tempting. For instance, one can hardly be a healthy male in this culture and not be tempted by the sexual images all around us. No healthy female is above being tempted by the retailing of relational trauma that fuels television, or fills drugstore novels with romantic intrigue that makes her own relationships seem sparkless. It is impossible to be in business and not be tempted to sacrifice people for profit. Government workers can be regularly tempted to forfeit integrity for promotions. A mother of multiple preschoolers will be tempted by this culture's priorities to think of herself as a victim of her family's needs.

These temptations and dozens more are common among us. We can be weakened in our ability to handle such temptations if we think that feeling tempted is a sign that our faith is false, our situation is abnormal, our soul is warped, or our compulsions are unrestrainable. Satan wants us to believe such lies, because if we believe that we are special cases, then we have a ready excuse to yield to the temptation with the rationalization that no one else has to face what we face.

Despite the frequent hiddenness of others' struggles, the Bible disputes any assumption that our temptations are isolated to us. No temptation is unique to us. The feelings and thoughts that simultaneously attack and attract us are shared by many. Millions of Christians around the world and through the ages have gone through similar temptations. Satan, our psyche, and others may try to convince us that we are peculiar, but what tempts us results from common human tendencies, desires, and fears.

As a seminary professor, I am tempted to believe that I have (or should have) risen above the common temptations that others face. This makes the appearance of sin in my life all the more disappointing and difficult to confess. I was made more ready to deal with my weaknesses, however, through the observations of another seminary professor:

> I write these words at the age of fifty-five. During the past ten or twelve years, I have often—and with greater seriousness than ever before—reflected upon the course of my life. Certain patterns of thought and attitude and conduct have come to light, some of them quite disturbing. I look back upon repeated failures in my efforts to subdue inner thoughts, conflicts and fears, to combat immaturity and self-centeredness, to build genuine and enriching relationships with other people, to conquer besetting sins, and to grow in holiness and communion with God. I now see that every period of my life has been marked by . . . struggle. But the persistence of the failures, together with a growing understanding of the past, has made the struggles of recent years exceptionally intense and painful.[2]

The man who wrote these words is widely respected for his godliness, yet he dares to speak with extraordinary humility and candor for the benefit of others. His words help rescue me from the despair of thinking that I am extraordinarily strange because, despite my position and background, I am still tempted even by what I find detestable. In knowing that I am not alone, I find that I can be more honest about what is in my heart and more willing to identify the wrong of which I must repent. Paul intends for these freeing dynamics to work in all our hearts when he tells us that what tempts us is common in humanity and is, in fact, part of being human.

Rescue from Arrogance

The idea that susceptibility to temptation is simply part of being human needs further comment because of the special way Paul phrases his thought. When he says that no temptation has seized us but such as is common to all humanity, Paul does not mean merely that what we are feeling exists somewhere in the world in others' hearts. Paul's wording is very precise. In the original Greek, the three words translated into our English, "common to man," are actually pressed into a single term. A more literal reading would be, "No temptation has seized you that is not *human*" (the Greek is *anthropinos*, i.e., manlike). As New Testament scholar Robert Yarbrough puts it, "There is no temptation that is not simply 'part of the fabric of being human.'"[3]

Now this I do not like to hear. I do not mind being told that what I feel others feel. But the reverse of this equation is quite upsetting. I find it very difficult, if not detestable, to accept the notion that the sinful tendencies of the perverse, the cruel, and the weak exist in me as well. Still, this is what the Bible says. The seeds of every sin are in me. I cannot break one commandment without being guilty of transgressing them all (James 2:10). Why does Scripture tell us this horrible truth about ourselves? It tells us this because understanding the commonness of sin not only rescues us from a sense of isolation, it also rescues us from the vulnerability of arrogance.

Whatever I observe of others in the world, I must confess, is not beyond me. Humorist Garrison Keillor says that a scandal is nothing more than a revelation of the humanity of our heroes. The scandal of Scripture, however, is nothing less than the revelation of our own humanity. However untouched by the world's corruptions we may believe ourselves to be, the Bible says our humanity makes us no more beyond the most detestable sins than was a king like David or an apostle like Peter. Though the Scriptures call David a man after God's own heart, the slayer of Goliath also committed adultery and murdered his friend to cover the crime. Though Peter walked on water through faith in his Lord, he also denied him three times in one night of fear.

Recent anniversary celebrations of the World War II liberation of Europe have again put before our eyes the victims and the heroes of the Holocaust. I was shaken to read a postwar account of Oskar Schindler, the daring German hustler and hero who daily risked his life employing his wealth and wiles to save the lives of twelve hundred Polish Jews. After the war this noble heart abandoned his wife, became a womanizer and a drunkard, and fell into destitution and dependence on others. For some schnapps he even pawned the commemorative gold ring that had been fashioned for him from the false teeth of those he had rescued. How could one so noble fall so far? Because there is no temptation *out there* in the world that does not find common chords of resonance *in* every human heart.

THE HORROR OF TEMPTATION

In light of the revelation of our common humanity, Paul also advises, "So, if you think you are standing firm, be careful that you don't fall" (1 Cor. 10:12). Unless we acknowledge how susceptible our humanity makes us, we are far more vulnerable to wrong than we think. The degree of our vulnerability compels us to consider more seriously the other measurement of temptation that Paul wants us to know: its horror. Paul puts the horror of temptation before us so that we will not use its commonness as a rationalization for allowing it into our lives. Lest we say, "Everyone struggles with temptation, so I need not be concerned about it," this chapter of 1 Corinthians details temptation's terrible power and terrifying effects.

Temptation's terrible power

Paul reveals temptation's power by reminding us of the histories of two groups of people. He first points to the Israelites at the time when God rescued them from Egypt (vv. 1-4). They had the wonderful privilege of being united to God in an act analogous to baptism when God led them through the Red Sea and passed over them in a cloud. Further, in a miracle foreshadowing the Lord's Supper, Israel drank life-giving water from the rock in the desert. These experiences so demonstrated for Israel the saving presence of God that Paul says those Old Testament people partook of the same spiritual provision as we who experience the New Testament blessing of Christ.

Yet, despite their great spiritual privileges, the people of Israel fell into terrible temptation. They turned to idolatry, pagan revelry, sexual immorality, and grumbling against God's care for them (vv. 6-10). By Israel's actions we learn how potent temptation is. It can even corrupt the hearts of God's covenant people who have witnessed his miraculous power. This is *not* just an ancient history lesson. Paul makes it clear that New Testament Christians are just as susceptible to the power of temptation. When he says to the Corinthians, "No temptation *has seized you* but such as is common," the tense of the verb makes it clear that some in the church have already been in temptation's grasp.

In another few verses Paul will reveal that he knows the Christians in Corinth have actually mixed pagan idolatry with their worship of God in the Lord's Supper. Initially we question how this could be. These New Testament Christians know of Christ's resurrection. They have the ministry of an apostle. They have seen the gospel rescue people from gross sins of idolatry. As a first-century church, how could they fall so quickly and so far? The answer lies in the terrible power of temptation. It can corrupt even the most spiritually privileged. That is part of its horror.

I began one Wednesday morning discussing the marital unfaithfulness of a minister with his counselor. The counselor, himself a minister in the same denomination, had been chosen by the regional board of their churches for this task because many years previously he had also fallen into such sin. By midmorning another minister came to visit me. His mission was to tell me of the infidelity of yet another man, who had been my childhood pastor. It was a devastating morning. I know all of these men very well. Part of me wanted to shake them by the shoulder and ask, "How could this happen? You men love the Lord. You have proclaimed his Word and have seen the miracle of converted souls. How could you do this?" But I know the answer to my questions in God's Word and in my own heart. Temptation has terrible power. Even those with great spiritual privilege are not immune to its influence.

Temptation's terrifying effects

Not only does Paul want us to know that no one is beyond the reach of temptation's power, he also wants us to know of its devastating effects. He cannot let us conclude that, because temptation is common and powerful, we might as well capitulate to it.

EFFECTS ON THE CHILDREN OF GOD. —— Paul needs to remind us that temptation unchecked has terrifying consequences. Thus he puts before us a historical scene more nightmarish than a Salvador Dali painting. Paul reminds us that when the Israelites succumbed to temptation, "God was not pleased with most of them; their bodies were scattered over the desert"

(1 Cor. 10:5). Due to their sexual immorality, twenty-three thousand died in one day (v. 8). Others were killed by snakes, and still others by the destroying angel (vv. 9-10). Paul says that these things happened as examples and warnings to us (vv. 6, 11). We must understand that when temptation results in transgression there can be awful consequences.

I considered these consequences on a street in a small village in Europe. There my son and I walked for hours with a friend who poured out his heart about his need to know how to parent. He told us how his father had purposely driven his mentally fragile mother into insanity in order to protect his affair with a married neighbor. So horrible was my friend's childhood that the memory of his earliest years was largely blanked out. He only had flashing recollections of his mother and father battling in the hall outside his bedroom.

As a consequence of his sad upbringing the man who now walked the streets with us confessed that he had no parental models to follow and no clear ideas how to nurture his own family. He was candid about the resultant difficulties with his wife, and he could see other effects beginning to touch his children. It was a tale of horror, as the consequences of the initial father's desire to have an affair first destroyed his family, then damaged his son, and now were affecting his son's children. The powerful consequences of the first sin were affecting three generations.

Such horror is magnified to almost unthinkable proportions when we read a book such as David Blankenhorn's *Fatherless America*. Blankenhorn contends that many of our society's worst ills are the result of 40 percent of America's children now growing up in homes without fathers.[4] In that one statistic the experience of my friend is horribly multiplied many times. Drug abuse, promiscuity, teen pregnancy, abortion, and crimes of many sorts are the fruit of hundreds of thousands of fathers yielding to temptation and abandoning responsibility for their families. The damaged lives being strewn over the desert of our society are those of our own children. Temptation can truly have terrifying effects that we as a nation will bear for generations to come.

Sadly, in considering the consequences of sin, we are not allowed to consider only one category of temptation. Immorality, rebellion, idolatry, materialism, and even grumbling are mentioned by Paul as he addresses the church. He challenges us to examine every dimension of our lives for vulnerability to temptation. As the representative of God's compassion, Paul cannot allow us to ignore temptation of any sort lest the terrifying consequences overwhelm us and our families.

EFFECTS ON THE CHILD OF GOD. —— Perhaps we would not consider Paul's warning compassionate if all God let us see were the consequences of sin. If God's love is so conditional that such extreme judgment awaits all of those who so fail him, then truly we would be left in despair. However, this is not the whole picture.

Paul explains that Israel's experiences were examples and a warning for us. God used the covenant people of old as an instrument of salvation for the entire world. The nation itself served as an example of what Christ would do. Israel's sacrifice became a means of warning and instructing us about the awfulness of sin and about our need of God's help when we fall prey to temptation.

Israel herself serves as a compassionate expression of God's desire to save us. God used his discipline upon his nation-child to turn her and all succeeding generations from the eternal dangers of idolatry. Through the inability of Israel's idols or good works to save her from the consequences of sin, we learn that we must trust in the eternal salvation offered by the divine Child of her own progeny. Ultimately we know of the horror of sin and the necessity of grace because the consequences that Israel experienced in an illustrative way actually fell upon God's Son.

As our eyes scan the accounts of the Israelite bodies fallen in the desert due to sin, our vision ultimately rests upon mention of another slain Son of Israel (vv. 15-17). Ultimately Paul leads his concern about temptation to a focus on Christ's body and blood represented in the Lord's Supper. The images remind us that God allowed his own Son to experience the consequences of *our* sin. Our "participation in the blood of Christ" and the need that "we all partake of the one loaf" (vv. 16-17) are more than statements of communion; they are reminders of our complicity. We are all participants in the wrong that required his life. In the Savior's death that we commemorate in our communion we ultimately measure the horror of temptation that has led to sin. As we consider the penalty for our sin paid upon the cross, we are reminded of the hymn writer's words:

> Ye who think of sin but lightly nor suppose the evil great
> here may view its nature rightly, here its guilt may estimate.[5]

By the horror of the cross we learn the full measure of temptation's terrifying effects. Those effects truly are larger than we can imagine, for
they required the death of God's divine Son. More than the arguments
we can muster about the awful consequences upon us when we yield to
temptation, the sight of what our sin caused our Savior to suffer should
convince us to turn from sin's path. Our God would not have paid so
dear a price to rescue us from temptation's consequences were not they
to be deeply feared.

LEARNING TEMPTATION'S MATCH: ——— HE IS BIGGER THAN IT IS ———

The Bible's warnings of the pervasiveness and power of temptation are
meant to alarm us but not to overwhelm us. We are forewarned to fore-
arm us against temptation's onslaughts. But how can we stand against so
formidable an enemy of our well-being? Paul answers by urging us to put
our faith in the divine forces at work in our favor. He identifies those forces
for us so that we will know how to face and fight the battles of temptation.

A SOVEREIGN PROMISE

Some of the most encouraging words in all of Scripture are these: "God
is faithful; he will not let you be tempted beyond what you can bear. But
when you are tempted, he will also provide a way out so that you can
stand up under it" (v. 13). God promises that our temptation is never
stronger than he is. Then he whose power created the universe and
controls the destiny of all things assures us of this grace: he will always
provide a way out.

God provides his solemn word and sovereign promise that he will
never allow us to be tempted beyond what we are able to resist. Satan will
try always to convince us otherwise. His evil will work in our hearts and
minds to convince us, "This temptation is bigger than you are. You cannot
resist this. You know the way you are. You have a weakness that makes
you more susceptible than others. And, after all, God made you this way,
so how could he blame you?"

God's promises destroy the foundation of Satan's lies. His promise to
provide "a way out" of temptation is translated as "a way of escape" in the
King James Version of the Bible. This translation helps us capture a key con-

cept of the original language. This expression would have brought a military image to the mind of ancient people, the image of a small troop surrounded by a larger, more powerful enemy and with no way out.

Paul describes this "Alamo" situation to help us envision how powerful are the forces of temptation that surround us. But he says, "There is a way out; God will always provide a way of escape." Though our spiritual enemies surround us, the cavalry will come, a secret passage will be discovered, an overpowering weapon will be supplied, or a weakness in the enemy lines will form. Somehow, God will provide an escape from the temptation.

God doesn't belittle our temptations. Through Paul he has already told us they are pervasive, actually common in our and other believers' experiences . . . past and present. Paul also affirms what our hearts must confess about the power of temptation: its tentacles are remarkably strong, having the ability to grasp us for years and to destroy those we love. Still, God promises that he will always provide the sovereign control of the situation so that the temptation will not be greater than our ability to resist, and that he will provide a way of escape. Now, of course, we ask, "What is the way of escape, and how do we plan to get there?"

A Saving Plan

We discover God's saving plan in the key words: "bear," "stand up," and "flee" (vv. 13, 14). The first two words communicate the idea of exerting energy against the force of temptation; the last refers to getting out of its way. Both concepts are critical. For they indicate that overcoming temptation is not a matter of simply sitting down on a sofa with a box of chocolates and telling God to make the way of escape from whatever sin is tempting us. By faith we believe that God will make a way of escape; by faith we believe that he has regenerated and secured us in Christ so that we have both the desire and the ability to use his means of rescue; *and,* by faith we act on his promises despite great opposition.

As should be obvious by Paul's battle language, acting on faith in God's gracious provision does not negate the need for effort on our part. The great Puritan writer John Owen explains,

> Let us consider what regard we ought to have to our own duty and to the grace of God. Some would separate these things as inconsistent. If holiness be our duty, they would say, there is no room for

grace; and if it be the result of grace there is no place for duty. But our duty and God's grace are nowhere opposed in the matter of sanctification; for one absolutely supposes the other. We cannot perform our duty without the grace of God; nor does God give his grace for any other purpose than that we may perform our duty.[6]

The fact that the Christian does not rely on simple willpower or discipline to overcome temptation does not mean that we are to disengage our energies from the process of escaping temptation.

Fight

The air war over Bosnia in the late 1990s made famous the escape of Scott O'Grady. The downed American flier evaded capture for days in enemy territory until rescue helicopters found him. When the helicopter landed in the clearing near where O'Grady was hiding, he didn't relax in the brush and say, "I wish that the pilot would have landed a little closer." He shook off his fatigue, fought through the bushes, drew his weapon and, with every ounce of energy he had, ran to the escape that had been provided for him. His actions parallel the engagement God requires of us in spiritual warfare. We should not assume that, because God promises to provide a way out of temptation, we have no role in our own rescue. God always provides a way of escape, but he may also require great effort from us.

We take advantage of the way of escape God provides by exerting every resource he gives us to fight the enemy. Sometimes he provides the way of escape by miraculous deliverance. For instance, there have been times in my life when I believe that if God had not taken away the opportunity to sin, I would have fallen to it. I praise him that, when I was weak, he removed the temptation that was greater than my will. Taking advantage of the rescue God provided in these circumstances simply required me to walk away from what God had already taken away.

While God has made these special provisions at times in my life, this is not always how God delivers us. To increase our faith and strengthen our character, God more often allows us to escape temptation by using the means of grace always available to us: conscientiously seeking God's power and instruction through prayer, meditation on his Word, and the counsel of mature Christians are never passive endeavors.

Using these ordinary means of grace to resist temptation will require so much of our heart, soul, and mind that we might well despair of securing our escape were it not for God's promise that it will be provided. The reasons that we may abandon the fight, however, relate not only to the expense of energy involved but also to the humility that may be required.

I know of a group of Christian businessmen who have recognized the commonness and power of temptation in their lives, and so they hold each other accountable with a set of questions that they ask each other at every gathering. The candor with which they acknowledge the temptations of their occupations is evident in the challenging nature of the first two questions: "Did you stay pure in your hotel room when you last traveled?" and "Did you stay honest on your expense report after you returned?"

What would cause respectable businessmen to subject themselves to answering honestly such embarrassing questions? They know that they are at war against a spiritual enemy. That enemy plots the corruption of their souls, the disruption of their lives, and the destruction of their families. Knowing the seriousness of the battle, these men are unwilling to sacrifice spiritual victory just to preserve personal pride. And if one of the men should try to embarrass another by asking, "You mean that you are tempted by something like that?" then the one being questioned need only reply, "Yes, I am, and don't you dare pretend that you are not. The Bible says that nothing tempts me that is not also common to man. What tempts me, tempts you too."

This fight against temptation will stretch us. The writer of Hebrews chides fellow believers who are buckling under pressure with the observation, "In your struggle against sin, you have not yet resisted to the point of shedding your blood" (Heb. 12:4). Victory over temptation ultimately will require us to use every resource God provides: constantly claiming the reality of his love for us, filling our mind with his Word, appealing to him in prayer, seeking Christian counsel, confessing our sin one to another, repenting of our failures.

Neither these efforts nor the faith that causes us to exert them are meritorious in themselves. The Bible carefully distinguishes between any *meritorious cause* of God's love and the *instrumental means* of his blessing. Louis Berkhof summarizes,

> Sanctification is a work of the triune God, but is ascribed more particularly to the Holy Spirit in scripture.... Though man is privileged to cooperate with the Spirit of God, he can do this only in virtue of the strength which the Spirit imparts to him from day to day. The

spiritual development of man is not a human achievement but a work of divine grace. Man deserves no credit whatsoever for that which he contributes to it instrumentally.[7]

God does not love us *because* we overcome temptation, and he does not cease to love us *because* we may have yielded to it. Still, our efforts are necessary *means* for us to grow in godliness.

A good analogy to help us understand the relationship between God's love and our progress in becoming Christlike (i.e., our progressive sanctification) is our children's obedience. My child's compliance with my standards and his resistance to counter impulses do not cause or deter my love. He is entirely my child, and has the affection of my whole heart solely as a consequence of that relationship. Still, in order for him to grow and to have the parental approval that every child desires, he must obey me.

This family analogy is imperfect because my parenting is imperfect, but God's covenant care of his children reflects perfectly the fatherly nurture that unites unconditional love with the obedience required for a child's good.[8] By keeping in mind both God's gracious love and his required standards, we utilize God's most powerful means for reflecting his holiness in our lives. Archibald Alexander, the first professor at Princeton Theological Seminary, explains the process while noting the dangers of omitting either element from the Christian life:

> To exercise unshaken confidence in the doctrine of gratuitous pardon is one of the most difficult things in the world; and to preach this doctrine fully without verging toward antinomianism [i.e., living without standards] is no easy task, and is therefore seldom done. But Christians cannot but be lean and feeble when deprived of their proper nutriment. It is by faith that the spiritual life is made to grow; and the doctrine of free grace, without any mixture of human merit, is the only true object of faith. . . . Here, I am persuaded, is the root of the evil; and until religious teachers inculcate clearly, fully, and practically the grace of God, as manifest in the Gospel, we shall have no vigorous growth of piety among professing Christians.[9]

Only by God's grace can we be holy. By his blood the Son washes us of the stain of sin, and by his Spirit he creates every righteous desire and enables every righteous action (2 Cor. 3:18; 1 Pet. 1:2). Jesus said, "Apart from me you can do nothing" (John 15:5). This truth takes away all grounds for boasting before God, but it does not encourage us to do nothing (cf. Rom. 3:27-28; 1 Cor. 4:7; 2 Cor. 10:17-18; Eph. 2:8-10).[10]

To mature in our faith and walk with God, we must realize that the standards of his Word are also gracious. By walking according to his paths we honor the One whom we love, love those that he loves and, while being kept from danger, discover the blessings of his loving ways. Our obedience does not merit God's care, but it is an instrumental means by which his care transforms our lives. Obedience may not be easy in the face of temptation, but God's promise to enable us to resist temptation equips us for the fight.

Flee

Still, even this plan of resistance may not be enough to escape temptation. So we should not miss the expanded plan contained in the key word "flee" (1 Cor. 10:14). Temptation is bigger than we are; but God is bigger than it is, so he will provide a way of escape. But when the way of escape is opened for us, we should not just stand idle. God says, "Run!" If God has placed us in a situation where we must endure temptation, then he will not give us more than we can bear. This promise does not mean, however, that we can intentionally or naively put ourselves in positions of temptation and remain unaffected.

The Bible clearly indicates that among God's gracious provisions for escaping temptation are feet! God provides us the ability to flee. Some people reading this book have trouble believing that this is true. Patterns of wrong have persisted for so long in their lives, or have such a strong hold on them, that they believe it is impossible for them to leave a sinful situation. However, God promises that "the one who is in you is greater than the one who is in the world" (1 John 4:4). Faith in the promised power of the Holy Spirit residing in us should enable us to pull ourselves from the molasses mire of temptation and command our feet, "Get out of there!"

God's Word commands us to flee temptation (1 Cor. 6:18; 10:14; 1 Tim. 6:11; 2 Tim. 2:22). As Joseph fled temptation when Potiphar's wife tried to seduce him, we must be willing to run from what we know tempts us (Gen. 39:12). The knowledge that we are able to flee should encourage us to examine all aspects of our lives with honesty and rigor. Those that are tempting us to disobey God and damage our fellowship with him, we must flee. We should not be dissuaded by the rationale that the activity does not seem to tempt others, or appears innocent to outsiders. If we know the matter tempts us, then it is out-of-bounds for us regardless of its impact on others. The Bible says, "Anyone, then, who knows the good he ought to do and doesn't do it, sins" (James 4:17).

God does not excuse us from fleeing what we know tempts us simply because others do not appear to struggle with the matter. God has made each of us unique, and it is very possible that certain movies, magazines, music, relationships, or ambitions may tempt us and not tempt others—or that others are simply willing to accept the temptation.

Getting away from what tempts us may involve putting actual distance between us and the temptation—not driving a certain route home from work, not going near someone's house, or avoiding a certain store. We may need to change a subscription, change a job, change schools, change friends, change a channel, honestly admit what an entertainment is doing to us, or throw something away. Each of these measures may seem embarrassing—even humiliating—but, lest we hang our heads in unrelenting shame, we must remember that no temptation seizes us "except what is common to man."

Additionally, we should remember that God does not warn us of the evil of temptation because he is an eternal killjoy. Faith gives us confidence that he warns and steers us from spiritual danger because he loves our well-being more than he loved his own life (Gal. 1:4; Titus 2:14). Courage to flee comes from the confidence that God's care lies in the design and destination of the way of escape.

We simply must not believe that we can dally with what tempts us and remain unaffected. The book of Proverbs reminds us that we are not to set our foot on the path of the wicked; we are not even to go near that path. Rather, we are to turn and go the other direction (Prov. 4:14-15). It probably is true that some will find themselves almost powerless against their compulsions when they get near certain temptations. Therefore the Bible tells us to flee their proximity. The old line, "By the time of choice most of the choosing is already done," harmonizes with Scripture that urges us to choose to stay far away from temptation.

We should seek to understand ourselves well enough to keep distant from situations where resistance will be very difficult for us. We should not despise the grace of Christian friends and counselors that God provides in his church to help us become accountable. Though the way of escape may not be easy or immediately evident, we have God's promise that the means are available for rescue from temptation.

THE SAVIOR'S LOVE

Though the means of escape are available, we still may not choose to employ them if we are convinced that the way out of sin is no better than the way in. For this reason, Paul moves directly from the command to flee sin to what would otherwise be a curiously placed discussion of communion (1 Cor. 10:16-17). Paul reminds the Corinthians that their celebration of the Lord's Supper is actually a commemoration of the body and the blood our Savior sacrificed for us. Why would Paul introduce this discussion? Surely one reason is that the Corinthians were profaning the Lord's Supper with idolatrous practices. Without a doubt correction of the Corinthians is on Paul's mind, but compassion is in his heart, and he intends for this love to motivate us as well.

In earlier verses Paul tells the Corinthians to flee the clutches of sin, but now he reminds them that they flee to the arms of their Savior. Paul uses the embracing love of the Savior's sacrifice to woo wandering souls from spiritual danger. The heart does not know a more powerful motivation.

Several years ago my wife, Kathy, and a friend gathered up their kids and made a trip to the St. Louis Zoo. A new attraction had just opened called "Big Cat Country," which took the lions and tigers out of their cages and allowed them to roam in large enclosures. Visitors observe the cats by walking on elevated skyways above the habitats. As my wife and her friend were taking the children up one of the skyway ramps, a blanket became entangled in the wheel of the friend's stroller. Kathy knelt to help untangle the wheel while our boys—roughly ages three and five—went ahead.

When next she looked up, Kathy discovered that the boys had innocently walked right through a child-sized gap in the fencing and had climbed up on the rocks some twenty or twenty-five feet above the lion pen. They had been told that they would be able to look down on the lions, and they were doing just that from their hazardous vantage point. Pointing to the lions below, they even called back to their mother, "Hey, Mom, we can see them!" They had no concept of how much danger they were in. Kathy saw immediately. But now what could she do? If she screamed she might startle the boys perched precariously above the lions. The gap in the fence was too small for her to get through. So she knelt down, spread out her arms, and said, "Boys, come get a hug." They came running for the love that saved them from danger greater than they could perceive.

With similar love our Savior beckons us from temptation that would devour us. Through the elements of the Lord's Supper we are reminded that he knelt down into this world of spiritual jeopardy, spread his arms upon a cross, and beckoned us to an embrace of eternal love that even now calls us from danger. To gaze upon that act of sacrifice is to measure again the matchless love of Jesus and, by its magnitude, to be drawn from the dangers of temptation into the security of his arms. We find powerfully motivating the warning, guidance, and instruction of him who loves us so. With much wisdom Charles Spurgeon said,

> While I regarded God as a tyrant I thought my sin a trifle; but when I knew him to be my Father, then I mourned that I could ever have kicked against him. When I thought God was hard, I found it easy to sin; but when I found God so kind, so good, so overflowing with compassion, I smote upon by breast that I could ever have rebelled against One who loved me so, and sought my good.[11]

Another church leader echoes, " . . . the man who comes to obey God will love him first . . . the love of God is the beginning of religion." Love of the Savior draws us from the lure of temptation.

Faith in the love that paid the penalty for our sin also provides powerful motivation to flee temptation. Were God merely a frowning tyrant—if all I feel when I face him is guilt and defeat—then I will never have the joy of my salvation that is spiritual strength. Yet because he has provided a way of escape from my guilt, I have reason to go to him in prayer to ask his forgiveness and to seek his aid. Gazing upon the cross, not fearing or fleeing from "the ogre in the sky," destroys the power of temptation. Its allures lose their power over me when I am resting in the arms of a Savior who makes me eternally secure in his love.

Jerry Bridges writes with deep insight into the power our security in Christ provides for our continuing sanctification:

> A legal mode of thinking gives indwelling sin an advantage, because nothing so cuts the nerve of the desire to pursue holiness as much as a sense of guilt. On the contrary, nothing so motivates us to deal with sin in our lives as does the understanding and the application of the two truths that our sins are forgiven and the dominion of sin is broken because of our union with Christ.
>
> Robert Haldane in his commentary on Romans . . . said, "No sin can be crucified in heart or life, unless it is first pardoned in con-

science. . . . If it be not mortified [put to death] in its guilt, it cannot be subdued in its power."[12]

Thus, faith in the great escape that our God provides from the guilt of sin is also the great escape from the power of sin. The assurance of my pardon provides the peace of heart that is the Spirit's ultimate weapon against temptation. After all, when I am perfectly satisfied, then what can tempt me? When I am perfectly loved, then what else do I desire? When I am eternally secure, then what can threaten me?

———— LOVE'S ESCAPE ————

A few years ago the Ooduck people of Sudan had to make their escape from an Islamic government that had forbidden their Christianity. Forty years earlier the Ooduck had learned of the love of Jesus from two single women who had served with Sudan Interior Mission before returning to America for health reasons. Unwilling to give up that faith, thirteen thousand of the Ooduck fled to a refugee camp in Ethiopia. Many starved en route. Even in the refugee camp their ration of food was initially only a handful of grain per person per day. The trials these Christians endured were greater than we might think any people could bear.

When a mission organization heard of the perseverance of the Ooduck, a return visit of the original two missionaries was arranged as a tribute to and encouragement for their faith. The impact of the now-elderly missionary women's visit to the refugees was as heart-rending as it was inspiring. The gratitude of the people for these spiritual mothers was so overwhelming that it resulted in an extraordinary gift: a box of eggs—not Easter eggs, just eggs.

With our grocery stores full of eggs of all grades among the milk, cream, and cheeses, we can hardly sense the significance and sacrifice of those eggs until we remember the diet of the Ooduck. They had only a handful of grain to eat each day. Yet even though their own children had red hair due to malnutrition, these people put aside their own needs and desires to give chickens enough grain to lay eggs as an expression of gratitude for the grace they had learned of through these two missionaries.

When they presented the eggs to the missionaries, the African Christians sang the song taught them so long ago, "Jesus Loves Me." Then they embraced their spiritual mothers and wept tears of joy. These believers had barely escaped with their lives, and might not now escape death, but they had already participated in a greater escape. They had been freed from the guilt of their sin, and in the full apprehension of the eternal significance of that blessing they had learned to put aside the desires of this world.

May God give us such a clear perspective of the ministry of our Savior! For with that vision we also will learn so to treasure the great escape from our sin that he provided by denying himself life. With Christ's sacrifice before our eyes, we too will sing "Jesus Loves Me" with a fervor enabling us to put aside the earthly temptations that would deny him. What tempts us is pervasive and powerful, but Christ's love is a match for it all, freeing us from sin's guilt and power as we survey the wondrous cross and embrace the great escape it provides.

Constrained by
the Law of Freedom

The youth pastor was in the youth room working on that evening's lesson for the teens. A mother of two, who was also responsible for providing snacks, came by early to arrange the food. As she was moving trays and arranging napkins she glanced at the pastor's notes marked on the white board at the front of the room. Then she stopped working. She focused on the board more intently and, still staring at the lesson about God's unconditional love that was written there, spoke to the youth pastor. With a firmness that betrayed a hint of anger she said, "My children don't need more talk about grace. They need rules."

The mother's words may sound unkind, judgmental, or even harsh, but the youth pastor reported, "She wasn't a crank." She was a mature, godly woman who was active in the church and concerned for the good of her children. In fact, this mother had been so supportive of the young pastor's ministry and was so sound in her faith that he knew he could not simply dismiss her concerns as being mean or petty. This was an informed, spiritually-minded mother who was genuinely worried that too much preaching on grace would lead her children to harm by encouraging them to disregard God's standards.

The mother's concern will be shared by many. Whenever we broadcast that God's unconditional love has provided an escape from the guilt and power of sin, fears arise that we will broaden the definition of what God allows. Many assume that teaching God's acceptance of people despite their sin will create the impression that God accepts sin. The questions are logical and legitimate: "Can the preaching of grace become an excuse for lawlessness?" Or, to put it technically, "If we talk about grace all the time, is there not a danger that we will encourage antinomianism . . . living without any standards under the presumption that God will forgive anything?"[1] The answer to these questions is yes. It is difficult to *say* plainly that our obedience does not qualify us for grace, without having some *hear* that obedience is no longer a requirement of God.

If we are not careful in our statements, if we are not biblical in our expressions, preaching that God loves us despite our sin can lead some to disregard their sin. In fact, there is a natural human inclination to take advantage of grace in order to excuse sin. The apostle Paul faced this concern, and directly asked the question many had about his own teaching: "Shall we go on sinning so that grace may increase?" (Rom. 6:1). His answer, of course, was, "By no means! We died to sin; how can we live in it any longer?" (v. 2). Still, Paul's need to clarify the demands of the Christian life for those in the church indicates that concern about grace undermining obedience is not just a mean-spirited objection raised by critical voices today.

In our churches it is possible to present grace in such a way that, if anyone specifically questions certain ungodly behaviors, entertainments, or patterns of speech, we can deflect any need to examine our hearts with the rationalization, "That's just 'legalism'." We can be so cavalier about our freedom in Christ that if anyone questions our irresponsibility or bad attitudes regarding our employment, financial obligations, or academic work, we are prepared to duck and to shoot back, "I thought you believed in grace."

Does grace release us from our scriptural obligations to God and to each other? Does grace keep us from being able to correct others or make them face the consequences of their wrong? Does God's acceptance of anyone mean that we should tolerate everything? Somehow we know the answers to these questions has to be no. Still, it is exceedingly hard to speak in the same breath of the unconditional love of God and of the unchanging requirements of godliness. How do we keep the wonders of grace and the standards of Scripture married—beautifully supporting each other? The answer lies in making sure that people know that grace is not contrary to holy living. Grace and holiness perfectly agree; the psalmist says they "kiss" (Ps. 85:9-10). They must, because both are from God. Grace does not preclude holiness, but makes it possible. Holiness springs from the fountain of grace. In chapters 2 and 3 of Colossians, Paul shows us how to drink from this fountain to strengthen our obedience to God.

OUR GOD REJECTS THE LAW OF MERIT

Paul reminds us of the great privileges grace provides by freeing us from the law of merit. The law of merit is the assumption that God will love us on the basis of our keeping legal standards of goodness. Mark Baker well explains the law of merit:

> As humans we seem to have a natural tendency to attempt to reach God or enter into a higher state through our own efforts. We seek through our actions to earn something from God or to appease God's wrath. . . . In day-to-day life people's worth and standing are measured by their merits. This is true in almost all aspects of life: economic, social, educational, etc. The law of merit, not the law of grace, reigns. Therefore people naturally operate according to the law of merit in relation to God and the church as well.[2]

By *focusing on God's action* in salvation, Paul makes it clear that our actions are not the basis of our standing with God. This foundational understanding of grace—that God loves us on the basis of his actions and through no accomplishment of our own—has two wonderfully freeing implications. Grace frees us from having to gain God's acceptance by our personal efforts to keep his law (I'll call this "ego-nomianism"), and from having to satisfy him by meeting new standards that others create for us (I'll call this "neo-nomianism").[3]

FREE FROM EGO-NOMIANISM (HUMAN LIMITATION)

Ego-nomianism operates on the presumption that "It's all up to me." Under this thinking a believer reasons, "I can or must fulfill the requirements of God's law in order to know his love." Paul quickly dispels this misconception:

COLOSSIANS 2:13-15

13When you were dead in your sins and in the uncircumcision of your sinful nature, God made you alive with Christ. He forgave us all our sins, 14having canceled the written code, with its regulations, that was against us and that stood opposed to us; he took it away, nailing it to

the cross. ¹⁵And having disarmed the powers and authorities, he made
a public spectacle of them, triumphing over them by the cross.

In these verses Paul reiterates the life-giving features of our union
with Christ. We were once spiritually dead in our sins and the defilement
of our sinful nature (signified by "uncircumcision," a term of spiritual
uncleanness for those with a Jewish background). Then, God made us
alive with Christ (v. 13). God saved us by a sovereign act of love since we
had no spiritual ability to respond to him. He did this by forgiving our
sinful actions, overcoming our sin nature, canceling the written code (or
penalizing sanctions) that were against us, and disarming the spiritual
forces that could overpower us (vv. 14-15). Our Savior's ultimate victory
over our enemies is evidenced by the public spectacle he made of them
when he triumphed over sin through his death and resurrection (v. 15).

Paul's brief recounting of the wonders of the gospel is meant to free us
from the ego-nomianism that presumes, or fears, that a relationship with
God depends entirely on our actions. Because divine actions alone liberate us from the clutches of sin, we are freed from the struggle to gain an
infinitely holy God's acceptance through our own finite goodness.

I recently heard Christian artist Don Tiemeier movingly explain the
import of being freed from human limitations in trying to please God. To
demonstrate how the gospel of God's pardoning grace had changed his
life, Tiemeier showed us two portraits. The first he drew when he was
a non-believer in search of life's meaning. The self-portrait showed two
reclusive eyes peering out of numerous shadows into a world of confusion. Tiemeier said the portrait displayed his hopelessness of finding
meaning and happiness in the various spheres he had tried: university
philosophy, personal pleasure, military life, and, finally, the dropout,
counterculture of the 60s and 70s.

The next portrait Tiemeier showed was an older, Romantic-era painting of Jesus. The lines were uniform, the face was perfectly featured, and
the mild contours of the gentle countenance were well formed. The initial
thought of all in the room was that Tiemeier would say that this idyllic
portrait of Christ's perfection was what brought the modern artist peace
of mind. He said that it did the opposite.

When he saw this picture of Jesus with every line and brush stroke
flawlessly executed, Tiemeier said that it filled him with fear. He knew that
he could never meet the standards of a God so depicted. What ultimately

comforted the artist was not any human portrait but the picture of Christ painted in the words of Scripture. Tiemeier said, "The picture of Christ that brought me peace was in the words, 'Christ died for the ungodly'" (Rom. 5:6). Jesus' willingness to act for us in the face of our inability to live for him was the message that freed the sensitive artist from his hopelessness.

The gospel frees us from ego-nomianism. We do not have to pretend to others or to ourselves that we are capable of making our own way to God. Writes Samuel Bolton, "[N]ow in the Gospel we are freed from impossibilities."[4] Our Savior overcame our human inability to achieve holiness by forgiving our sin, removing our guilt, and overcoming the spiritual opposition that we could not.

Our freedom from performance standards of all types as the basis for gaining God's acceptance should convince us of the revolutionary and unique character of Christian faith. To demonstrate the truly revolutionary nature of the gospel, I regularly draw a spectrum on the blackboard for my seminary students. At one polar end I write the word "legalism" and at the other end I write "liberalism." Then, I ask where mature Christianity falls on this spectrum between the perceived restrictiveness and licentiousness of the two extremes.

Our tendency, of course, is to try to put mature faith somewhere in the middle of the spectrum. But this will not work. For, if we were to ask what a legalist thinks makes us right with God, the answer would be works such as abstaining from alcohol, tobacco, and sensual entertainments. On the other hand, a theological liberal would contend that what makes us right with God are works of charity, generosity, and tolerance.

While the types of works differ, each of these religious systems assumes that adherence to a system of human goodness will make us right with God. The ends of the spectrum that originally seem so far apart actually fold into each other, since each is a theological system of earning God's acceptance. Paul contends that mature Christianity cannot be found on this spectrum. No amount or type of good works will justify us with God. Because this basic Christian truth so easily eludes us, the great theologian B. B. Warfield took pains to express it plainly:

> [T]here is nothing in us or done by us at any stage of our earthly development because of which we are acceptable to God. We must always be accepted for Christ's sake or we cannot ever be accepted at all. This is not true of us only "when we believe," it is just as true

after we have believed. It will continue to be true as long as we live. . . . It is always, on His "blood and righteousness" alone that we can rest. There is never anything that we are or have or do that can take His place or that take a place along with Him. We are always unworthy, and all that we have or do of good is always of pure grace.[5]

We must seek our justification through means other than obeying God's law. But the thought that our destiny is not in our own hands is so counterintuitive, and so humbling, that the human tendency is always to devise new methods, systems, or standards that will allow us to make ourselves right with God.

FREE FROM NEO-NOMIANISM (HUMAN LEGISLATION)

Because our relationship with God is forged by his actions rather than our own, not only are we freed from our human limitations, we are also freed from human legislation. Apparently some at Colosse were contending that what made them right with God, or at least gave them higher standing with him, was what they would or would not consume, or their honoring of certain festival or Sabbath days, or even their worship of angels (Col. 2:16-18). Without specifying what each of these practices involved, Paul rejects the premise that they will reconcile us to God.

Paul gives the reasons that honoring these regulations could not make us right with God. Some of the standards are the continuance of Old Testament practices that only foreshadowed the reality of spiritual good that is in Christ (v. 17).[6] Thus, they held no spiritual power in themselves, but only pointed toward the One who does.

Advocates of these practices presume that they, rather than union with Christ, are the cause of spiritual life. Paul reminds us that spiritual life cannot be maintained apart from Christ, any more than the body can survive without its head (vv. 18-19). These regulations only reflect the worldly perspective that we gain standing with God by our performance, a principle contrary to the gospel of grace (v. 20).

Finally, and most significantly, these regulations in their present form are not from God, but are of human origin (vv. 21-23). Only God has the prerogative to establish standards of holiness. No earthly being has the right to make up new rules to determine what will make me right with God.[7] Paul says that we are *not* subject to human legislation. Thus, God's grace also liberates from neo-nomianism, having to earn favor with God on the basis of new laws of human design.

In principle, most of us readily agree that the rules that humans make up do not make us acceptable to God. However, our desire to please God, combined with the human bent to prove our acceptance by comparison with and control of others, makes us factories of human legislation. For example, a pastor recently told of how a controversy erupted in his church over whether members should use the artificial sweetener in the blue or the pink packets. The controversy ended mercifully and quickly, however, when the pastor pointed out that the controversy had already been settled in the words of a song that the congregation regularly sang: "I heard Jesus whisper, *sweet and low* . . ."[8]

I cite this humorous (and of course fictitious!) account to prepare for what actually is a very serious and difficult examination of human legislation. Neo-nomianism is hardly a laughing matter in the church. Mark Baker writes of his experience in a South American church:

> Evangelicals are best known in Las Mesetas for their strict observance of rules such as no drinking, no dancing, no drugs and no smoking. Members are required to tithe their earnings and attend all church services—six or seven nights a week in most churches. Churches will not baptize anyone in a common-law marriage (the status of thirty-eight percent of the households in Las Mesetas). Some churches prohibit men from wearing jeans or shorts. Most churches do not allow women to wear pants, shorts or short skirts. They also prohibit women from wearing jewelry, using makeup or cutting their hair. A number of churches require women to wear head coverings in church. . . .
>
> Legalism certainly helps some people not to drink, but it also forces people to live with questions and burdens like . . . when a woman in Las Mesetas said to me, "My friend told me that I have lost my salvation since I cut my hair."[9]

Neither the experience nor many of the issues Baker describes are foreign to most of us in North American evangelical churches. Concerns about earning God's regard or appeasing his wrath typically create a church culture that has roots in biblical morality but manifests its current character in community-specific codes that supposedly become the distinguishing marks of "serious" Christians.

We tease that the codes of Christian legalism specify, "Don't smoke, or drink, or chew, or go with the girls that do," but the expectations of neo-nomianism may not be so obvious. Baker astutely and candidly reports,

> I thought I had come a long way from my high school legalism until I . . . watched the professor put my life on the board.
>
> He drew a line that angled uphill: "Many evangelical students see their life as a progression from legalism of their youth to more mature Christianity that stresses issues of lifestyle and justice and explores authentic Christianity. It appears that they have moved forward." Then he drew a circle and wrote "legalism," "simple life-style," "freedom to drink," and "issues of justice" at different points. "They move along, but they are not going anywhere. They just change one means of judging themselves superior for another."[10]

Newly concocted church rules come camouflaged in good intentions and legitimate concerns that blind us to their potential spiritual danger and divisiveness. Most of the battles that have erupted in the churches I have pastored or attended have involved good people dividing over neo-nomian issues. All of the Christians involved would have agreed that we should not make up rules that are not biblical, but we were often unable to see our own rule-making tendencies.

Some of the battles were quite localized. We debated whether in cold weather women should be allowed to wear pants in worship, or whether in warm weather men should be able to wear shorts in evening church. The issue of whether to put cushions on pews led some to consider leaving the church. The biblical principles at stake seemed obvious to the parties involved. The "cushionites" were accused of not really being concerned for biblical worship because they were willing to muffle the music with sound-absorbing cushions. The "non-cushionites" were accused of unbiblical callousness in their lack of care for elder members' lower extremities.

Some of the battles have been generational. For example, issues relating to movie attendance and music preferences clearly divide many evangelicals along age lines. Historically, codes of expected conduct in such areas develop as a practical means to differentiate believers from nominal churchgoers or to separate them from sinful activities. Over time, however, rigorous adherence to the means, rather than separation from the wrong, can become the measure of faithfulness. The generation that develops the means may assume that they are the "uniform" that real Christians wear.

Subsequent generations, however, typically find the uniform less appealing—and in taking it off they may well fail to maintain the distance from evil that the uniform automatically created. The generational conflict, thus, is succeeded by experimentation with the original evil, which leads to observable harm that will cause the later generation to design its own Christian uniform for future generations to debate.

Some of the battles are cultural. My friend and fellow pastor Petros Roukas reports that when he first came to the United States from Greece, many evangelicals were sure that he was not a Christian because he drank wine with his meals. In Greek culture such concerns were truly foreign even among Bible-believing Christians. But the cultural tensions between Greece and the United States did not travel a one-way street. Petros himself was horrified that women who identified themselves as Christians in this country wore makeup. In Greece only women of the streets wore makeup, and Petros had trouble accepting the fact that women in America who wore makeup could really be serious about their faith.

Some of the battles are current, often based on strongly held preferences difficult to prove absolutely from Scripture. Consider what divides us so deeply and readily: worship styles, whether to tithe on net or gross income (or whether to tithe at all), length and pattern of personal devotions, schooling choices, political choices, racial reconciliation measures, child-discipline philosophies, economic theories, and methods of evangelism.

Some of the battles are embarrassingly personal. I want my children to "dress up" for church in order to display respect for their Lord. But what degree of "Sunday best" is appropriate given my tastes, their tastes, their need to be a good example to their friends, and their need to be able to relate to their friends? How can I insist on this standard for my children and, at the same time, expect them to be entirely non-judgmental of others who believe that it is better to "dress down" on Sunday rather than wear the daily "power suits" that stratify people in the business world? And, by the way, why do my standards change so much between Sunday morning and Sunday evening?

Making prudential choices and giving spiritual advice based on scriptural principles is the calling of every Christian.[11] However, to rule other people's lives based on what we cannot definitely establish from Scripture is dangerous for those we lead, and for us. Recently a pastoral friend of mine called for advice on how to deal with a woman going through a difficult marriage separation. The woman was leaving because of her husband's infidelity. However, her attitudes and actions prior to and after her husband's unfaithfulness had not been exemplary either. The pastor was particularly upset with her at this moment because she had ignored his advice about how she should respond to her husband's sin. The pastor was considering convening a church court to discipline the woman.

The hard question I had to ask my friend was whether his desire to discipline her was his response to her definite transgression of a biblical standard, or her definite disregard of his advice. After careful thought, he humbly acknowledged that it was the latter. He dropped thoughts of discipline and displayed great character in continuing to counsel the wife and her husband as they sought to resolve their difficulties.

It is very hard, but biblically necessary, *not* to judge others because of their disagreement with our judgment regarding scripturally uncertain issues. An "Aha! moment" occurred for me in ministry when I learned to ask a key question about advising others: Is it more wrong to allow what God prohibits, or to prohibit what God allows? This is actually a trick question because both alternatives are equally wrong. Either alternative would put me in the position of the Lawgiver. God allows only himself the prerogative to determine holy standards.

When, in an effort to "err on the side of caution," we forbid what God allows, then we actually break the commandment against creating other gods. We put ourselves in God's position when we forbid what we cannot prove God prohibits. Before we use our positions to control others' lives and decisions, we had best be very sure of our biblical grounds for doing so.

We must learn to advise, counsel, and judge within the limits of the authority and wisdom God has given us. Cautioning on the basis of our judgment, parenting on the basis of greater experience, making decisions where conclusions are not certain, and offering advice in times of trouble are duties demanded of mature Christians. Still, part of our maturity is the wisdom to discern the difference between a good idea and a biblical mandate. We must differentiate our best judgment on which *we must act* from God's will that *others must heed.*

We do not abandon our responsibility when we confess uncertainty and act charitably toward those who differ with us regarding prudential choices. In fact, this is our biblical responsibility (cf. Rom. 14:1; Col. 2:16). Grace frees us from having to earn God's acceptance by meeting others' expectations, and it also frees us from the unholy pride and prejudice of determining others' acceptance by God on the basis of our own wisdom.

OUR GOD AFFIRMS
THE LAW OF LOVE

God's actions in our behalf free us from human limitations in satisfying his law, and from obligations to human legislation. Our acceptance with God does not hinge on our meeting legal standards of any sort, divine or human. We naturally wonder, does this unconditional acceptance mean that God has no concern for standards? Are we free from all divine law? The apostle Paul answers by saying that, though God rejects the law of merit, he affirms the law of love.[12] In this understanding, Paul echoes Jesus' words: "If you love me, you will obey what I command" (John 14:15).

In the third chapter of his letter to the Colossians, Paul explains what those commandments are and how they coincide with the principles of love. Here, however, the focus is not so much on God's actions through Christ but rather on our union with him. Our union with the Savior is spelled out in terms of past, present, and future realities that we have already examined in preceding chapters of this book.

In the past, we have been raised with Christ (Col. 3:1). The ultimate consequences of sin have no power over us, since we are already in union with the risen and reigning Lord Jesus who sits at the right hand of God.

In the present, our lives are hidden with Christ in God (v. 3). In contrast to the way Adam and Eve once hid from God because of their sin, we are now hidden with Christ in God despite our sin. His goodness and perfection cover us despite our faults and frailties.

In the future, as a result of these past and present realities, when the Savior who is our life appears, we will have the privilege of appearing with Christ in glory (v. 4). There is no "if, and, or but" here. Rather, there is the glorious assurance that, despite our sin, those who entrust their lives to the Savior are secure in his love. Paul uses this confidence of our security to show us that, just as we are free from ego-nomianism and neo-nomianism, we are also free from antinomianism.

FREE FROM ANTINOMIANISM

Antinomianism reasons, "Since God accepts me as I am, I need not be very particular when it comes to the law. And since I already have been fully forgiven from eternity, it doesn't really matter how I live."[13] Paul's reasoning is precisely the reverse. He says that, as a consequence of our union with our Savior, we desire to walk in the way that he provides, both to benefit our union and to provide for our safety. This desire does not mean that no duty of God will ever seem irksome, nor that we will not at times struggle deeply to do as he commands. Still, the person united to Christ's heart longs for the home of God's embrace even when spiritually trespassing in a far country.[14]

As a piano string can take up a harmonic resonance with the string struck beside it, so when we are in union with Christ our lives begin to resonate with his holy character. The Scriptures do not leave us wondering what this holy character involves. In the context of the new nature God has given us, Paul writes,

COLOSSIANS 3:5-9

5Put to death, therefore, whatever belongs to your earthly nature: sexual immorality, impurity, lust, evil desires and greed, which is idolatry. 6Because of these, the wrath of God is coming. 7You used to walk in these ways, in the life you once lived. 8But now you must rid yourselves of all such things as these: anger, rage, malice, slander, and filthy language from your lips. 9Do not lie to each other, since you have taken off your old self with its practices.

This portion of Colossians, immediately following Paul's reaffirmation of our union with Christ by his grace alone (see Col. 3:3-4), contains a "New Testament Decalogue." Paul reiterates virtually all of the Ten Commandments.[15] He could not more clearly demonstrate that grace does not annul God's concern for holiness, nor should it ours.

Paul's specificity regarding God's standards for believers indicates not only that the renewed heart desires to please God but also that the Bible does not leave us wondering what God expects. It would be a cruel father who said to his children, "You must please me or I will not love you." God's grace assures us that he will not say that. But it would also be a cruel father who would say, "You can please me, but I will not tell you how to do so." God's law assures us that he will not say this. Ernest Reisinger explains,

Biblical love is never an autonomous, self-directing force capable of defining its own norms and standards of behavior. . . . Likewise, the true Christian does not let his own heart—even though it is a renewed heart—spontaneously decide what is right. That heart must be directed by God's law. Indeed the Spirit writes the law on the hearts and minds of all who are born again (Heb. 8:10; 10:16).

Does that mean that we come to the law simply by reading an inscription on our hearts? No. The teaching of Hebrews 8:10 and 10:16 is that the renewed heart has an affinity with, and love for, the law of God, resulting in cheerful, loving obedience. "For this is the love of God, that we keep His commandments. And His commandments are not burdensome" (1 John 5:3). "I delight in the law of God" (Rom 7:22). Here again we see an important bond between God's law and love.[16]

Freedom from our fog

Prior to our faith in the pardoning grace of the cross, the Law ultimately could only be a condemnation code specifying the reasons for our death penalty.[17] Now that Christ has paid that penalty, however, the Law is a map of blessing showing how those God has made right with himself can further experience his love, bring honor to the One they love, and share his love with others. Understanding that the Law no longer condemns but guides us to spiritual safety, worship, and fellowship makes its standards a delight, and indicates why antinomianism shackles God's people to unhappiness.[18] Denying people access to God's path of spiritual safety is a contradiction of grace.

Each summer our family attends a Christian family camp in Colorado. During one day of the camp, I usually hike with friends up the steep slopes of Horn Peak, a climb that approaches fourteen thousand feet. One hike stands out in particular. We started out on a sunny day in late June. About the time we reached the tree line, clouds had come over the mountain. Still the peak was visible, and I had climbed the mountain enough times in past years to have no real concern about locating the landmarks that would lead us back home. My lack of concern proved very wrong.

We ultimately reached the peak, but as we came down the mountain, dense fog enveloped my fellow climber and me. The trees and rock formations that we regularly used to navigate our way back were totally hidden. Our vision became obscured beyond a few feet. The only directions we definitely knew were up and down. We followed the sound of rushing water for a while, assuming that it was a creek we had followed on our way up. However, the rushing water we eventually found in the fog was not the creek but a waterfall plunging into a steep canyon whose floor was hundreds of feet below.

Without any path to guide us, we traversed the waterfall and tried to get down one side of the mountain only to be blocked by a glacier bank.

We hiked the opposite direction only to run into another glacier bank. Then we slowly began to edge straight down the mountain only to discover hours later that in the fog we had angled wrong. As a result, we had descended the wrong face and were hemmed in by other mountains.

The only choice left to us was to climb back up to the original peak in order to descend another slope, hoping that it would lead down the correct face. We climbed back up the mountain, but now the fog was even more dense. Clouds mixed with fog began to drop rain on us, and then snow. We were dressed for a summer climb, fatigued from hours of climbing, in danger of hypothermia, and didn't know where we were. When we reached the summit again and began our descent, the fog was creating an early dusk. We began to plan for how we might survive the night.

Finally, as we were squinting to find our footing in the last minutes of daylight, we came across a climbing path on the mountain that had been abandoned because it was so deeply rutted through years of climbing. I had used the path years before and recognized it.

Now, when we came across that well-worn path, I did *not* say, "Oh, that trail is too constraining. The ruts will not allow us much freedom to climb how and where we want." No, I said, "Hallelujah! This is the path we need!" The cold and darkness that had enveloped us made the path that God so graciously provided and plainly marked exactly the one that we wanted to travel. We knew that we were "home free" on that course.

Similarly, when we have been trapped by the cold darkness of wandering apart from God's paths, we do not doubt that the path marked by his commands is freeing. The law of God frees us from the antinomian fog of having no guidance in a dark, confusing, and spiritually dangerous world. The safe path that God provides out of concern for our good liberates us from anxiety and danger. Paul says that without God's guidance we become "slaves to sin" (Rom. 6:20-22). Candid assessment of the imprisoning destinations to which our sinful desires and compulsions have led us affirm Scripture's declaration that a person without God's law is not free.

A pastor friend writes of the bondage of disregard for God's law among those he serves in an urban setting:

> These all love the Lord and are looking forward to what he will do
> in their lives:

José—Living with a woman. Claims he is sleeping in the living room. The other day she had to come downstairs however. Her tanned body is in skimpy shorts. José knows that he should get out, but he doesn't have enough money to afford the kind of place that he wants. He has kicked his addiction, however, and is looking forward to God doing great things in his life.

Charles—He is jumping parole from another city. He does not want to do the prison time he will have to do if they catch him. When told by his small group leader that the church will help him get some change in his parole in light of his confession of faith (he came forward last Sunday), he stated that he has given his past to God, and that God will take care of it. He will not take the risk that the authorities will listen. He just wants to get an apartment, a car, and nice things. He is trusting God to help him get those things.

Herbert—"Praise the Lord, He is good," in one sentence; a curse in the next. It does not even cross Herbert's mind that there may be something inconsistent here. He knows he is free in Christ though. He doesn't have to change a thing.

Marie—She has just heard a preacher on TV complete a series of teachings on how God wants us to be rich so that we can give freely to God's work. When instructed by a Christian friend that what the preacher lady said was not true, Marie counters that her heavenly Father lets her know what's right and what's not. She is going to "reap a harvest by sowing a seed" in that preacher lady's ministry.

All of them live raunchy lives as addicts and drug pushers in violent, hard-hearted, and broken relationships. Their testimonies of coming to Christ are not mainly because they realized that they were in rebellion against a holy God, disobedient to his law, deserving hell, and accountable for their actions. Rather they tell of the horror of life on the streets—the pain, the emptiness and cheapness of life— the horrible pit that Jesus is supposed to lift them out of. They do not deny being displeasing to God, but have little understanding of God's purposes for their lives and what holy living requires. Why is it not obvious that some kind of clear guidance is needed in our society today? How can it be argued that the law has no ongoing place in the lives of believers?[19]

The consequences of disobedience to God's law that these urban dwellers experience is only more obvious but no more enslaving than what others in very different social contexts face. The businessman carrying on an affair while praying that God will bless his business knows that his affluence has not freed him from anxiety and guilt. The soccer mom yelling at the youth pastor for his mistakes with her children while hiding her drinking problem knows bondage also.

Antinomianism is not freedom. Only in obedience to God's commands do we discover release from the shame of infidelity, the worries of dishonesty, the emptiness of materialism, the web of gossip, the poison of hatred, the compulsions of our addictions, the embarrassment of anger, the hollow victories of ambition, and the remorse for time wasted on self. We are free from the curse of the Law but thankfully not lacking its guidance.[20]

Freedom for our duty

Understanding the freedom from darkness that God's law provides helps us reconcile biblical calls to duty with the gospel promises of grace (1 John 2:7-11). Affirming that God doesn't love us on the basis of our keeping within his paths does not require us to act as though he has left us without good direction. In church circles where the beauties of grace are passionately proclaimed, some people inevitably will worry whether a gospel emphasis opens the door to licentiousness. However, others will begin to wonder if it is any longer appropriate to challenge one another to be holy, or to correct anyone who does not follow Scripture's mandates. Grace does *not* forbid giving directions, promises, corrections, and warnings. Only cruelty would forbid such help.

While obedience to God's law will not sanctify us, we must understand that not all attempts to apply the Bible to modern life are "legalism." James Buchanan writes, "Man's method of sanctification is by law, God's method of sanctification is by the Gospel; the former is by works, the latter is by faith, unto works."[21] If we only tell people their duty, then we wrongly communicate that human works will heal their souls. But if we never specify the duties that God's Word requires, then we deny God's people the blessings he wants them to know and multiply through their obedience to his law.[22]

The following guidelines can help us consider how to talk about biblical duty without denying grace:

How can talk about duty be gracious?

1. To help rescue from an empty way of life is gracious.

The apostle Peter reminds us that living according to our own codes, however religious or proper they may seem, commits our lives to vain endeavors (1 Pet. 1:18). It is not gracious to leave people to the pursuit of emptiness.

2. To teach to say no to ungodliness is gracious.
Paul reminds us that grace "teaches us to say 'No' to ungodliness and worldly passions" (Titus 2:12). Grace is not a universal solvent to wash away God's standards. Understanding the character of the God who lovingly pardons us teaches us to say no to what denies him and damages us.

3. To lead to the blessings of obedience is gracious.
The psalmist and our Savior tell us that blessing accompanies the one who walks in God's ways (Ps. 1; Matt. 5:3-12). If we do not specify what these ways are, then we obscure the path others must walk to God's fountains of blessing.

4. To teach that there is discipline for disobedience is gracious.
The writer of Hebrews says that God will discipline us, rather than allowing us to continue down dangerous paths, because he loves us (Heb. 12:6). Hebrews also tells us that no discipline is pleasant (12:11). Warning others, to prevent them from experiencing such discipline, is a gracious act.

How can talk about duty be ungracious?

1. To teach that there is merit in obedience is ungracious.
Jesus himself teaches that when we have done all that we should, we are still unworthy of his household (Luke 17:10). To teach that we can earn God's affection through our "filthy rags" of righteousness, or that doing our duty somehow fulfills our infinite debt to him, damages the foundations of faith in Christ's once-for-all, full, and complete payment for sin (Rom. 6:10-14; Heb. 10:10; 1 Pet. 3:18).

2. To teach that God rejects for unrighteousness is ungracious.
God's mercy would not be merciful if it applied only to the righteous. The kindness of God will lead to repentance when we understand that our wrong does not cause him to turn his back on us (Rom. 2:4). While the prodigal son of Jesus' parable was still "a long way off" the father ran to him (Luke 15). Our wandering does not send God away.

3. To teach that God does not require holiness is ungracious.

We have been redeemed from the curse of the law—it can no longer condemn those forgiven by Christ—but God has not left us without guidance for how to please him and protect ourselves from spiritual harm (Rom. 8:2; Gal. 5:13-15). Genuine love for God is intensely preoccupied with doing his will, and the regenerated heart cannot be satisfied without it (Rom. 7:22).

4. To teach the Law apart from grace is ungracious.
Simply to tell people to do good and not do wrong, leaves them with the understanding that their work wins God's love. Even though it is taught with the best intentions of improving conduct, a "sola boot-strapsa" (human striving alone) message undermines the gospel and leads away from the true basis of holiness (Eph. 2:8-9).[23]

We must not ignore God's grace or his standards for our lives. Nor can we fail to emphasize the order of their functioning for the Christian. Herman Ridderbos provides wonderful insight into Paul's explanation of the relationship between our conduct and God's acceptance of us:

> [S]triking in this respect is Colossians 3:3ff., where in response to "For you have died and your life is hid in God," the command at once resounds: "Put to death therefore your members that are upon the earth: fornication, uncleanness," etc. Having once died to Christ does not render superfluous putting to death the members that are upon the earth, but is precisely the great urgent reason for it. . . . [I]t is immediately clear that the imperative rests on the indicative and that this order is not reversible.[24]

Pointing to the commands that follow Paul's great attestation of our union with Christ, Ridderbos notes that the relationship that God establishes with us by his grace does not erase his commands but is precisely the reason for them. Thus, "the imperative [what we are to do] rests on the indicative [*who we are* by virtue of our union with Christ] and . . . this order is not reversible." We are *not* in a relationship with God because of what we do (God's imperatives); what we do results from who we are (God's children) by his grace alone.

In colloquial terms, we must understand how to separate our "who" from our "do." What we *do* does not gain us God's affection. Who we are by virtue of his unconditional love constrains us through the power of our gratitude to obey him. If we ever invert these relationships (as is the instinctive, natural impulse of all humanity) by assuming that who we are before

God is a consequence of what we do for him, then we make God's love conditional and our security questionable. Yet when we grasp the wonder of how conduct can flow from love rather than secure it, then the gospel has the power profoundly to affect every relationship in our lives.

Freedom for our families

When the truths of grace began to touch my wife and me, we needed to change the way that we talked to our children. I used to say to my son, "Colin, because of what you did you are a bad boy." I would characterize him by his actions. But then I recognized that this is not the way God treats me. The grace that identifies me as God's child is not based on my actions. He characterizes me based on my relationship with him, not on the basis of what I have done. My union with Christ (the indicative of who I am) precedes and motivates my obedience (the imperative). Thus, to treat our children as God treats us, my wife and I put ourselves under the discipline of saying to our son, "Colin, don't do that, because you are my child." In essence, we urged our son, "Be what you are, our beloved," rather than, "Do, so you will be beloved."

We made sure that the imperative (the command) rested on the indicative (the relationship), and that the order was not reversible. As we have attempted to reflect the truths of the gospel in our home, we have assured our children that their relationship with us hinges on the fact that they are our children, not on their conduct (cf. Rom. 8:12-15; 1 Thess. 5:5-8). Such assurance does not annul the need for discipline, but it keeps correction from damaging a child's heart or creating doubt about his security in his family (cf. Heb. 12:5-11).

The grace that can change our parenting should affect every other relationship in our lives: spouses, friends, coworkers, and even enemies. This is not easy. For instance, when my wife has done something that frustrates me, my tendency is to punish her for it through silence, anger, or shame. My natural reflex is to relate to her on the basis of her actions rather than on the basis of our covenant relationship. A marriage that reflects Christ's love for the church operates under different principles (Eph. 5:21-33). I do not abandon all of my expectations, but neither do I imply that my affection rests on her meeting them. She must relate to me in the same way regarding her expectations of me. In a healthy Christian home, the imperatives must always rest on the indicative of a relationship, and the order is not reversible.

While we always struggle to live out completely the beauty of these truths, we do not despair. Rather we take strength and instruction from remembering that God does not let our failures to keep his imperatives erase the indicative of his love for us.

Freedom for God's family

Since we are in union with Christ, we become more like him, putting off our old tendencies and putting on our new self that is progressively becoming more like our Lord (Col. 3:9b-10). These changes do not only influence us individually. Because all those in union with Christ are becoming more like him, the differences among them should melt away. Of those in the church, Paul says, "Here there is no Greek or Jew, circumcised or uncircumcised, barbarian, Scythian, slave or free" (v. 11). Not only should our conduct toward one another reflect Christ's purity and integrity, but the pride and partiality that mark our differences should also disappear.

This dynamic of disappearing differences can be compared to the way some couples who have been married for many years actually grow to look like each other. Though we understand how shared experiences, expressions, and environments can cause this homogenizing of appearances, the blending of characteristics remains an amazing dynamic. The differences of the husband and wife were originally so great: different sexes, different sizes, different families, different backgrounds, different personalities, and different DNA—they were separate individuals with separate concerns. Of course, each individual retains a unique personality and complementary gifts for the marriage relationship. Yet as their thoughts, concerns, diet, lifestyle, joys, and pains are increasingly shared, their identities and appearances converge.

Similarly, when we are in union with Christ, although our personalities remain intact, we become more like him in character. His holiness begins to characterize more of us, and our differences with others united to him diminish.

The Spirit enables each member of the church family to reflect the features of his image that minimize our respective differences and heighten our mutual love.

FREE FROM AUTONOMIANISM

By uniting us to each other in our walk of faith, our union with Christ ultimately frees us from what I will call "autonomianism." Autonomianism is not so much being a law unto oneself (i.e., antinomianism), but rather living for self alone. We may tend to think of the gospel in very individualistic terms: "Jesus saved *me. I* am free from *my* sin. He will take care of *me. I* will be with him in glory." Paul's words force a broader perspective.

Grace not only rescues individuals from their personal sin; it also creates a new community where the barriers of pretense and pride have been razed because of our mutual dependence on Christ. Our responsibilities for and in this community provide freedoms not found in any other setting. Baker writes,

> The present evil age offers autonomy and independence; the gospel of Jesus Christ offers freedom for covenant community. It is a freedom from alienation from God and hence a freedom from our self-alienation, freedom from the hiding we do to cover up our finite humanity and the grasping we do to try to become more than just finite humans. It is freedom from the powers of this evil age, such as materialism, racism, sexism and individualism, that alienate us from ourselves and others. The cross of Jesus Christ produces a new creation where one is freer to express loving commitment to others and thus experience his or her true personhood.[25]

The Bible never isolates us from concern for others, even when it frees us from a performance standard for gaining or keeping God's love. "But wait," we may be tempted to ask, "I thought that we were free from *having* to follow God's standards." We are free from the law of merit (i.e., having to earn God's affection), but we are not free from the law of love. The law of love is the safe path that God marks for all those in his care. We can wander from this path and still have his love; but we cannot depart from this path—which we travel with others he loves—and still be confident of the blessings that free us from this world's anxieties and animosities.

Those in a covenant community of God's love do not merely absorb Christ's love individually, their changed lives also reflect his love corporately. We live the law of love because our union with Christ creates community responsibilities, even though fulfilling our responsibilities is not what qualifies us for his covenant love.[26]

We are no more free from the law of love than we are from the law of gravity. The law of gravity says that if we jump off a building, we will get hurt. The law of love says that if we jump from the safe paths lovingly laid by our God, we jeopardize our well-being and that of those who follow us. Our peril is not eternal, but neither is it without earthly consequences. If we depart from telling the truth, we destroy the unity that makes community life secure and productive. If we abandon faithfulness, we wreck our family relationships that make all other pursuits either rewarding or empty. Through the law of love, God warns of such destructive paths and gives guidance for safer, more blessed courses to follow.

As we enjoy our freedom in Christ, the law of love obliges us to consider the needs and weaknesses of others (cf. Rom. 15:1-6). Though this obligation may initially seem to bind us to others' priorities and weaknesses, our exercise of concern for them frees us from the unrewarding self-preoccupation of autonomianism.[27] Since the ultimate goal of our sanctification is the praise of God that will reach its zenith in the new creation, today's Christian obedience gives us and others a foretaste of heavenly blessings.[28] Through the benefits and blessings of his grace, God enables us to bring the benefits of heaven earthward for others and, in the process, to experience them more fully ourselves (Rom. 8:17; Eph. 2:7).

We impoverish our own souls when we so hoard the privileges of grace that we forget graciousness. Being unconcerned for the feelings, sensibilities, and concerns of others ultimately denies us experiential knowledge of the Lord's care for us. No one can know the deep rewards of being a pastor, parent, counselor, or friend who is not willing to show concern for the good of another at the cost of personal disadvantage or limitation.

We do not consider the needs of others above our own simply because they need to be coddled. We do so because: 1) their special concerns may reflect wisdom from God that has not occurred to us; or, 2) forging ahead without such consideration may put them in spiritual danger (1 Cor. 8:13); and, 3) giving up our privileges for the sake of others reveals more of the mysteries of Christ's passion to our own hearts (Phil. 3:10). Others' desires must not rule over our decisions, lest their weaknesses become controlling idols of our own lives (Rom. 14:16); but absence of regard for others' weaknesses deprives us of the mind of Christ (Phil. 2:1-5).

Because love for Christ makes us care for those whom he loves, we must consider the needs of those whom our lives touch when determining our own paths.[29] While I have no desire to expose the dark shadows that exist in the church, at times I wish every believer could share a pastor's perspective of how terribly messy are the lives of most people in our covenant communities. A realistic exposure to the frequency and commonness of the spiritual ills hidden beneath the surface of propriety and courtesy would help force us to consider how the solely self-concerned exercise of our own freedoms can damage others. On a hiking trip with my children I must consider not only how close to the edge of the bluff I can walk without danger, but also how well the path I tread will secure the safety of the children with various levels of maturity who follow me. Leaders of God's covenant family must similarly consider his children's safety.

FREEDOM FROM FEAR

Love of grace should not make us any less on guard against the assaults of Satan that damage us and others when we move from the safety of God's paths. There is a danger in preaching a kind of grace that is only a reaction against legalism and gives no thought to licentiousness. Grace protects from both errors by keeping us from the despair of believing that we must merit God's love, and from the danger of thinking that God has given us no guidance for how to love him and one another.

A wonderfully warm and fresh breeze of grace is currently blowing over large portions of the evangelical church where ice storms of legalism have paralyzed many for most of the last century. The progress is profoundly encouraging but will continue only if we herald the full message of the gospel. The danger of a grace movement growing in churches whose history is largely influenced by the fundamentalist/modernist controversy of the twentieth century is that we grasp grace only as a way of reacting to legalism.

Many of us resonate deeply with the message of grace that rightly corrects the artificial constraints and condemning attitudes of legalism. We should recognize, however, that grace also frees us from the bondage of antinomianism and autonomianism. We must be aware of the pitfalls of licentiousness as well as legalism. Legalism will lead to despair, but lawlessness leads to a darkness that is no less dangerous. Our message must be of the grace that frees us from both.

Missionary statesman Myron Klaus spent many years in Costa Rica with the poorest of the poor. His mission focused on orphaned urban children who took shelter and food from the country's garbage dumps. Taking these abandoned children from such a living horror and trying to educate them for survival in the world has been a mammoth task. The children have lived as animals, and making them understand the dignity and worth that Christ gives has stretched every educational technique the mission has tried.

One fairly successful technique involves training these children in public speaking and entering them in local competitions. One boy did particularly well, advanced to regional competition, and eventually won the national tournament.

As the national champion he had the privilege of addressing the president and his wife at a state dinner. The trash-heap boy took the opportunity to speak of his faith in Jesus Christ. Bravely and unabashedly the youngster spoke of the grace that had saved him when he had no hope of rescuing himself from the horrors of his daily life in the garbage.

Then, in a final act of courage, the young man addressed the president personally. In that culture, calling an elder by the first name was not disrespectful but a demonstration of affection. Thus, facing the president whose country was confronted by many imposing challenges, the boy said, "José Mario, if you follow the commandments of the Lord Jesus Christ, you have nothing to fear."

The boy's words by themselves may sound quite legalistic if interpreted to mean, "You just obey, and God will take care of you." But when we put the words in context, their proclamation of the richness of God's grace is unmistakable! The child had already said, "When there was no good and no life worth living in me—when I was on the garbage heap—Jesus saved me. I know how great is his care because I know how great is his grace." It is in the light of the grace so remarkably evident in the life of the child that he could speak so confidently of God's care by saying, "If you walk in his ways you have nothing to fear."

In the testimony of a child the greatness of grace became the foundation and motivation for obedience. May this little child lead our understanding, so that our message is as gracious for others . . . telling them that because God loves them without condition, they should walk in his ways without fear, knowing the hand that marked that path is full of unswerving grace.

SIX

Fighting with All His Might

I have seen the wall where the ink left its stain. A spattered shadow still appears where Martin Luther is reputed to have thrown his inkwell at the Devil because the Reformer so vividly perceived his presence. The story is famous for its dramatic features but important to us for its reflection of the spiritual warfare we may face. Luther was not running from God or pursuing an evil path when the powerful temptation confronted him. The spiritual assault came when Luther was translating the New Testament.

After enduring great personal sacrifice and while engaging in a religious effort that would change the face of the Western world, Luther's faith was severely tested. The attack of the spiritual enemy was intense despite Luther's noble activity. At the time of great spiritual endeavor, Satan seemed more real than ever.

Luther's experience teaches us that we are not immune to spiritual assault even when we have personally sacrificed and deeply immersed ourselves in noble spiritual endeavor. In fact, such moments may bring the most intense spiritual battles. Neither personal resolve nor church walls insulate us from Satan's threats.

The realities of spiritual warfare remain in every spiritual condition. Consider the pressures that face modern Christians despite centuries of refining biblical thought and fighting for biblical principles. The fortresses of fundamentalism that artificially kept potential temptations at arm's length by demonizing all forms of alcohol, tobacco, card playing, and theatre going are crumbling throughout the evangelical world. At the same time, the accessibility and allurement of the Internet have put sexual temptation, material indulgence, gambling entertainment, personal disengagement, and ungodly communication within a mouse-click of persons of every age and social station. The expectations of business travel, the interactivity of genders in the workplace, the "freedoms" of the pill, the isolation provided by our closed-apartment lifestyles (even when living in million-dollar homes), the personal anonymity allowed by multi-thousand seat worship centers, the enticements of consumerism endlessly promoted by amoral Western prosperity—all combine to create a culture where sin is nearer to the door of even the most socially respectable than ever before.

At the same time that these winds of external change blast us, changing patterns of family and church relationships make our spiritual footing unsure. A short list of the cultural gales that have swept over our traditional centers of spiritual development would include: divorce frequency, domestic partnership acceptability, single-parent families, two-parent paychecks, abortion availability, day care, the busyness of soccer-moms and career- or hobby-dads, the media preoccupation of teens, the recreation orientation of Sundays, and the decline of biblical literacy. The breakdown of traditional structures that nurture faith not only have robbed us of models of how to live godly lives, but also have removed even from Christians the ordinary restraints against temptation that past generations of believers had built (sometimes through inappropriate legalism) into their lives.

Combating this cultural mix of libertine tendencies with the gospel of God's unconditional love is counterintuitive. Strong assurance of God's unearned affection would seem almost assured to lead to the abuse (and excuse) of grace in order to pursue freedoms contrary to Scripture. When religious opponents argued with John Bunyan in prison, they urged him not to assure his Christian friends of God's unswerving love. "If you keep assuring the people of God's love," the opponents argued, "they will do whatever they want." Replied Bunyan, "If I assure God's people of his love, then they will do whatever he wants."

Of course, there are those who will try to take advantage of God's mercy to excuse their wrongdoing. However, those who truly love God and have their renewed hearts continually warmed by reminders of his mercy, desire to please him. Due to the limitations of our humanity this desire does ebb, but it is refueled both by the scriptural promises of God's care and by the observation of what occurs to those who depart from his ways.

The consequences of wandering from God's path are evident in the moral "freedoms" of our fracturing society. With all of this personal liberty, we have discovered great bondage—not merely to occasional temptation, but to ingrained patterns of biblical violation, unhealthy thought, and spiritually destructive behavior. Our slavery becomes apparent in our prayers for release from compulsive, addictive, and repeated sin. We pray, "God, please help me to stop . . . to stand against this temptation . . . to resist this sin . . . to change this habit . . . to act differently . . . to be rid of this compulsion . . . not to fall again, to yield again, or to be this way again . . ."

Our release from the perception that we must live according to the law of merit does not end our longing for freedom from personal indulgence and selfishness. We want our identity in Christ to become the foundation of a life that is not shackled to the world's empty promises of happiness, pleasure, and fulfillment.

In theological terms, hearts truly renewed by the Spirit want our positional (or definitive) sanctification in Christ to become an ever-greater reality in our lives. It is not enough that we know God's law of love. We want faith in our sanctifying union with Christ to push back the dead husk of self-destructive patterns in order to yield the fruit of new life—progressive sanctification.[1] We desire to decrease in order that Christ's reality might increase in us. But how do we stop the impulses that so powerfully war against our righteous resolve? How do we progress in the battle against sin and self when Satan attacks us through our own lusts, weaknesses, and ambitions? The apostle Paul provides this answer:

EPHESIANS 6:10-18

10Finally, be strong in the Lord and in his mighty power. 11Put on the full armor of God so that you can take your stand against the devil's schemes. 12For our struggle is not against flesh and blood, but against the rulers, against the authorities, against the powers of this dark world and against the spiritual forces of evil in the heavenly realms. 13Therefore put on the full armor of God, so that when the day of evil comes, you may be able to stand your ground, and after you have done everything, to stand. 14Stand firm then, with the belt of truth buckled around your waist, with the breastplate of righteousness in place, 15and with your feet fitted with the readiness that comes from the gospel of peace. 16In addition to all this, take up the shield of faith, with which you can extinguish all the flaming arrows of the evil one. 17Take the helmet of salvation and the sword of the Spirit, which is the word of God.

¹⁸And pray in the Spirit on all occasions with all kinds of prayers and requests. With this in mind, be alert and always keep on praying for all the saints.

With these words Paul equips us for spiritual warfare. He assures us that *we can stand* against the Devil's schemes (v. 11). There is hope of spiritual victory when with Paul's help we understand the nature of our enablement, our enemy, and our weaponry.

—— OUR ENABLEMENT ——

With the simple word "Finally" (v. 10) Paul reminds us that this plan for spiritual battle presumes previous instructions. This battle plan of Ephesians 6 cannot operate in isolation from a grasp of matters previously addressed in the letter. These matters include an understanding of: the divine source of our relationship with God who eternally loved us and made us his own (chapters 1–2); the need for a unified relationship with, and prayerful dependence on, others in the church with their various gifts (chapters 3–4); and, the beauty of loving and sacrificial relationships in our families that help us incorporate and reflect Christ's grace (chapters 5–6). Implicit in these preceding instructions are all the patterns of belief and behavior that equip us for godly living.

GODLY PATTERNS

There are no shortcuts to spiritual victory identified here, but thankfully there is no mystery either. Putting ourselves under sound teaching, seeking prayerful association with and accountability to others in the church, and serving one another in healthy family relationships are enabling means by which Christlikeness grows in us. Identifying these well-worn paths to godliness grants us confidence for Christian living. Ours is not a magic religion full of mysterious incantations, secret handshakes, and arcane codes. Thus, we have a duty to challenge others and ourselves to be faithful in these ordinary patterns of spiritual preparation, if we are to persevere in spiritual growth as God intends.

One of my more meaningful automobile trips came when a church elder drove me from the airport to his church to preach. He said he had discovered that his own walk with the Lord could be charted according to his level of accountability to other Christians. He said, "I have discovered in

the Christian life that you are moving either toward or away from accountability." Very few healthy things in the Christian life happen in secret. If
you cannot or will not tell your spouse, your peers, or your superiors about
something, then accountability falters. Our immersion in and integrity
with these patterns of Christian association and accountability are ordinary
means by which we grow in godliness.[2]

Of course, we dread and fear that these ordinary means of growth are
not enough. And in truth they are not. If all we are depending on to help us
overcome Satan are our own right beliefs and accountable behaviors, then
we are in grave danger. Perhaps we have discovered this when we have
altered our patterns and renewed our personal resolve to master a sinful
practice in our lives, only to struggle and fall again. Then what should we
do? Having reminded us of the necessity of godly patterns in our lives, Paul
places those patterns in their proper context.

GODLY POWER

God's power alone enables us to pursue the patterns of godliness his Word
commands. God expresses this power by embracing us and energizing us
so that we can do as he requires.

His embrace

We can begin thinking how this strengthening process works by acknowledging our reservations about the accountability measures we have considered. We feel cautious about this ordinary means of grace not simply
because we doubt that it will work but also because we fear being found
out or embarrassed. But the Bible's instruction to confess our sins to one
another (James 5:16) does not require that we confess our sins to *all*
others. While all Christians should readily acknowledge their inherent
need of grace, certain types of accountability require "safe" persons (e.g.,
spouses, pastors, or close friends) who have the spiritual maturity to
handle our confidences with discretion and compassion.

The importance to us of finding a person who is "safe" underscores
how caring the Lord's words are as he lays out his plan for our battle preparation. Paul begins his instruction by urging us, "Be strong in the Lord . . ."
(Eph. 6:10). "In the Lord" is Paul's common way of referring to our being
in a right relationship with God through our union with Christ.[3] We are
in him: covered by his blood, robed in his righteousness, members of his
household, sons and daughters, in union with him, beloved. We may be

weakened by dread of how people will react to the exposure of our sin and our battle against it, so Paul reminds us of the strength of our relationship with our God. Because we are in him, embraced by the One who reigns over all, we should not fear the bruises to our ego that the comments and opinions of lesser beings may inflict.

My five-year-old daughter decided to play soccer with her much older siblings and cousins at a recent Thanksgiving gathering. She accidentally but quickly tripped and got trampled. In tears she ran off the field, determined to enter the fray no more. So I picked her up, hugged her to my chest, and from that position she shrieked laughter and aggression toward her opponents. We played the rest of the game with her in my arms. Knowing that she was in my embrace renewed her zeal for the battle. In a similar way we gain strength for spiritual battle from knowing that even if we have failed and fallen, we are "in the Lord." Because knowledge of our unchanging relationship grants us the will to fight and the zeal to reenter the fray when we have fallen, we understand why Paul first urges that we "Be strong in the Lord."

His energy

After these words of relational encouragement, Paul identifies the source of the power that we will need for spiritual battle: "Be strong in the Lord, and in his mighty power" (literally, "the power of his might") (v. 10). God provides not only support but also the actual strength we need for spiritual battle. This strength that comes from God is not mere internal energy, as though God were promising to dispense spiritual vitamins or pep pills. Paul's specific wording indicates that God does not merely want us to supplement our strength with his; rather he wants so to invigorate the new life he has given us that he *is* our strength.

The phrase Paul uses to refer to God's "might," he has used previously in this letter. In the first chapter, Paul writes that he wants the saints to know God's "incomparably great power for us who believe" (1:19a). That incomparable power Paul then describes as "the working of his mighty power" (1:19b) that God "exerted in Christ when he raised him from the dead and seated him at his right hand in the heavenly realms" (1:20). Then Paul goes on to say that this power also "made us alive with Christ even when we were dead in our transgressions. . . . And God raised us up with Christ and seated us with him in the heavenly realms in Christ Jesus" (2:5-6). All of this background makes it clear that the "mighty power" in which

Paul urges us to "be strong" is resurrection power—the divine power that makes the dead live and reign in heaven.[4]

The effects of this power have been carefully described in the early passages of Ephesians. Because of the power of God's might, we who were once dead in our transgressions and sins are now alive (2:1, 5). Once we followed the ways of this world and were under the dominion of the ruler of the kingdom of darkness, but now by virtue of the definiteness of his sovereign choice we reign with Christ in the heavenly realms (cf. 2:2, 6). Once we were by nature objects of wrath, but we are now his glorious inheritance (cf. 2:3 and 1:18). Once we were foreigners and aliens, but now we are fellow citizens with God's people and members of God's household (2:19). We can further understand the power of God's mighty work in us by identifying the differences that distinguish our past spiritual status (before Christ indwelt us) from our present status (due to his indwelling Spirit):

ONCE WE WERE	NOW WE ARE
Dead (2:1)	*Alive (2:5)*
Under the dominion of Satan (2:2)	*Seated in heavenly realms (2:6)*
Objects of wrath (2:3)	*His glorious inheritance (1:18)*
Separate (2:12)	*Brought near (2:13)*
Foreigners (2:19)	*Fellow citizens (2:19)*
Aliens (2:19)	*Household members (2:19)*

These contrasting descriptions reiterate with startling clarity that God's resurrection power has made us fundamentally different creatures than we were in our unregenerate state.[5]

Through the power of God's might, we have a new nature. Whereas the old nature was not able to resist the wiles of Satan and the lusts of our flesh, the new nature operates with the power of the risen Lord and, thus, has abilities never before attainable or apprehensible. Sinclair Ferguson summarizes,

> . . . [W]hile we continue to be influenced by our past life, "in the flesh," it is no longer the dominating influence in our present existence. We are no longer in the flesh but in the Spirit (Rom. 8:9). Christ's past (if we may so speak) is now dominant. Our past is a past "in Adam"; our present existence is "in Christ," in the Spirit. This implies not only that we have fellowship with him in the communion

of the Spirit, but that in him our past guilt is dealt with, and our bondage to sin, the law, and death has been brought to an end.[6]

Biblical truths already examined in this book now ring with greater
clarity and significance. Greater is he that is in us than he that is in the
world because Christ's resurrection power is at work in us (see 1 John 4:4).
We enter spiritual warfare with strength borne of the confidence that no
temptation will assault us that is greater than we can bear—because we
bear the pressures of our trials with that same indomitable force that raised
Christ from the dead (1 Cor. 10:13). Isaac Watts wrote of the resurrection
victory that we have over Satan's attacks:

> Hell and your sins resist your course;
> but hell and sin are vanquished foes:
> your Jesus nailed them to the cross,
> and sang the triumph when he rose.[7]

Our minds protest, "This is not the way I feel. I feel that I am not able
to resist. I have fallen before and have resolved with all my willpower that
I will not fall again, but then I have. I do not feel that this resurrection
power is mine." We feel this way because no greater vestige of our former
nature clings to us than the doubt that our new nature is real and that the
God who gave it is more powerful than any foe. That is why Paul prepares
us for spiritual battle with the truth of God's certain relationship and the
reality of our resurrection power. Faith in these is essential if we are to
enter the battlefield with confidence. As Walter Marshall wrote long ago,

"We must first receive the comforts of the Gospel, that we may be able to
sincerely perform the duties of the law."[8]

Faith that God has made us new, has made us his, and has made us
able are essential before we will experience God's victory over compelling and compulsive sin. I thought of these truths as I listened recently to
my wife working with a thirteen-year-old doing an algebra problem. The
answer was not coming easily, and before too long my straight-A-student
daughter was crying, "I will never get this. I can't do it. I'm so dumb."

My wife, with a voice made stern enough to cut through the tears, said,
"You are not dumb, and I never want to hear you say that. Now look back
two pages in your book and see what you already know is right and, then,
come back to this problem." Our daughter is not dumb. The sternness in
her mother's voice was actually a loving affirmation of our daughter's true

nature and ability. Only the lack of confidence that she could handle the problem kept her from pushing through to the answer. When her mother refused to allow this child to characterize herself by that powerless nature, the capability our daughter actually had came to the fore and she solved the problem.

God speaks in a similar fashion to his children through the apostle Paul. The Lord hears us crying, "I am so weak, evil, stupid, and incapable that I cannot overcome this sin." We are lovingly corrected: "'Be strong in the Lord and his mighty power.' The One who has loved you gives you a nature that makes you capable. You must have faith in the power of his might. Your Adversary, who says that you cannot resist, lies and seeks your harm. Do not believe him."

——— OUR ADVERSARY ———

So able is our Adversary that Paul takes some time to describe him. The Devil schemes (Eph. 6:11).[9] He also uses forces beyond mere flesh and blood as his instruments. Since we are new creatures in Christ Jesus, our struggle is not fundamentally against our own impulses anymore. Christians wrestle "against the rulers, against the authorities, against the powers of this dark world" (v. 12).

HIS NATURE

Many attempts have been made to classify the demonic forces of darkness Paul identifies. Most of these classifications are speculative and based on traditions clouded by history. What seems clear, however, is that Paul wants us to know that Satan works through evil forces that are in "this dark world" before our eyes: wicked leaders, decadent pursuits, poverty, injustice, racism, promiscuity, materialism. The Evil One who parades as an angel of light blinds us to the devastating effects of these forces. He deludes or distracts us with selfish interests to convince us that we must accept these evils for the sake of the personal liberty, pleasure, and power that are supposed to bring happiness.

Still, Paul does not limit the evil of Satan to the world we know. Instead, he adds that we are also wrestling against "spiritual forces of evil in the heavenly realms" (v. 12). We are not used to thinking of evil in the "heavenly realms." Paul uses this term broadly to characterize the spiritual world where evil schemes develop to ensnare the heart, confuse the mind, and entrap the soul.[10] Our natural, physical orientation does not normally allow us to perceive this unseen world, and yet the Devil is so clever and able that he operates on both the worldly and the spiritual plane in his endeavor to destroy God's kingdom and people. The Bible therefore alerts us that Satan's deceit powerfully and pervasively influences every sphere of life.

OUR CONCERN

Characterizing the delusions of evil is quite painful but necessary.

At the cultural level: women and children are abused while our entertainments are filled with sexual stimulation that supposedly hurts no one. Racism retreats from the national agenda while one in five young black men is in prison. Recreational spending increases while rogue nations with nuclear arms multiply. Care for other nations increasingly becomes an imposition while our own economy flourishes.

At the family level: pursuit of higher incomes causes parents to decrease their involvement with the children whose lives they are supposedly improving. In hopes of finding financial heaven in a jackpot, our nation now spends more on gambling than on food. In the pursuit of personal freedom divorce, promiscuity, AIDS, and abortion mercilessly entangle the lives of virtually every family.

At the spiritual level: more open attitudes toward enjoying the freedoms of Christian liberties—fueled by accelerating changes in societal norms and the erosion of family and church authority—make struggle with compulsive, secret sin more common among us each year. These pursuits further stimulate the selfishness and insecurities that impoverish our relationships and lead to greater family and community breakdown.

When I entered seminary twenty-five years ago, our Old Testament professor said that he knew of no graduate of our institution who had ever gotten a divorce. Yet I have lost count of the broken marriages that have occurred among our seminary graduates since that time. I know of no evangelical seminary president who would say otherwise. We plan courses and curriculums to deal with marital stress while blaming the societal, family, and church failures that have led to this too frequent sadness. But when we think of the tears shed, the compulsions battled, the pain caused, the testimonies damaged, and the families shattered, Paul's words will not allow us to see the problems solely in terms of factors in this world. All of this pain, fear, frustration, and disappointment is part of Satan's scheming in the spiritual as well as the material world.

The Bible attributes such power to our Adversary to make us regard him with proper seriousness and ourselves with proper significance. At the location of the ink-stained wall of Martin Luther, the current curators of the historical site have hung a little monkey with pointed ears and tail to represent "the Devil" Luther supposedly resisted. How convenient were it so. We could then dispense with any real concern about the Adversary who has lived for thousands of years and has known the counsels of heaven. We only invite harm to ourselves by making our Adversary small and unintimidating. Kent Hughes writes,

> I am no genius at mathematics, but even with my limited capabilities I could be terrific at math if I worked on it for 100 years (maybe!). If I labored at it for 1,000 years and read all the learned theories, I would be a Newton or an Einstein. Or what if I had 10,000 years? Given that time, any of us could become the world's greatest philosopher or psychologist or theologian or linguist. . . . Satan has had multiple millennia to study and master the human disciplines, and when it comes to human subversion, he is the ultimate manipulator.[11]

Beyond these capabilities, the certainty of Satan's attack (v. 13) and the viciousness of his fiery assault (v. 16) add to our causes for concern. If Satan is so capable and his evil is so definite and destructive, then we had better regard him seriously. We must also recognize our limitations in confronting him. No one is ready for spiritual warfare until, in view of the nature of this Adversary, we freely confess that apart from God we cannot repel his assaults. This is the second great need of spiritual warfare: along with faith in our new nature, we must confess our helplessness without God.

——— OUR WEAPONRY ———

Confession of our helplessness prepares us—even compels us—to don the weapons of spiritual warfare. Paul identifies two major aspects of this arming process: putting on the full armor of God, and praying in the Spirit. We humbly seek these heavenly provisions when recognition of our enemy's potency rightly erodes our confidence in our own resources to repel him.

PUTTING ON GOD'S ARMOR

Confession of our helplessness apart from God must precede putting on our armor, lest our preparations be perceived as righteous works that qualify us to resist Satan. As Rose Marie Miller writes,

> The first "real enemy" in your life is always your own unsubmitted self-life (James 4:1-10). To struggle against your own agendas and passions is at the heart of spiritual warfare. The second "real enemy" is Satan. The one who hates you without compromise is always the power of darkness (Eph. 6:12). Wherever there is self-praising pride the Devil has much, much influence.[12]

The "steel" of God's armor is not a product of our energies and efforts, although we can unearth much erroneous teaching that implies otherwise.

Taking our stand

Paul carefully identifies the source of the strength in our armor. He says, "[B]e strong in the Lord and in *his* mighty power" (v. 10, emphasis mine). How are we to be strong in his power? We "put on the full armor *of God*" (v. 11, emphasis mine). After identifying the magnitude of Satan's power, Paul again tells us to "put on the full armor *of God*" (v. 13, emphasis mine). He repeatedly emphasizes the divine source of our protection. We take our "stand against the devil's schemes" (v. 11) and "stand [our] ground" (v. 13) not primarily by more vigorous performance of good deeds nor by greater exercise of our willpower and resolve, but through confidence in God's provision.

This perspective does not encourage spiritual sloth. Paul says, "[A]fter you have done everything" that is needed, God's armor enables the stand that spiritual warfare still requires (v. 13). These instructions maintain the importance and necessity of our labors, but keep us from believing that our works are sufficient to protect us from Satan's assaults. No matter how excellent his preparation in terms of diet and exercise, we would not expect a soldier to do well in battle if his armor were insufficient. In a similar way the spiritual disciplines God provides for us help prepare us for battle against our Adversary, but we are still totally exposed and vulnerable to attack without armor. Our armor is faith in what God has already provided for us.

Though there is a great human inclination to do so, if we interpret "putting on the full armor of God" as greater human righteousness or resolve, then Paul's metaphor will ultimately fail. That failure becomes apparent when we consider each instruction of Paul as it is sometimes taught with a well-intended (but misguided) zeal to equip Christians to battle Satan with human effort. Paul says, "Stand firm . . .

- "with the belt of truth buckled around your waist" (v. 14). This is often interpreted either as studying the truth so that you know it well, or speaking the truth with integrity.

- "with the breastplate of righteousness in place" (v. 14). This may be interpreted as acting righteously in as many situations as possible.

- "with your feet fitted with the readiness that comes from the gospel of peace" (v. 15). This, of course, commends proclaiming the gospel in as many places and ways as possible.

- " . . . take up the shield of faith, with which you can extinguish all the flaming arrows of the evil one" (v.16). Interpreters find various ways to demonstrate that these words require stirring up as much internal sureness, willpower, or belief as we can, so that Satan cannot penetrate our psyche with doubt or our lives with harm through a chink in our faith.

This kind of interpretation, however, becomes quite troubling when we read the instructions that immediately follow. Paul next says, "Take the helmet of salvation and the sword of the Spirit, which is the word of God" (v. 17). But how do we supply the helmet of salvation and the sword of the Spirit, which is the Word of God? Yes, I can quote from Scripture, as Jesus did to resist Satan, but I do not provide the Spirit. And eternal salvation is certainly not something that my hands supply.

How can we equip ourselves with salvation and the Spirit? The solution lies in discovering that such interpretations—whereby we arm ourselves by our own actions—miss Paul's point. His point eludes us when we ask, "*How* can *I* provide truth, righteousness, the Gospel of peace, faith, salvation, and the Spirit?" His point becomes evident when we ask, "*Who* supplies truth, righteousness, the Gospel of peace, faith, salvation, and the Spirit?" The answer is, our God supplies it.

Trusting our armor

Our God, not our hand, supplies these weapons against evil. Paul's precise language furthers this understanding. A literal translation indicates that we put on the full armor of God and stand, *"having* the belt of truth buckled" about our waist, and *"having* the breastplate of righteousness in place," and so on.[13] God has already put the armor in place. We stand firm *because* God has already supplied our armor, not *in order to receive* the armor.

This was the point from the beginning: we stand firm against the assaults of Satan because we have strength "in the power of God's might." God provides the power that enables us to stand against Satan's attacks (cf. Rom. 13:12; 1 Thess. 5:8). The Old Testament passage that stimulates Paul's thought on these images makes it clear that these pieces of armor are God's (see Isa. 59:17). Thus, we stand firm in the confidence that we are protected—armored—by his truth, by his righteousness, and with the gospel of peace, with the faith, with the salvation, and with the Spirit that are from him.

HIS PROVISION. —— Because God provides each aspect of our armor, we need not fear its failure against Satan's attacks. Our confidence is not in our ability to stand but in the ability of our armor to withstand assault. Whenever we begin to point to our godly practices as the source of our spiritual protection, our virtues become tools of unbelief in which we deny the need of grace and assert the rule of self.[14] We do not put on the armor of God by trusting in the more vigorous performance of our duties, but by relying on God's provision for our protection. We gain the confidence to rely on God's armor when, on Scripture's authority, we perceive his protection to be as real as the armor Paul observed on the soldier guarding him in prison while he penned these words.

Thus, when the day of evil comes and our temptation is great, we should not say, "Satan can't touch me, because I have been truthful, righteous, and faithful." Rather we should say, "I am protected by the truth that though I feel weak, I am strong; though I may fall, I possess Christ's righteousness.[15] And, though I am not perfect, I have peace with my God who has provided the faith I could not conjure (for faith, too, is a gift of God[16]), the salvation I could not earn, and the Spirit I daily need."

The way I visualize this truth—that we are enabled by confidence in the armor God provides—follows very precisely the imagery of Paul. I can imagine looking out through the faceplate of the helmet of salvation that God has given me. Coming toward me I see the assaulting forces of the Evil One with all his dominions, powers, and authorities. Simply seeing the approaching cloud of darkness from this mighty enemy, I fear that I cannot stand. The ground shakes, and my knees begin to buckle.

Then, the apostle Paul—like a general on the field of battle—calls out, "Steady now. Do not retreat. Take your stand. Be strong, in the power of his might. Forget the strength you thought you could provide. Remember the might of the armor God has given you. Resurrection power has given you a breastplate of his righteousness, the shield of faith, feet that are shod with readiness that comes from being at peace with the Sovereign of the universe. Beyond all of these defenses, he has given you an ultimate weapon, the sword of the Spirit that is the Word of God. Now, confident of the strength and integrity of the armor that you have been given, stand firm."

OUR EFFORT. ⎯⎯ Is there any degree of human effort in resisting sin? Yes, of course there is.[17] Already we have discussed the faith, church, and family patterns that are God's means of nurturing Christian health. In addition, study of God's Word, commitment to righteousness, and the proclamation of the gospel are means by which we are readied to repel Satan. Richard Foster personally articulates the responsibility that every maturing believer assumes:

> [T]hrough the Holy Spirit's guidance and strength, I will order my life according to an overall pattern that conforms to the way of Christ. Over time this process will develop deeply ingrained habits in me so that, at the moment of crisis, inner resources to act in a Christlike manner are available.[18]

Our habitual godliness is a means the Holy Spirit uses to increase our faith, inform our minds, and strengthen our wills for God's purposes. We cannot neglect the daily disciplines of holiness and expect to be well-muscled for spiritual warfare.[19]

Still, the core steel of our resistance "when we have done everything else" (cf. v. 16) is to take up "the shield of faith" in what God has provided so that we can withstand the fiery darts of the Devil. "Satan has not changed his strategies. *His approach is always to insinuate that God is not good, and that he is not for us.*"[20] Thus, our primary power in spiritual warfare resides in faith because, as Don Matzat writes,

> It is the primary task of the Devil to remove from us the Word of God, primarily the good news of the Gospel. He attacks our faith. In the parable of the sower, our Lord Jesus identified the birds who steal the

newly sown seed as the Devil. He does not want us to believe, confess, and stand upon the Word of God.[21]

Satan wants to rob us of confidence in our acceptance by God on the basis of
Christ's righteousness alone, knowing that the freedom, joy, and courage provided by the unyielding love of God unleashes the Spirit's power in our lives.

PRAYING IN GOD'S SPIRIT

Since the power to stand is ours, why do we not stand? The gospel answer
is not that our enemy is too strong, because Satan is defeated. Neither is
the answer that we are too weak, because resurrection power indwells
us. Rather the answer is that we do not have sufficient desire to resist. It
sounds contrary to the cry of the heart to say that we do not have a desire
to stand. We desperately desire the dismissal of the sin from our lives. Yes,
we want it gone, but until then we still want it. The sin still appeals. Our
armor is not too weak to withstand Satan's attacks unless we let him in, but
we do. For this reason, Paul's final instruction is not to add more armor
but rather to seek to stir within us the will to use it.

Why we pray in the Spirit

Having discussed the armor that we should put on, Paul urges us to do one
more thing: pray in the Spirit . . . first for ourselves and then for others (v.
18). As Ferguson explains, "Praying in the Spirit is prayer that conforms
to the will and purpose of the Spirit."[22] As we humbly submit our wills
and desires to God's, the Spirit takes our limited wisdom and zeal as finite
creatures and uses them with infinite wisdom and power to work all things
together for good (cf. Rom. 8:26-38).[23] In terms of our sanctification, the
"good" the Spirit brings is accomplished by transforming us continually
into Christ's likeness (Rom. 8:29).

What do we seek when praying in the Spirit for ourselves and others?
Such prayer is not a plea for magical power so much as it is a prayer for the
Spirit to stir up within us a greater zeal for God, an inner stirring to stand for
his purposes when the enemy approaches. We utter this prayer when we sing,

> Breathe, O breathe thy loving Spirit into ev'ry troubled breast;
> let us all in thee inherit, let us find the promised rest:
> take away the love of sinning; Alpha and Omega be;
> End of faith as its Beginning, set our hearts at liberty.[24]

We understand why Paul urges such prayer in the context of spiritual warfare when we discover where the concept of praying in the Spirit receives fuller explanation in Ephesians. While Paul is now urging *the people* of God to pray for the Spirit's work, *the apostle* has previously prayed the same in their behalf:

EPHESIANS 3:14-19

[14]For this reason I kneel before the Father, [15]from whom his whole family in heaven and on earth derives its name. [16]I pray that out of his glorious riches he may strengthen you with power through his Spirit in your inner being, [17]so that Christ may dwell in your hearts through faith. And I pray that you, being rooted and established in love, [18]may have power, together with all the saints, to grasp how wide and long and high and deep is the love of Christ, [19]and to know this love that surpasses knowledge—that you may be filled to the measure of all the fullness of God.

Paul's prayer culminates with the petition that the Ephesians would be strengthened with power by the Spirit in their inner being. This power will enable them to grasp how high and long and wide and deep is the love of Christ, so that through this love they will be filled with the fullness of God.

The power that the Spirit communicates comes as a result of the love he stirs in our hearts. Our desires are transformed by what Thomas Chalmers (1780–1847) called "the expulsive power of a new affection."[25] The Spirit renews and cleanses our desires, creating an appetite for a closer and more mature relationship with God. By the Spirit's work in us this appetite overwhelms and drives out unhealthy, previous appetites. As Ezekiel beautifully expressed it, those in whom the Spirit works become "careful to do" the Lord's will.[26] Samuel Bolton explains the radical changes the Spirit effects in our affections:

This, then is the reason why a godly man conducts himself well in duty, not merely because it is commanded but because he has the nature which truly and rightly responds to the command. The law of God which is in the Book is transcribed into his heart; it is his nature, his new nature. So that he acts his own nature renewed as he acts obedience. The eye needs no command to see, nor the ear to hear; it is their nature to see and hear. . . . So far as the heart is renewed, it is as natural for it to obey as for the eye to see or the ear to hear. . . . So far as the law of God is its nature, so far does it find delight in obedience.[27]

The Holy Spirit takes hearts that are hard and softens them toward God (Ezek. 11:19-20; 36:25-27). The Spirit changes our priorities, our affections, our cravings—and gives us a love for God that is greater than a love for the things of the world that attack us even as they attract us.

Hearts formerly cold toward God do not become warm toward his people and purposes by a mere act of willpower.[28] While we can will a change in behavior, we do not by an act of will change what we find attractive, appealing, and lovely. The Spirit accomplishes what willpower cannot in reconstructing the affections of our hearts. This is a supernatural work that is facilitated by the means of grace, but that cannot be accomplished by them apart from the Spirit.[29] We should understand that there is many a cold heart ritualistically praying and reading Scripture in the vain expectation that the labor itself will produce godly love and spiritual power. We pray in the Spirit because we believe that the Spirit alone can so radically change the heart as to make it truly desire the things of God.[30]

As I am writing, three oak trees outside my back window are waving their leaves in the cold midwinter winds. The waving is a sign of their obstinate nature. All of the other trees in our neighborhood have long since shed their leaves. These oaks, however, will keep the brown, shriveled vestiges of their former life all winter. While the winter blasts and freezes will strip the leaves from some stems and even make bald some sections of their limbs, the trees will not entirely shed the deadness that clings to them.

Only when the warmth of spring activates the hidden energies in the oaks will the new leaves push out the old. "The expulsive power of our new affections" operates similarly. As the vestiges of our old nature cling to us through the shriveled but still potent desires of a past way of life, no amount of natural effort will eradicate their presence. Though the rigor of our disciplines may remove some habits and change the appearance of large portions of our lives, only forces within us stimulated by the Spirit of God will truly replace vestiges of the old life with the vitality of the new.[31]

The human will is engaged in spiritual warfare, but it is not human willpower that defeats the forces of Satan.[32] Rather it is the supernatural process by which the Spirit makes his will our will by renewing within us a consuming, overwhelming, compelling love of God. Then, as the forces of evil come and we need the weapons (means) of grace that Paul has described, we willingly take up our arms with the confidence that God has provided everything we need to do what he requires.

Love for God provides the zeal we need to employ the weapons he provides. This does not mean that the battle will be without effort or without pain. It is, after all, spiritual *warfare*. But with the faith that God has given us sufficient armor to resist Satan, we can stand so long as we truly desire to do so. That desire is also the gift of God, as his Spirit for which we pray stirs within us the love for God that is more compelling than the love for sin.

How we change through the Spirit

As we try to explain to people how God can help them overcome entangling sins, we must help them see that *the why is the how*. Engaging in spiritual warfare *because of* a compelling love for God is *how* we secure victory over sin. A love for God made vital and vigorous by sensing deeply his compassion toward us is the primary means that enables believers to resist Satan.

A COMPELLING LOVE. —— Simply telling people what to do is not enough for spiritual victory. This becomes apparent when we consider how overmatched we are by our Adversary. Certainly, we must help people apply Scripture to their lives, and in that sense we must tell them what to do. But telling drowning people to "swim" will not rescue them from the waves.

People drowning in destructive habits are not rescued by simply urging them to act more like Christians—reading their Bibles more, praying more, and becoming accountable to fellow believers. These are all good and necessary steps. They may result in some behavior changes and even a reorientation of worldly desires, but in themselves these disciplines will not rescue from the sinews of sin that surround and infiltrate the heart. Just as secular psychology may change some people's habits by sophisticated behavioral techniques, the diligent pursuit of Christian disciplines can cause changes in us that have healthy aspects but do not reflect true spiritual change. So we must ask, how do we help people change at the core levels of their being?

We must keep in mind that, until the heart is changed, sinful compulsions may be redirected into more socially and personally acceptable practices, but their spiritually suffocating essence persists. Thus, the hardest question remains: Having dismantled works as the basis for our standing before God, how do we implore (or "leverage") people to use the needed disciplines of grace to combat Satan? We believe that such disciplines are powerful weapons for holiness in spiritual warfare. Still, the power and willingness to use these means comes from a constraining love for God that replaces our affections for the world. That change of affections, that reconstruction of heart, is the supernatural work of the Spirit for which we pray. We facilitate this work of the Spirit when we teach others the reasons *why* we love Jesus.

A CONSISTENT ADULATION. —— Spiritual change is more a consequence of what our hearts love than of what our hands do. The spiritual disciplines are important, but not as important as developing a heart for God. Hands and hearts coordinate and reinforce each other's functions in the biblical model of sanctification, but the heart is the command center for every battle (Prov. 4:23). As Steve Smallman writes, "We are quick to tell people who profess Christ what they need to be doing. But the apostle Paul, it seems to me, did not begin with 'doing' as much as 'knowing'. That was usually his first point of stress when he prayed for the churches."[33]

Full and consistent apprehension of why we love God is the most effective piece of armor in the Christian arsenal, because the Devil always begins his attack with an alienation of our affections. Thus, our most powerful spiritual weapon is consistent adulation of the mercy of God revealed in Christ. We "preach the Gospel to our own hearts,"[34] telling others and ourselves of God's eternal love, of Christ's humble birth, sinless life, selfless sacrifice, victorious resurrection, and coming glory. We provide the power of the gospel to other believers by reminding them of the manifold ways in which an infinitely loving Father has made the wonders of heaven the certain inheritance of children as wayward as we. Knowing that our adulation of Christ is our most powerful transforming tool gives focus and purpose to our preaching, sacrament practices, prayers, parenting, witness, and life endeavors.

As the Spirit uses the revelation of God's grace to change hearts, then affections change, lives change, and disciplines are willingly and lovingly exercised.[35] John Murray beautifully summarizes,

> The Holy Spirit is the Spirit of truth and therefore as the Spirit of love he captivates our hearts by the love of God and of Christ to us. In the diffusion of that love there flows also love to one another. "Beloved, if God so loved us, we ought to love one another" (1 John 4:11). The

biblical ethic knows no fulfilment [sic] of its demands other than that produced by the constraint and claim of Christ's redeeming love (cf. 2 Corinthians 5:14, 15; Galatians 2:20). Our love is always ignited by the flame of Christ's love. And it is the Holy Spirit who sheds abroad in our hearts the igniting flame of the love of God in Christ Jesus. The love that is ignited is the fruit of the Spirit.[36]

The Word of God is the sword of the Spirit not because the Bible has magical power to charm Satan, but because its content from beginning to end is the revelation of God's love that compels the human heart to seek him (Eph. 3:17).[37] The message of grace is the instrument of power in spiritual warfare.

In light of the importance of the Spirit's work to stir up new affections within us, what does spiritual warfare look like in real life? Should we practice spiritual disciplines? Yes, we should. But we should do so with the recognition that these disciplines are primarily means of polishing the armor that God has provided, so that we see his power more clearly (Rom. 13:12). Practicing these habits in order to overpower Satan by our own discipline and diligence actually makes us more spiritually vulnerable.[38] We don the armor of God by faith, repenting of our own weaknesses and believing that each element of divine protection can resist the assaults of Satan as God has promised.[39] And, having received the promises represented by each aspect of the armor, we relish and rely upon the love of God to stir up within us a large and loving heart for his glory and purposes. Then we act as that heart inspires and enables.

This vision of the true nature of spiritual warfare explains why there must be such an emphasis on God's grace in our lives and in our ministries. We do not proclaim grace so that anyone will make light of sin or of our duty to resist it. We herald God's amazing mercy in order to join with the Spirit in stirring up in his people such a love for God that, when the day of evil comes, they will gladly put on the full armor he provides. Then, despite the hardships and the pain God's people may face in the battle, they will stand strong in the power of his might.

——— EMPOWERING LOVE ———

I enjoy watching "iron man" competitions on television. Watching those who swim, bike, and run multiple-marathon distances in the grueling triathlon makes me dream of what I might be able to do if I had more time and opportunity, and a different body. More inspiring to me than the usual stories of the big-name competitors, however, was the 1999 account of the father-and-son team, Dick and Ricky Hoyt. The two have run together in more than eight hundred races.

More remarkable than the fellowship this father and son enjoy is the fact that the now adult son, Ricky, was born with cerebral palsy. To race, he must be pulled, pushed, or carried by his father. There is a part of us that might jump to the conclusion that Ricky does not race at all . . . that his father does all the work. But tens of thousands of viewers saw the son's role in this competition when wind, cold, and an equipment failure made progress hard on Ricky, even though his father was the one pedaling the modified tandem bike. Dick knelt down to his son, contorted and trembling in the cold, as the two were still facing many more miles of race on the defective bike. Said the father to the child belted to the bicycle seat, "Do you want to keep going, Son?"

The father would be the one enabling and providing the means to overcome, but the son still had to have the heart to finish. To the son was given the privilege and responsibility to desire to continue the race. Though the example is not perfect, it explains much of what the Bible teaches about our spiritual battles. We have a Father who has already given us the power to resist all the challenges of our Adversary. We can prevail through the means and strength our Father provides, but we must still have the heart to do so.

Because we need a heart that beats for him, our God bids us seek the Spirit, who opens our minds with the Word of God to the knowledge of the Savior and renews our will with a compelling love for him. By God's Spirit we desire to run with him (and to him) more than anything else in the world. His grace enables us "to grasp how wide and long and high and deep is the love of Christ, and to know this love that surpasses knowledge—that [we] may be filled to the measure of all the fullness of God" (Eph. 3:18-19).

Part Three

MOTIVES
of
LOVE

What's Discipline
Got to Do with It?

The young man called late at night and asked if the pastor would meet with him the next morning. The pastor did not want to pry but did want to prepare for the meeting, so he asked, "What may I pray about in preparation for our time together?" The man chose not to answer the question, but responded simply that what he wanted to discuss was "very serious." They made arrangements to have breakfast at a nearby restaurant.

The next morning the young man told his pastor that on a recent business trip he had stayed too late at the hotel bar with a woman colleague. The alcohol, distance from home, and easy laughter the two shared had led to the obvious. They ended up in bed together. "Now what?" asked the man.

The pastor took a deep breath. He thought of the young wife and small children whose lives could be so terribly affected by a night of indiscretion. To preserve the family, he briefly considered advising the young man to cover up the error, but then the eternal consequences of establishing such a spiritual pattern convinced him that simple honesty was the path to follow. To make the young man think biblically about what he must do, the minister asked him a series of questions:

- Had he prayed to ask God's forgiveness and pardon?

- Had he confessed his sin to the young woman involved and told her that the intimacy would never happen again?

- Had he confessed his wrong to his wife and asked her forgiveness?

- And, if he was not yet ready to do this, had he at least arranged to have an AIDS test? For until he had been tested, he could not approach the marriage bed without endangering his wife and the child she was expecting.

The young man listened to each of the questions without expression or comment. When the pastor finished, the young man pushed his breakfast plate away from him, leaned back in his seat, and said, "I came for grace, not for discipline. You disappoint me, pastor."

The words cut the pastor to the heart. He did not wonder if what he had said on this occasion was wrong. He wondered, rather, what he had said in the past that would lead an intelligent, capable man such as this to believe that the promises of grace mean we will never have to face any consequences for wrongdoing. Even after confessing his infidelity, the young businessman seemed to be more interested in accusing the pastor of hypocrisy than of assuming any responsibility for his own actions. He said to the pastor, "You say you believe in grace, but you judge people according to their works just like the rest of the world."

In essence the businessman was saying, "God and those who communicate his grace must do their part to make sure that life does not become difficult or inconvenient for me no matter what I do." This, we must make clear, is not the nature of biblical grace. As much as we might at times wish that God's free pardon permitted freedom from all his requirements and our responsibilities, God makes no such promise. Instead he assures us that he will discipline those he loves in order to make them more conscious of his requirements, more careful of his standards, and safe from future, more serious error.

In our childishness we may say to God, "If you really loved me, then you would not bother me, or limit me, or make demands on me." However, we should understand that such requests are really demanding God's absence from our lives, since his commands are an expression of his character and care in our lives. God will not grant such requests, because he promises never to leave or forsake us. When God says, "I will not leave you alone," he is not only promising his continuing presence, he is promising holy confrontation when we abandon him.

God desires to draw ever nearer to our hearts and to draw us ever nearer to himself. He accomplishes this by proclaiming and exercising his love toward us. But we should understand clearly that such love requires him, to strip away our predilections and propensities for wrongdoing in order that our lives may more fully embrace his holiness.

This shedding of the husk of our humanity is not painless, but neither is it punitive. God's discipline is always loving in its intent. The love goal of discipline makes it gracious, but this is not easy to understand if and when pain is involved. The writer of Hebrews takes care to explain the grace of God's discipline so that we will not despair ("not lose heart," are his words) when this severe mercy comes.

HEBREWS 12:4-11

[4]In your struggle against sin, you have not yet resisted to the point of shedding your blood. [5]And you have forgotten that word of encouragement that addresses you as sons:

> "My son, do not make light of the Lord's discipline,
>   and do not lose heart when he rebukes you,
> [6]because the Lord disciplines those he loves,
>   and he punishes everyone he accepts as a son."

[7]Endure hardship as discipline; God is treating you as sons. For what son is not disciplined by his father? [8]If you are not disciplined (and everyone undergoes discipline), then you are illegitimate children and not true sons. [9]Moreover, we have all had human fathers who disciplined us and we respected them for it. How much more should we submit to the Father of our spirits and live! [10]Our fathers disciplined us for a little while as they thought best; but God disciplines us for our good, that we may share in his holiness. [11]No discipline seems pleasant at the time, but painful. Later on, however, it produces a harvest of righteousness and peace for those who have been trained by it.

The writer addresses a church that in some measure has already faltered in the face of persecution. His goal is to prepare God's people for greater trials ahead. In preceding chapters of Hebrews that preparation took the form of citing the example of God's own Son who endured persecution for the sake of God's purposes, and of recalling others in the past who remained faithful in trial (chapters 10–11). Now, those to whom this letter is addressed must prepare their hearts for their own present and future spiritual warfare. To prepare them, the writer speaks unambiguously concerning a necessary feature of spiritual equipping that they probably do not want to hear: God's discipline. In the course of this discussion he answers a simple but difficult question that comes from the depths of our souls: what good does God's discipline do?

DISCIPLINE
EXPLAINS HARDSHIP

"Endure hardship as discipline," says the writer of Hebrews (12:7). When we experience difficulty we are to understand that it is, at least in part, God's process of making us what he wants us to be. This understanding is important for two reasons: it teaches that hardship is neither punitive nor pointless.

NOT PUNITIVE

Saying that discipline is not punitive does not mean that it is without pain. The Bible does not anesthetize us to God's discipline, but keeps the pain from overwhelming us by promising that the purpose of God's discipline is never to impose a penalty or to damage us. Nine times in this passage from Hebrews 12 the term for discipline refers to the correction or training of children. It includes not only reaction to wrong but also preparation for future challenges and character development. One commentator says that the meaning of this discipline is "to put someone in a state of good order so that he can function as intended."

The goal of God's discipline is to correct, or to set right, or to improve, not to make someone suffer as an act of vengeance or retribution (cf. v. 11c). Samuel Bolton explains:

> If Christ has borne whatever our sins deserved, and by doing so has satisfied God's justice to the full, then God cannot, in justice, punish us for sin, for that would require the full payment from Christ and yet demand part of it from us. . . .
>
> God does not chastise us as a means of satisfaction for sin, but for rebuke and caution, to bring us to mourn for sin committed, and to beware of the like.
>
> It must always be remembered that, although Christ has borne the punishment of sin, and although God has forgiven the saints for their sins, yet God may God-fatherly correct His people for sin.

Christ endured the great shower of wrath, the black and dismal hours of displeasure for sin. That which falls upon us is as a sunshine shower, warmth with wet, wet with the warmth of His love to make us fruitful and humble. . . . That which the believer suffers for sin is not penal, arising from vindictive justice, but medicinal, arising from a fatherly love. It is his medicine, not his punishment; his chastisement, not his sentence; his correction, not his condemnation.[1]

Our hearts warm to these words that make such good theoretical and relational sense, but are they biblically defensible? This same passage in Hebrews says that God "*punishes* everyone he accepts as a son" (quoting from Prov. 3:11-12, emphasis mine). Since the word *punishment* can carry the connotation of imposing a penalty, it is very important to determine just what this New Testament writer means. The translators of the *New International Version* of Scripture that I have quoted are attempting to be gentle with our sensibilities in their use of the word *punishment*. The root word being translated is actually a term for "whipping." This word initially sounds even worse than "punishment," but the precise meaning is important because it indicates that the author is describing the *means*, not the *motive*, of divine discipline.

Though the means of God's actions may be quite painful, his motive is never to "punish" his children in the sense that he makes them pay some penalty for their sin. We need to remember that the writer of Hebrews urges us to "fix our eyes on Jesus, the author and perfecter of our faith, who for the joy set before him endured the cross" (Heb. 12:2a). After he had suffered for us, our Savior then "sat down" as our High Priest at the right hand of God to signify that his atoning work was finished (v. 2b). The penalty for our sin God has fully and completely put upon his own Son (see also Heb. 7:27; 9:24-28; 10:10; 1 Pet. 3:18).

For two thousand years Israel's priests offered atoning sacrifices for sin. The Bible describes in intricate detail the altar, candlesticks, robes, curtains, laver, and tables involved in the temple ceremonies. However, there is no description of a chair for the priests. They did not sit down, because their work was never done. But when Jesus acted as our great High Priest, offering his body in sacrifice for our sin, no other sacrifice would be needed, and so he sat down. His posture signals that his work is finished. Now we can rest in his finished work, with no need to offer additional sacrifices for our wrong.

What was necessary to satisfy divine justice and reconcile us to God, the author and *perfecter* of our faith fully supplied. God does not now demand some additional penalty or penance or pain to make us right with him. The prophet Isaiah says, "The punishment that brought us peace was upon him" (Isa. 53:5). We are at peace with God by virtue of Christ's assuming fully the penalty that our sins deserve.

 Since God's justice has been fully satisfied, the remaining purposes of his discipline are to help those dear to him to know more of the riches of his grace, and to grow more like him.[2] As indicated by the loving motives of the heart that administers it, divine discipline is intended to benefit the wayward rather than to exact retribution for wrong. Very simply put, understanding the difference between punishment and discipline enables us to consider God as a Father in heaven rather than an ogre in the sky.

 I once left a hospital room with an elder whose son had been seriously injured in a freakish flying accident. The boy was hanging between life and death, and though the family was gathered around, the father of the boy wanted to speak to me in the hallway. Through tears he said, "I know what is going on. God is punishing my son for my sin."

 The father's comments shocked me. He was a wonderful man of faith, but in this time of hardship the only God he seemed to know was an ogre who was demanding his pound of flesh. I don't know how God gave me words to reply, but the ones that came to mind have helped me in my own times of hardship since. I replied to this grieving father, "God is not putting the penalty of your sin on your son, because our Father put the penalty for your sin on *his* Son."

 The hardship we face can be disciplinary, but it is not punitive. Our heavenly Father can use hardship to correct and to train, but he is never an ogre who delights in harming those he calls his own children. They are so precious to him that he purchased them with the life of his own Son. God will not damage treasure so costly (cf. Deut. 7:7; Eph. 1:14; 1 Pet. 2:9).

NOT POINTLESS

If hardship is not punitive, then why does God allow it? The writer of Hebrews answers, "God disciplines us for our good, that we may share in his holiness" (Heb. 12:10). He also tells us why the Hebrew Christians needed this reassurance. They were being tempted to let down in their fight against evil. He gently chides their weakness, saying, "In your struggle against sin, you have not yet resisted to the point of shedding your blood" (v. 4).[3] Still, he does not want their hardship to cause them to give up and give in to sin. So he encourages them to remember that hardship is not a sign of God's abandonment but of his activity (vv. 5-6; cf. Rev. 3:19). By teaching the believers to recognize temporal hardship as discipline rather than desertion, the writer equips them to convert such hardship into a tool for resisting sin and its spiritual threats.

The writer assures the Hebrew Christians that God has no desire to harm them but, in a manner similar to an earthly father, wants to train them in character and conduct that will lead to future blessing (vv. 7-10). Through discipline God "produces a harvest of righteousness and peace for those who have been trained by it" (v. 11). These training aspects of discipline need to be kept in mind, lest we think that all hardship is God's response to some wrong in our lives.

Discipline can be preparatory as well as corrective. God may use a fiery trial to prepare us for greater usefulness or as a means to turn us from sin, or as a combination of both of these purposes. As he knows is best in his fatherly love, God uses the disciplines of difficulty to make us both more tender and more hard than we have been.

Making tender

Affliction and trial conform our nature more to Christ's. As he is able to sympathize with us through his suffering (Heb. 4:15), we are able to sympathize with his heart by *our* suffering. When our goal is *not* simply taking care of ourselves, our hearts begin to beat with his heart's concerns (Acts 20:35; Rom. 12:15; Gal. 6:2; Col. 3:12-15). Solely because Christ cares for them, we begin to care for people and purposes that benefit us nothing.

Once when our church's leadership council met to discuss our outreach efforts, the leader of the meeting asked who had taken the time to speak to two young women who had visited the preceding Sunday. The two friends "stuck out" because they were so unattractive physically and were dressed so shabbily. All had noticed the pair, but no one had spoken to them. Then our leader dared to ask why no one had spoken to them. With equal daring a sensitive elder replied, "Because it was not to the benefit of anyone here to speak to them. May God forgive us!"

When we have experienced loneliness, disdain, poverty, abuse, unfair accusation, fear, betrayal, heartache, fatigue, and trial, then our hearts remain tender toward those facing similar difficulties. Even when there is no benefit to us, the discipline we experience enables us to sympathize with those who suffer and, consequently, maintain a biblical concern that:

- Some African cities have a 50 percent AIDS infection rate.

- Some American cities have high schools where not one graduating student is able to pass a standardized achievement test.

- In our nation's capital, one of every two births is out of wedlock.

- One in five African-American males between 18 and 29 years of age is in jail.

- In some parts of this country, abortions equal live births.

- Civil wars now rage in many countries throughout the world, with ethnic and religious fighting accounting for tens of thousands of deaths each year.

- A third of the Christian church in the world today must operate in secrecy, under the threat of persecution and extermination.

- Throughout the world hundreds of millions do not know the love of Jesus.

There is no advantage for us in knowing these facts. No benefit accrues to us in caring about the people involved. No reward will come for sacrificing our life to do something because we care for such people. Yet we *will* care when we have experienced enough tears to keep us tender toward God's people and purposes.

The apostle Paul wrote to the Christians at Colosse, "Now I rejoice in what was suffered for you, and I fill up in my flesh what is still lacking in regard to Christ's afflictions, for the sake of his body, which is the church" (Col. 1:24). His words remind us that not only do our sufferings enable us to identify with Christ, but also they give us his heart. By suffering as he suffered we learn to love as he loved. Life becomes less obsessed with what we can get out of it when we learn to die to self. We become sympathetic with those afflicted rather than remaining obsessed with avoiding personal disadvantage or inconvenience.

Making hard

The discipline of affliction also hardens us, in that it relaxes our grasp on this world. We learn that the cruelties and vagaries of this temporal existence are real and, thus, we are less inclined to live for what this world offers. We walk through life as our Savior did—as pilgrims with eyes and energies focused on future glory—because we have been stripped of the delusion that this world can offer any satisfaction that is not always in jeopardy.

Because the pleasures and glamour of this world charm us less, we come less under their influence. By learning that the best of this world's delights can vanish in a moment, prove false, or bring great pain, we become unwilling to sacrifice ourselves on their altars. We simply stop being persuaded or distracted by this world's promises and as a result the rewards, pleasures, and pains of this world lose their power over us. As we become hardened to this world's powers, we subsequently become empowered by the next world's priorities and promises.

Knowing that God intends to use suffering for the purposes of both making tender our hearts and hardening our resolve enables us to face difficulties with greater endurance. A minister (who prefers to remain anonymous) recently wrote:

> After being in a pastorate for only two years, I have faced several adulteries among the leaders of my church, I have dealt with multiple, terminal illnesses—tragedies of young and old, I have tried to navigate through intense political and generational battles rocking our church, and I have wondered how much more I could take. Then, a few weeks ago, the Lord put me within hearing of a conversation a young woman in our church was having with my wife. The woman simply said, "I wonder what God is preparing your husband to do that requires him to face so much so early in his ministry."
>
> The implicit question in her words had a profound effect on my heart that has given me great strength. I was reminded by her question that God lets nothing go to waste in our lives. He is preparing me for more service, both by making me tender in learning to care for those who were suffering and in making me hard so that I could endure their and my pain. Knowing that there is a purpose in God's plan and in my difficulties enables me to serve God with more courage and conviction. I again feel that I can endure because I know that God is in my suffering.

Because the hardship Christians face is discipline, it is not pointless.

Knowing that God has a purpose for our hardship, we will neither "make light of the Lord's discipline" nor "lose heart" when it comes (v. 5). The pain never means that God wants our harm. His intention is always to bring an ultimate good, even if his discipline requires temporary hurt. Knowing this enables us to endure what we must without making light of the difficulty or despising the God who uses it.

The story is told of a mother who took her son to the doctor because of a fever. The doctor decided that the child would need a shot. To put her child at ease about the coming pain, the mother tried to make light of the shot. "Don't worry, Johnny," she said, "this won't hurt a bit." The doctor, who knew it surely would hurt, prepared the child with an honesty that would build trust and encouragement in the midst of pain. Said the doctor, "Son, I may hurt you, but I will not harm you." These are God's words to us so that we will not grow discouraged or despise the Lord's discipline. For our good in the war against evil, and to preserve us against spiritual damage, our God may allow our hurt. But he will not harm us.

NOT PASSIONLESS

We are God's children, and for that reason when we face difficulty we need not despair that his care is lacking. His discipline only designs to heal, to help, and to bring us back into his loving embrace.

Knowing him through our trials

Faith in the purposes of his discipline grants strength to endure and to grow in the trials that are sure to come to both the faithful and the wayward. God passionately promotes the ultimate welfare of his children, and promises for each what the centuries-old hymn "How Firm a Foundation" teaches:

> "When through the deep waters I call you to go,
> the rivers of sorrow shall not overflow;
> for I will be with you, your troubles to bless,
> and sanctify to you your deepest distress.

> "When through fiery trials your pathway shall lie,
> my grace, all sufficient, shall be your supply;
> the flame shall not hurt you; I only design
> your dross to consume and your gold to refine.

"The soul that on Jesus has leaned for repose,
I will not, I will not desert to his foes;
that soul, though all hell should endeavor to shake,
I'll never, no never, no never forsake."[4]

The discipline of the Father who sent Jesus is not punitive and is not pointless but is full of grace. We cannot always prove this by the facts available to the human eye in a fallen world. Still, Scripture gives us eyes of faith to see that God's plans are to benefit us and not to harm us; to give us a hope and a future (cf. Jer. 29:11).

Looking only at our temporal situations and immediate difficulties will cloud our vision, but when we focus on God's character rather than our circumstances, our sight clears. He who did not spare his own Son but delivered him up for us all will along with that gift provide whatever is needed for our eternal well being (Rom. 8:32).

Debbie Trickett writes with the clear vision that faith in Christ's love provides as she describes the darkness of her childlessness:

> Nothing else in my life has been as baffling to me as not being able to conceive a child. My emotions hide even from myself, spilling out in tears at times of sadness or anger at the most inopportune times. There have been no days of real clarity, no time when a light has come on to show the way—not even a little. But the mysterious and marvelous mercy of God has convinced me of one thing in all this; it is dark because I am in that deep hidden place under God's wing. . . .
>
> My heart cries out, "Why, O God, will you not answer this prayer?" . . . When this happens, God in His time and in His various graceful ways, comes to me to remind me that I am not alone.
>
> He has given His best to me, His own beautiful, beloved child. Will he withhold any good thing from me? No, never. Is Jesus enough to make up this aching void in my soul? I do not always feel that it is so. But it is. Jesus loves me . . . this I know.[5]

So that we will perceive the reality of God's affection despite the real afflictions we must endure in this world, the Bible makes the ministry of Jesus its theme from the first page to the last. Every page of its history— every character, event, and teaching—unfolds the mystery that God has loved his people from eternity, and has sent his Son to redeem them from their weakness and to fit them for heaven.[6]

So great is God's passion to save and sanctify his children that it takes priority for him over all our other comforts, pursuits, and affections. This is not to imply that God always conforms us to his purposes by discipline alone. To the contrary, his ordinary way of molding our hearts and affections is by overwhelming blessing with things dearest in human experience: loving families, provision of all that we need (not all our desires, which would be unhealthy for us), providential control of all circumstances for our good, and joy in him.

Why then does God allow the trials that discipline us? Probably the answer lies in the way we let blessings and comforts dull our perceptions to our greater need of finding ultimate and eternal fulfillment in him. God loves us too much for us to become deaf to his voice. Thus, as C. S. Lewis says, "God whispers to us in our pleasures . . . but shouts in our pains."[7] For our good, God disciplines (i.e., trains) through treasures and trials, by joys and sorrows, through denial of vain desires, as well as by blessing beyond what we can ask or even imagine (Eph. 3:20). All we experience and all our heavenly Father allows he carefully designs to promote our spiritual good, eternal salvation, and ultimate fulfillment through the joy of knowing him (Rom. 8:28).[8]

Knowing him through the trials of others

I was shocked when I looked down the line of friends graduating with me. The realization suddenly hit me that every one of my close friends had been through a major life challenge while in seminary. Why, I wondered, had going through seminary been so hard? While I still cannot answer with certainty these twenty-five years later, I have little doubt that the suffering we experienced was necessary for us to understand the God we were preparing to proclaim.

Suffering cannot be avoided if we are really to know Christ. Since the Bible says that he became like us in order to sympathize and understand our condition (Heb. 4:15; 5:2), the converse must also be true. We must know his suffering in order to know him. The apostle Paul writes, "I want to know Christ and the power of his resurrection and the fellowship of his sufferings, becoming like him in his death" (Phil. 3:10). If even an apostle would only know Christ through suffering, then I must recognize that the Christian disciplines that reveal him include Scripture reading, prayer, communion with fellow believers—and sharing in the fellowship of his suffering.

But what is the nature of Christ's suffering that we must share, in order fully to know his fellowship? His suffering included poverty and humiliation, pain and death. All of these he endured for us. We must not forget this altruistic dimension of his afflictions. He suffered to take on himself the guilt and the consequences of the sins of others. Thus, if we are to know him through like suffering, we will not merely have to experience the difficulty of nameless forces and circumstances; we must also experience what it means to suffer for the sins of others. We must be willing to endure and love the damaged and damaging personalities who make us suffer. This is Luther's theology of the cross—the understanding that our deepest knowing of the One who bore the cross for us in some measure depends on our own cross-bearing of the miseries of this world and even of the miserableness of others.[9]

In Sudan, a radical Muslim regime has targeted Christians for mandatory conversion or extermination. Selective starvation and bombing of the Christian villages have been traditional tactics used to accomplish these purposes. But human rights organizations have reported that another newer method of conversion involves taking Christians, in groups of fifty, many miles into the desert. There our brothers and sisters in Christ are left without food or water. Every couple of days government trucks return to the site with offers to rescue those who are ready to deny their faith. The trucks keep coming back every few days to renew the offer until there are no more Christians living. Then the trucks take the next group of fifty into the desert.

This is a horror beyond the ability of most reading this book to fathom. Yet amid such suffering there is a deep spiritual blessing. Those brothers and sisters—by their suffering of deprivation and by their suffering for the evil of others—know something more of what Christ was willing to endure for them when with a whisper and a blink he could have called upon heaven's avenging angels to rescue him.

When we face the pressures of finances, when illnesses ravage our families, when dear friends become our critics, when trusted workers undermine our leadership, when governments act unfairly, when people to whom we have given ourselves turn on us, and when those we count on remove their support—there is still cause for joy. Whether we suffer under the weight of circumstances or under the weightiness of bearing the consequences of the sins of others—these disciplines teach us more of what Christ endured for us. As a result, we know him to a degree and depth not available through any other means of study or contemplation.

The discipline of suffering shows us how tender and tenacious was Christ's care for us. The body blows that come, the accusations, the deprivations, the betrayals—in each we can say, "Ah, Lord Jesus, now I understand more deeply who you are and how much you loved me, for you endured this when you could have escaped it all. You suffered so for my sake and that of countless others who caused you pain. Ah, Jesus, now I know you."

Though we should never seek suffering in morbid or meritorious self-indulgence, knowledge that temporal discipline deepens our knowledge of our Lord makes us more willing and able to endure it. I occasionally think to myself that it would be nice to be rid of all of the headaches, irritating details, and distracting pressures of my office. I yearn for opportunities to write sermons and books without distraction and with adequate time. I think if I could just get free of daily entanglements, then I could really do something significant. All such thoughts I know are ultimately folly, for what sermons do people want to hear from a preacher who lives without challenge or difficulty? Apart from trials of life there is no deep knowledge of the Savior worth sharing. The testing of our faith is what produces the perseverance that makes us mature and complete (see James 1:3).

When we understand that God has *not* called us to freedom from all difficulty, his grace begins to flow through us in the most profound ways. Knowing that he communicates himself through suffering, we find ourselves willing—for the sake of others—to pursue opportunities that are less prestigious, stay in positions with fewer perks, go to fields of service where the people cannot adequately compensate us, and endure people whose insensitivities and ingratitude cause us to suffer.

When knowing Christ is our highest goal, then escaping suffering will not be a chief motivation of our lives. Instead, the deeper purposes and power of God will dominate us. Thus, through the example of his own Son, the Father tells us that sufferings should not surprise us. In fact, they help us to know him better by making us more like him in priority and purpose.

DISCIPLINE
CONFIRMS SONSHIP

To this point I probably have not written much about divine discipline that will be seen as news. I have simply said that God's discipline—though it may seem unpleasant—is intended for our good. In this I have probably seemed much like a mother urging her children to eat their vegetables or take their vitamins: "I know that you don't like it, but take it anyway because it's good for you." But divine discipline has a health-driven purpose greater than vegetables or vitamins.

We need to understand this higher purpose so that we will gain strength from our trials rather than being overwhelmed by them (cf. Heb. 12:5; Isa. 43:1-7). Discipline is a means to gain a special vision of God's love—a means of seeing special things about ourselves and about God (Heb. 12:6).

A few years ago a seminary student came to me confessing his anger with God. The student had struggled with tight finances throughout his studies. His grades were marginal though he worked extraordinarily hard. The combination of tight finances that required him to work long hours outside the home, along with long hours of study away from his family, were creating tensions in his marriage. This was particularly burdensome because the couple was expecting a baby, and they already had a handicapped child who had drained them physically, emotionally, and financially.

The student catalogued his difficulties and then asked, "Why does God treat me this way? I wouldn't treat my child like this." His question makes sense. If God really loves us, then why does he allow us to go through such pain? Curiously the answer the Bible provides is that such actions confirm his love and our status as his children.

Why Discipline Starts

If we were not his children, then God's discipline would not start. Sometimes when my children think that I am being too strict in forbidding them to do something, they will respond by saying something like, "Dad, why won't you let us? Jason's parents don't care."

Of course, such statements grant me the opportunity to ask my children to consider their words. Those other parents' lack of discipline indicates in some measure that they "don't care." The Bible actually says that parents who will not discipline "hate" their children. This is because children without discipline have inadequate guidance to build their character and keep them from danger (Lev. 26:23-24; Prov. 5:23; 19:18). Parents who will not discipline are treating their children with such lack of care that the results are as bad as if the parents hated their children.

God's willingness to discipline us confirms that we are children for whom he cares (Prov. 13:24). As an earthly father's neglect of discipline indicates that he has prioritized other matters above his children, God's attention to discipline proves he has no higher priorities than us (Heb.12:7-9). The mark of the unregenerate is that God lets them have their own way (Rom. 1:24, 26, 28); the mark of those in union with Christ is that God turns them to his way.

Discipline does not indicate that God has abandoned or despised us. We live in a fallen world where hardship exists for all. Even Jesus, the Son of Man, did not live without pain. We do great damage to others' faith when we imply or teach that "real" Christians do not experience affliction. Great purposes call for great training, and this may involve intense discipline even where no flagrant sin exists:

- Jesus said to his disciples, "Blessed are those who are persecuted because of righteousness" (Matt. 5:10); "No one who has left home or brothers or sisters or mother or father or children or fields for me and the gospel will fail to receive a hundred times as much in this present age (homes, brothers, sisters, mothers, children and fields—and with them, persecutions) and in the age to come, eternal life" (Mark 10:29-30; see also John 15:18-19).

- Paul said to those at Philippi, "For it has been granted to you on behalf of Christ not only to believe on him, but also to suffer for him" (Phil. 1:29); and to Timothy, "[E]veryone who wants to live a godly life in Christ Jesus will be persecuted" (2 Tim. 3:12).

- Peter said to the persecuted church, "Dear friends, do not be surprised at the painful trial you are suffering, as though something strange were happening to you. But rejoice that you participate in the sufferings of Christ, so that you may be overjoyed when his glory is revealed" (1 Pet. 4:12).

- John said to the church in Smyrna, "Do not be afraid of what you are about to suffer. I tell you, the devil will put some of you in prison to test you, and you will suffer persecution for ten days. Be faithful, even to the point of death, and I will give you the crown of life" (Rev. 2:10).

God's discipline is confirmation of our calling and purpose, for without trial the realities of God are hidden to us. By his discipline God frees us from the attractions of the world and the attentions to self that keep us distant from him and his purposes. Edith Stein insightfully identifies the importance of loosening our grasp on this world to claim the realities of the eternal. She writes, "I believe that the more deeply someone is drawn into God, the more one must also come out of oneself; that is, come out into the world, in order to carry divine life into it."[10] As God redirects our priorities through discipline, it becomes our will to do God's will. We find our life not in our priorities but in his, not in our pursuits but in his purposes.

In essence, discipline enfolds us into God's embrace and makes all worldly noises, desires, and distractions only background. We feast on the milk of his presence, and in discovering that he is our portion we also find how precious a child we are to him (Ps. 73:26). Jesus said, "If anyone would come after me, he must deny himself and take up his cross and follow me. For whoever wants to save his life will lose it, but whoever loses his life for me will find it" (Matt. 16:24-25). Through our faith that God's discipline is motivated by his love, he enables us both to lose and to find our lives. The Spirit supernaturally creates a disposition of the will to live for Christ, and in doing so gives us his life as our own. Dietrich Bonhoeffer, who died in a Nazi prison camp, writes,

> If we refuse to take up our cross and submit to suffering and rejection at the hands of men, we forfeit our fellowship with Christ and have ceased to follow him. But if we lose our lives in his service and carry our cross, we shall find our lives again in the fellowship of the cross with Christ. . . . To bear the cross proves to be the only way of triumphing over suffering. This is true of all who follow Christ, because it was true for him.[11]

WHEN DISCIPLINE STOPS

Because we are God's children we experience his discipline, but also because we are his children there is a limited duration to divine discipline. The writer of Hebrews compares God's discipline to that of earthly fathers who discipline for "a little while." And though this discipline does not seem pleasant "at the time," "later on" it "produces a harvest of righteousness and peace" (Heb. 12:10-11).

Discipline may persist at great length in earthly time, but on the eternal clock its duration is short. This is evidence of great mercy. When we who have been saved through the death of Christ trample on the blood of

God's own Son by deliberate sin or negligence of holiness, God has every right to infinite rage. Yet his discipline is metered for our good.

The truth of God's measured discipline is important for those who flee discipline for fear that God will never let up. I know of those who refuse to pray for divine discipline for their own wayward children because they do not trust God's restraint. The mother says, "I'm afraid to pray for God to correct my son, for I fear the pain needed to correct him will destroy him." For such fear we need the Bible's reminder that, because God is concerned for the spiritual growth and health of his children, his discipline brings life.

The "harvest" analogy of the writer of Hebrews should help us remember that God's husbandry will not destroy us (v. 11). To make the plants that he cherishes produce as they should, God will sometimes prune. But he knows the effects of pruning and never loses sight of his purposes. For this reason he does not always prune. Rather, he also abundantly waters and nourishes our growth. God's corrective discipline mercifully stops when he knows it has accomplished the growth and training he desires.

The fact that God's discipline will stop—despite the punishment our sins deserve—evidences his mercy and our status as his children. Neither the discipline nor our acceptance of it makes us God's children. Still, faith in the good purpose of whatever God's hand brings allows us to experience the benefits of his fatherly love even when we face this world's harshest realities. Such realities include the discipline that ends only when we enter Christ's heavenly presence.

During China's Boxer Rebellion at the beginning of the last century, a young American woman named Lizzie Atwater demonstrated the power of such faith to sustain us in life's harshest trials. She wrote with childlike confidence in her heavenly Father's love while awaiting her own execution:

> Dear Ones, I long for the sight of your dear faces, but I fear we shall not meet on earth. . . . I am preparing for the end very quietly and calmly. The Lord is wonderfully near, he will not fail me. I was very restless and excited while there seemed to be a chance of life, but God has taken away that feeling, and now I just pray for grace to meet the terrible end bravely. The pain will soon be over, and oh the sweetness of the welcome above. . . .
>
> I cannot imagine the Savior's welcome. Oh, that will compensate for all these days of suspense. Dear ones, live near to God and cling less closely to earth. There is no other way by which we can receive the peace that passeth understanding.[12]

In the expanse of eternity, those who have suffered long on this earth will still rejoice that their discipline was so brief relative to their embrace by the Savior. Knowledge of his timeless affection enables us to experience temporal discipline with peace.

—— DISCIPLINE REVEALS GOD ——

Faith in the loving nature of God's discipline not only gives us a clear vision of our status with him, it also gives us a clearer vision of him. The writer of Hebrews makes it clear both that the goal of discipline is our holiness (Heb. 12:10), and that "without holiness no one will see the Lord" (v. 14). The connection is clear. Through the holiness that our discipline nurtures, we gain a clearer vision of God.

By bending our will to his in discipline, the Lord removes the obstructions in our souls to a clear vision of him. He then fills and becomes our vision as earthly priorities and distractions are removed. Such discipline can easily place us in a desert of the soul and make us question both the reality and the benefits of God's mercy. But as we see stars more clearly in the desert where there is no competing light, so in a seeming desert of discipline God wipes away what competes for our attention. As Stephen, when being stoned, saw the heavens open to reveal God (Acts 7:55), our chastenings clarify our vision of God. Through his discipline we can learn to see through the heavens to perceive the very heart and hands of God.

His Heart

Our God's willingness to discipline shows that he is more concerned about our sanctification than we are. We care about success; he cares about holiness. We care about temporary pleasures; he cares about eternal consequences. We covet others' experiences like teenagers longing to taste more of the world; he longs for a closer embrace like a parent seeking to keep a family together.

God cares so much about our holiness—including our avoidance of spiritual dangers and disorders that we might be willing to risk—that he will use discipline to extricate us from present or potential spiritual harm that we may not even perceive. His measures may make us question his goodness, but Scripture confirms his faithfulness. God puts our regard for him at risk rather than allowing us to continue in courses that would damage us spiritually.

The theme that discipline is an act of love (v. 6) challenges our trust in God, showing once again that our pursuit of holiness requires faith. By faith we believe that when we experience the worst of divine discipline our heavenly Father loves us no less. Faith in the character of God, confirmed in the ministry of his Son, gives us confidence that a kind hand guides divine discipline, with the goal of turning us from lasting harm. We endure discipline by the faith that love motivates God, we resist bitterness by the faith that good purposes move him, and we repent of the known causes for our discipline through the assurance that he will receive us again (Rom. 2:4).

God's instruction will only accomplish its aims regarding our wrongdoing when we know that kindness fills the heart of the One who corrects us. The most mature spiritual response to divine discipline is like that of a child who, being too young for sophisticated rebellion and having just been spanked for dumping spaghetti onto the carpet, still reaches out for comfort from the very parent who just administered the correction. Such a child has no question but that love remains in the heart of the one whose hand disciplined. Perhaps this is why God so clearly shows us his heart in this passage where his hand of discipline is so detailed.

So that we will accept that the discipline is an act of love, God not only tells us that he loves us but he also shows the pain his own heart endured for us (Heb. 12:2). With tender care God shows us his own heart's pain in the suffering of his Son, even as he says that our pain is for our good. This combination of pain felt as well as pain administered assures us of his love and makes his discipline more evidence of his grace.

A pastor friend of mine has a very intelligent son who brought home a midterm report indicating that he was not applying himself to his studies. The father warned his son that he needed to correct his habits and warned that discipline would follow if he did not do better by the time final grades came. When the report card did come, it showed deterioration rather than improvement.

The father was true to his word. He took the son into the bathroom, shut the door, sat on the tub, bent the boy over his knee, and gave the promised spanking. When the spanking was over the boy did something he had never before done after such discipline. He stood up and fell on his father's neck in a crying hug. Through his tears the child said over and over, "Oh, Daddy, I love you, I love you, I love you."

Though appreciating the embrace, the father could not help but worry about what had caused such an overwrought reaction. The father put his hands on the boy's shoulders, straightened him up, and looked him in the eye. "Son," he said, "why are you now saying that you love me so?" Said the boy, "Because I watched your face in the mirror on the back of the door as you spanked me. I never before saw how much it hurt you to discipline me."

God shows us such pain in this passage where he promises his discipline. Lest we think that he exacts some strange pleasure by punishing his children, God shows us the pain of his love when he allowed our punishment to fall on his own Son. To save us eternally, our Lord took the pain of our punishment on himself. Knowing the heart that disciplines us is the same that bruised his Son in our behalf assures us of his continuing love (cf. Gen. 3:15; Isa. 53:10; Acts 2:23). Discipline from this heart can only evidence a care that will not let us indulge or pursue what would do us greater harm.

His Hand

Understanding (and appreciation) of divine discipline grows when we also see that God's discipline is not merely a revelation of his heart but is one of the clearest evidences of his sovereign hand in our lives. A clear and recurrent theme of the book of Hebrews is the rule of God over all creation. He brought the world into being and continues to uphold it by the word of his power (Heb. 1:2-3). We should be awed that such a majestic God, who could be so concerned about so many other things, would come to deal with us personally.

God could preoccupy himself with many other concerns than our petty rebelliousness and coldness to himself, but he loves us too much to look past us. With the emphasis of the present tense the writer of Hebrews says, "God is treating you as sons," showing us the continuing care of the Creator and Sustainer of the universe (12:7).

The special nature of discipline from a sovereign hand may be most evident when we believe that we are being disciplined for a specific sin (though, again, not all discipline/training is the result of our sin). In such cases (where sin is involved) we should recognize that God would have the right to turn away from us in frustration, disappointment, or even lack of concern. Instead, through discipline he demonstrates his presence.

Sin and Satan deceive our hearts with lies that God is distant. His hand

of discipline declares he is never nearer. He comes crashing across the stars
and heavens into our universe in such a way that we recognize he is right
here with us, caring enough to confront. Such confrontation is *not* without
pain, but there is comfort, encouragement—even wonder—in becoming
aware that he sees our condition and comes to save us from ourselves.

One of the most powerful images of my wife's childhood came when she
and a neighbor girl were playing in some woods behind their homes. The
girls wandered from the path and stepped into a nest of ground bees. As the
bees began to swarm and sting, the girls began to scream for help. Suddenly,
out of nowhere—"like Superman," my wife says—her dad came crashing
through the woods, leaping over fallen logs, hurdling vines and bushes. He
swooped up a girl under each arm and tore through the woods at full speed
to get them away from the bees. As he ran, the father's grip bruised the children's arms, branches scratched their thighs, and thorns grabbed at their
clothes and skin. The rescue hurt, but it was better than the bees.

The image is not so unlike our heavenly Father's work. He sees the
danger and, at times even before we call out, comes crashing into our
worlds. From some throne above the universe, he hurdles galaxies and the
infinite expanse of time to enter our realities and take us from spiritual
danger. His rescue may hurt us, but the goal is always our safety and the
motive is always his love.

——— DISCIPLINE IS GRACE ———

Discipline is evidence of God entering our world to rescue us from spiritual danger that we could not or would not handle on our own. Thus,
God's discipline is not contrary to grace but, in fact, *is* grace. Grace is
always God's unmerited work in our behalf, and discipline is just that.
True, it is divine work that we find unpleasant—but it remains just as
necessary—for its goals are our conformity to Christ's image and God's
revelation of his very self to accomplish this.

By power beyond ourselves, and for reasons beyond our righteousness, God leads us in paths that take us to the fruits of righteousness and
peace. Partaking of these fruits, we not only find confirmation of our status
as children but, in an amazing way, we discover that these fruits of discipline have the power to open our eyes to God. In the moments of greatest
discipline we see these truths and we see our God most clearly.

The vision of God that divine discipline reveals was reflected in the closing moments of Bronwyn Leonard's life. The adult daughter of the founding president of Covenant Seminary, Bronwyn valiantly warred against cancer for years before it claimed her life. Her brother, the Rev. Dr. Rob Rayburn, recorded her final hours in journal form:

> Sunday evening: It was growing clearer by dinner time that the end was near. . . . Her breathing was becoming labored; her color was changing. . . .
>
> Everyone [came] back into the room to sing. "How Sweet the Name of Jesus Sounds"; "My Jesus I Love Thee"; "None Other Lamb"; "Jesus Lives and So Shall I."
>
> Then Bronwyn began to breathe with greater difficulty. She cried out a number of times, "Help me; help me; help me. . . ." That was a horrible moment. Then it was that Steve and Linnea [her husband and daughter] helped her sit up straighter in bed to help her breathe. . . . Her head was turned toward Linnea, and Linnea said to her, "This is your very own Pilgrim's Progress—i.e., crossing the river. You get to do it first. . . . You're going to see Samantha [a child of Bronwyn's who was stillborn in 1978], and Papa [Bronwyn's father who died of cancer in 1990]." In response to Linnea's words, Bronwyn seemed to be trying to speak.
>
> Then Bronwyn said, in a clear voice, loud enough for anyone in the room to hear—though before for the last few days one had to have one's ear at her mouth to hear anything she might try to say—"Everybody's here. Jesus is here. Samantha is here. Paul, Mark, Joshua." Linnea said, "Joshy is next to you." Bronwyn shook that off, as if to say that she didn't mean her son, Joshua. Then, grasping the apparent meaning in her mother's words, Linnea said, "And John Donne?" Bronwyn responded with eyes wide open, "And Donne." She kept saying, "Hallelujah," and "Everybody's here." The sense of some in the room was that she was not speaking to those in the room but to those she had named who were before her eye. This period of her speaking lasted only four or five minutes. . . .
>
> As they laid her back on the bed, she did not return to the struggle to breathe, but took shorter gasps further apart until the breathing stopped completely.

What did Bronwyn see in those final moments? Had she already crossed over the river of life to heaven's threshold, or did the Lord grant to her the strength and peace of faith made real by images he put in her mind?

We will not know until we, too, are with the Lord. Still, we do know that when life brought its greatest discipline, God was never more clear, present, and real to this woman of faith.

God's discipline always works such grace in the lives of believers as we perceive the heart and hand of One who comes crashing through space and time to rescue us from powers greater than we can oppose on our own. The eyes of faith see this. And when they do, though the discipline will not seem pleasant in the moment, we must not lose heart. The discipline will produce in us a harvest of righteousness and peace when through faith we see that it is only a facet of God's grace, showing us more and more of his love and of him.

The Power of Mercy

She took her children to the park to break the monotony of schoolchildren now homebound for the summer, and instead she broke her own heart. She had watched her children run to the playground equipment as another car drove into the parking lot. The new car ground to a quick stop in the gravel. A young, attractive woman with a beaming smile leaped out of the driver's seat and virtually skipped to a secluded picnic table near an adjoining lake.

The mother's imagination began to race. Who could this attractive young woman be meeting in such a secluded spot with so much enthusiasm? Was this a long-awaited and carefully planned rendezvous with an over-busy husband, a lunch date with a best friend, or a tryst between secret lovers? She determined to stay on the lookout for whoever got out of the next car that parked.

No one else came immediately. The mother soon grew preoccupied with her children, and forgot to watch for whomever the young woman was meeting. When she did finally glance again at the secluded woman, what the mother saw made her own heart hurt. The attractive, young woman was reading a Bible. The person she had leapt from the car to meet with such enthusiasm was the Lord.

The mother recognized—with pain that penetrated her spirit—that she no longer had that same enthusiasm. Once the excitement of her relationship with the Lord overwhelmed her. Once the joy of her salvation burned warm and bright. But the fervor was gone. Faith had become dreary duty. God had become a detached, frowning bystander. Something had happened over the years of her walk with the Lord. She didn't know what it was, but she did know that she was not now the kind of person who would skip to meet him. She had lost something wonderful, and she wept there in the park for her loss.

Many Christians can identify with this young mother's loss. We know what it means for our worship to seem terribly important but painfully dull. We sympathize with those learning more and more about God but seeming to care less and less. We are trying to serve God and combat Satan, but increasingly we enter the battle with bowed neck, gritted teeth, and weary resolve. We know that we should do much more for the kingdom; but duty has become drudgery, God distant, and our love cold.

Long-term lives of faith do not have to be this way. God wants his work to excite us. He wants us to delight in his purposes with a warm love and burning zeal. But how do we find these motives? The apostle Paul answers with words of encouragement to rekindle our *desire* and our *ability* to serve God:

ROMANS 12:1-2

1Therefore, I urge you, brothers, in view of God's mercy, to offer your bodies as living sacrifices, holy and pleasing to God—this is your spiritual act of worship. 2Do not conform any longer to the pattern of this world, but be transformed by the renewing of your mind. Then you will be able to test and approve what God's will is—his good, pleasing and perfect will.

———— THE DESIRE OF MERCY ————

God expects us to do so much. Paul says that we are not to be conformed to the pattern of this crooked world, but rather are to be transformed so that we can know God's will (v. 2). We are to know God's will so that we will do it. God expects our transformation to impact our world. Paul's following instructions indicate how much God expects us to do in the construction of his kingdom on earth. He tells us our corporate responsibilities as a body of believers (12:3-7), then he gives us our individual work assignments (12:8-21). Because God does not limit his kingdom to the church, Paul next tells us our civic responsibilities (13:1-7). And finally he details our moral duties in society (13:8-14).

THE EXHORTATION OF MERCY

God gives us so much to do that we might lose heart. Paul must have known the likelihood of our discouragement, so he precedes all these work assignments with this exhortation: "I urge you, brothers, in view of God's mercy" to serve him (v. 1). Paul wants to make sure our hearts are in our work, so he encourages us with God's loving mercy above all other motivations.[1] We know the importance of such motivation from our own life experiences.

When as a child I learned a little bit of woodworking from my dad, nothing pleased me more than using a carpenter's plane. It seemed almost like magic to take a crooked, rough piece of lumber and, by waving this tool back and forth over it, take away its defects. Curly ribbons of paper-thin wood rose almost effortlessly from the blade, and before my eyes the board was transformed, becoming straight and smooth as silk. It was great fun. So when a professional carpenter came to my office recently to install a door, I could not help reminiscing a bit as he took out his plane.

When he began making those curly ribbons of wood, I said, "Isn't that the funniest thing in the world?" He looked at me as though I were nuts.

"Not when you have done it every day for twenty years," he said gruffly. "It's been a long time since I considered this fun."

Of course, then I felt foolish for asking. I also felt sorry for the carpenter who apparently took so little joy in his work. His lack of enthusiasm showed. When he left that day and I tried out my new door, it stuck! He had not planed it properly. The task that he took so little joy in, he did not do well. This was no surprise, of course, because whenever our hearts are not in our duties, the work suffers. The same is true of our spiritual duties. Samuel Bolton writes, "If the law is merely our command we cannot delight to do the will of God. We can perform duties but cannot delight in them, though we may think them needful as something necessary for glory and for heaven."[2] The inevitable consequence of obedience without delight is the erosion of holiness.

We cannot continue to do our duty to God if we have no love for the task or the Taskgiver. We can sense the importance of Paul's opening exhortation by imagining other words Paul might have used. Paul did *not* say, "I urge you by the guilt you will assume if you are negligent . . ." He did *not* say, "I urge you by the rejection you will face if you fail . . ." He did *not* threaten: "I urge you by the love you will lose if you fail . . ." Paul knew that if we serve God out of guilt—what the seventeenth-century Reformers called "servile duty" or "slavish fear"—then our labors will not be joyful, or strong, or long.[3]

Our own work experiences can confirm the wisdom of Paul's approach.

We may have worked for a boss who just could not be satisfied. No matter what we did it was never quite good enough. As a result, we approached every new task with a sense of dread and fear, questioning and self-doubt. Working for such a boss may cause us to stay on our toes for a while, but eventually we wear out, or grow hard, or avoid the boss. Our work suffers because we have no heart for it or for the one who assigns it. God doesn't want us to serve him that way. "Serve me," he says, "by keeping in view not my anger nor your shame . . . but my mercy."

THE ABUNDANCE OF MERCY

Even the word *mercy* is special. The translators of the *King James Version* of the Bible rendered the word in the plural as a reflection of the term's Old Testament heritage.[4] As a result, many Christians have grown up memorizing this text as, "I beseech you therefore, brethren, by the mercies of God . . ." The contemporary translations that render the word as a singular noun are not spoiling for an argument; they add an important richness to our understanding.

The word for "mercy" with which the translators wrestle communicates the truth that Paul presents in the preceding chapter (11:27). There Paul contends that in his grace God made a covenant to take away sins. Once it applied to the Jews only; now it applies to all who claim the gospel of Jesus Christ. God's mercy now applies to many. The mercy has multiplied (see 11:30-32). One word can hardly contain so much love. This rich, overflowing, and abundant grace is "a mercy of mercies."

The abundance of God's mercy that challenges the translators should overwhelm us. We should delight to serve him who has worked throughout time and in our hearts to provide so much for us. Yet because we so struggle to keep his mercy in view, God graciously gives us opportunity after opportunity to see the wonder of his love if we will but open our eyes.

I saw this mercy afresh during one of the most difficult weeks that Kathy and I have ever faced. That week we heard a word applied to one of our children that we had dreaded ever being used to describe any of them. That word was asthma.

Our son coughed a little during a Saturday night. At church the next day he started running a fever and, as his temperature went up, he started having trouble breathing. We left the service early and by nightfall he was struggling to draw each breath.

No doctor had officially labeled the problem yet, but I knew what was happening. I grew up with asthma. I know all about the days missed from school, the constant medication, and the innumerable trips to the doctor. I have known the bitter disappointment of preparing for months for a sports event only to experience a sudden attack that robs strength, breath, and the opportunity to compete.

I thought of all of this as I tried to help my son get to sleep that night. I rubbed between his shoulders that were hunched in the way that I know asthmatics naturally roll their shoulders to take pressure off their lungs. I listened to him inhale in wheezing misery and exhale through lips pursed as his body instinctively tried to create back pressure to expand bronchial tubes another micro-millimeter.

My son was miserable, but the difficulty he was having was not greater than the pain I was feeling. I had already experienced each of these asthma reactions a thousand times. I knew the life that lay ahead for my son, and my heart was crying out, "Oh, my child, how I wish I could spare you what I went through."

It was in those moments of heartbreak for my son that I thought of the mercy. I remembered another who went through such misery that it took his breath away. I thought of other shoulders rolled in suffering against the wood of a cross. I recalled the One whose weight hung on nails so cruel that each breath was a torture. He willingly took the agony my sins deserve, all so that his lips pursed with pain could express, "Oh, my child, now I will spare you what I go through" (1 Pet. 2:24-25; 1 John 2:1-2).

"How great is the love the Father has lavished on us, that we should be called children of God!" (1 John 3:1). Such mercy eclipses all other motivations for our service for him. His mercy should so fill our vision that gratitude fills our hearts with the longing to do his will. If thankfulness does not move us to serve God, then we do not truly understand who our God is and what he has done in our behalf. Without gratitude for Christ's sacrificial love, our duty will become nothing more than drudgery and our God nothing more than a dissatisfied boss. This is why Paul tells us at the outset to serve "in view of God's mercy."

THE CHALLENGE OF MERCY

Despite God's overwhelming love, mercy can quickly fade from view. Other motivations that make our service to God distasteful and destructive all too easily preoccupy us. We can begin to focus on reasons to serve God that spoil our view of the cross almost without our ever really intending it.

Our spiritual health requires us to confess the difficulty we have in keeping the mercy fully in view. I have struggled more than once over two decades of pastoring to keep mercy as the means I use for motivating others. I had been a pastor for about five years before I began really to admit that so many Christians, including those in the church I served, seemed so far from the Lord.

Recognition of the spiritual emptiness so many were experiencing was all the more surprising because both churches I have pastored are well over a hundred years old. Many of the families in those churches have been members for generations. There was nothing in their outward actions that signaled any problems. After being in church so long almost everyone knew very well how Christians should act. They faithfully observed a code of community conduct dictating that most were faithful to their spouses and did not smoke or drink to excess nor use profanity in polite company. Outwardly, so much seemed okay.

Failure to adhere to the code was not the problem, nor was ignorance of the Bible. Almost everyone took their Bibles to church, and many could put me to shame with their Bible knowledge. What I could not understand was how people who were so religious in habit and so knowledgeable of God could be so bitter, guilt-ridden, depressed, cold to each other, and intolerant of the faults of newer Christians. These longtime church people said they were followers of Jesus (and many of their outward actions gave their professions credence), yet love, joy, peace, patience, and long-suffering seemed so far from so many. I used to get so angry at those people for their hard-hearted attitudes and their coldness to the Word that they said they loved. Then I began to realize the problem was not so much them as it was I, and others like me.

If you are responsible for the spiritual welfare of others—if you are a preacher, a teacher, a parent, a spouse, a committed Christian in any walk of life—you know that God gives us a difficult task. The Word of God tells us to exhort sinful people to change even though they may choose to resist. We are supposed to instruct them to stop doing what is dishonoring to God. We often wonder how to do this, and probably all of us at some point in our attempts to change others discover a very effective tool called guilt. All parents know this tool. Preachers, teachers, employers, and friends know it, too.

There is nothing more *effective* than guilt to get people to obey God's standards, and nothing less *efficacious* in sanctifying them to God. If we make people feel bad and ashamed enough, then many will change their conduct. When it comes to changing people's behavior, nothing is more efficient than motivating by guilt. However, the Bible teaches that the liberty Christ has purchased for us consists in our freedom from the guilt of sin, the condemning wrath of God, and the curse of the moral law (cf. Rom. 8:1; Gal. 3:10; 1 Thess. 1:10).[5]

There is a proper role for what theologians call subjective guilt (how I feel). This feeling of remorse for wrong is a result of the Holy Spirit revealing our sin to our consciences (this we call "conviction"). However, amid our feelings of remorse we must remember that our objective guilt (the judgment that God imposes for our sin) has been entirely satisfied by Christ (Eph. 2:14-16; Col. 1:19-20). Simply making others or ourselves feel bad for a long time does not satisfy God nor stimulate true holiness.

Early in my ministry I didn't recognize how damaging it is to threaten people with God's judgment (or my disapproval) as the primary means for motivating Christian obedience. I used lots of this kind of guilt as a pastor. And I saw people's behaviors change . . . for a while. Still, I often discovered later that the people who did change simply because I had made them feel guilty did not mature.

Those whom I pressured with guilt did not grow in faith nor seem more spiritually whole even though their outward actions may have changed. For instance, I might deal with a married couple whose relationship was coming apart because they were not being faithful to each other. I would tell them that if they changed their behaviors God would bless them, but as long as they pursued sinful relationships they could not expect him to love them.

With this threatening advice, such a couple might very well cease their immoral activities, but I would later see that their abandonment of the immorality did not necessarily better their lives spiritually. A year or two down the road these same people were often locked into depression, pursuing other addictive behaviors, or were simply disinterested in godly priorities.

It took me a few years (we preachers can be notoriously dense), but finally I figured out what was happening. I was telling people that the way to get rid of their guilt before God, and to assure his blessing, was to change their behaviors. But what did this imply? If people expect behavior change to get rid of their guilt, then whom are they trusting to take their guilt away? Themselves!

I was forcing each individual to ask, "What action of mine will make me right with an easily angered, never-satisfied, vengeful God?" No wonder their faith did not mature. Their faith was in what they could do to fix their own situations with God. I had caused them to lose sight of the mercy.

I was encouraging people to look to themselves rather than to the cross as the place for guilt's erasure. Only Christ can remove the guilt of our sin. By letting people think that what they did made them right with God, I was driving a wedge of human works between them and God. The people who listened to me, though they may have changed some aspect of their lives to get my approval and to secure God's affection, were actually further away from God spiritually than when I began to "minister" to them.

When mercy got out of view, grace went away and a works-righteousness jumped into its place before I even knew it. My words were making people try to become acceptable to God by being good enough. But they could not be good enough for a holy God. Something in them knew that. That is why they were so hard and bitter and cold.

I was teaching that if people just did things right, they could make things right with God. How foolish was my instruction. The Bible says that when we have done all we can do, we are still unworthy servants (Luke 17:10), and our best works are only filthy rags to God (Isa. 64:6).[6] I was teaching people that if they just offered God more filthy rags he would favor them more, or smile more, or love them more. What an eccentric and cruel God I painted for them!

I denied people grace by teaching them that God's love was dependent on their goodness. It was I who had made them intolerant of less mature believers. By listening to me, they had to gauge their holiness by their works. And what better way is there to confirm your own righteousness than by finding fault in others! If the people in my church had bad attitudes and had lost interest in matters of faith, I had no one to blame but myself. I was the one who had veiled the mercy.

THE GOD OF MERCY

We should know from our own family experiences how unproductive is obedience motivated by guilt. What happens to a child who obeys only out fear of parental rejection—a child who stays good to stay loved? He may obey when he is young, but he is scarred for life. Because such parental love is never more certain than the child's actions, acceptance is always in doubt. As a result the child grows up callused or weakened—hating his parents and doubting himself. Many of us know these truths very well because we were manipulated by guilt as children and we may still bear the scars.

We hate what makes us feel guilt to gain favor. Family relations expert Karen Sanheim tells of a teenage daughter who was given a new hair dryer by her mother. But even as the mother presented the gift, she said, "Your father and I give up so much so that you will have things like this to enjoy." The girl later said that at that moment she wanted to take the new hair dryer and throw it through the window. She knew that every time she used it she would have to face the guilt of depriving her parents. Of course, she didn't throw out the hair dryer. That would only hurt her mother and lead to another round of guilt. Instead of getting rid of the hair dryer, the daughter cut off her hair! She did what she had to do to keep from feeling guilty. She punished herself.[7]

Many Christians respond in the same way. They punish themselves to get rid of their guilt. These same people feel that it is their preacher's job to beat them about the head and shoulders with the condemnations of Scripture, and that it is their job to take it. Their guilty feelings are the penance that they think God requires of them in order to renew his love for them. As a consequence they do not want to be denied their guilt. They will offer God the gifts of their own depression and self-hatred to satisfy his wrath.

All of this longing for guilt comes from the conviction that, if we will make ourselves feel bad enough and carrying a burden of remorse long enough, we will merit God's grace. But who really wants us pressed down and paralyzed by a burden of guilt? Satan. He is our accuser (see Rev. 12:10). Nothing pleases him more than for Christians to beat themselves down into paralyzing depression or unproductive despair. The Bible does not say our guilty feelings or compensating recriminations will make us right with God. God makes us right with God. He does not want us bowed down in despair. He is the lifter of our heads (Ps. 3:3).

We cannot offer loving service to a God who loves us only when we are good. If God's love is conditional, if he is only waiting to get us if we step out of line, if avoidance of his rejection or relief of our guilt is our reason for serving him, then we may obey him for a time, but we will not like him very much. Unfortunately, such a failure to love God will only make us feel more guilty and force us into a downward spiral of greater despair and more futile resolve to make things right with him. When we sin we will decide to let the guilt consume us more and will wallow in our guilt to punish ourselves with it. We may also intensify our disciplines of Bible reading, prayer, and church attendance so that God will forgive us.

Yet, despite all these well-intended attempts to bribe God with our despondency and discipline, we will find that we love this unappeasable God less and less even as we try to please him more and more. Eventually it all becomes meaningless. We become hard, cynical, judgmental, bitter, or despairing, because we have made God what he could never be—a heavenly ogre intent on extracting his pound of flesh from whomever crosses him.

Paul exhorts us to keep the mercy in view because grace alone will keep us serving our Lord. If we try to compensate for the guilt that only Christ can remove, then we will lose the capacity to love him and to serve him rightly. God doesn't want us to punish ourselves to erase our guilt. He punished his Son to cancel our guilt. God will not build his kingdom on our pain because he is building it on his mercy.

THE GRATITUDE OF MERCY

Remorse for sin does have a place in the Christian life, but we should be very sure what function it serves. Guilt should drive us to the cross, but grace must lead us from it. Guilt makes us seek Christ, but gratitude should make us serve him. Guilt should lead to confession, but without a response of love as the motive of renewed obedience, true repentance never matures.

The kindness of God motivates the repentance that truly promotes changed lives (Rom. 2:4). The love of Christ constrains and compels us to do his will (2 Cor. 5:14; Titus 2:11-12). We won't discover the joy that is our strength for Christian service if we have not claimed the mercy that frees us from all guilt at the cross. Thus, Luther taught that remorse prior to approaching the cross is of God, but after true repentance beneath the cross such self-reproach is of Satan. Our Adversary wants us to believe that Christ's blood is not sufficient to cleanse confessed sin. We become susceptible to his lie when we begin to doubt the power of the cross fully to cancel our guilt, for then we will begin to live (and fall) in the strength of our own efforts.

Mercy stimulates the gratitude that is the only enduring motivation for effective Christian service. Gratitude recognizes the love that never fades and restores confidence in our eternal relationship that is the only true source of Christian power. We cannot exercise this power if we are paralyzed with dread, beaten down with unrelenting remorse, burdened by constant guilt, miserable, and sad. Thus, God intends for us to take all of the sin and guilt that is ours, bring it to the foot of the cross, and lay it down. Then, God wants us to stand up, lift our head, rejoice in his pardon, and powerfully serve him without the weight of our past burden. Satan, on the other hand, wants us to try to serve God with a burden of unrelenting guilt on our back.

Lasting service comes when we serve God from his acceptance, not for his acceptance.[8] The former kind of service rejoices in his mercy; the latter seeks to merit (or purchase) his approval. When we confuse these motives, we inevitably begin to serve God out of selfish motives that will not sustain faith or service. J. I. Packer explains,

> The secular world never understands Christian motivation. Faced with the question of what makes Christians tick, unbelievers maintain that Christianity is practiced only out of self-serving purposes. They see Christians as fearing the consequences of not being Christians (religion as fire insurance), or feeling the need of help and support to achieve their goals (religion as crutch), or wishing to sustain a social identity (religion as badge of respectability). No doubt all these motivations can be found among the membership of churches: it would be futile to dispute that. But just as a horse brought into a house is not thereby made human, so a self-seeking motivation brought into the church is not thereby made Christian, nor will holiness ever be the right name for religious routines thus motivated. From the plan of salvation I learn that the true driving force in authentic Christian living is, and ever must be, not the hope of gain, but the heart of gratitude.[9]

There is a longing for heaven and a fear of hell that are of Satan, because the goal of each has been mutated in the soul from a desire to respond to God's love to mere acquisition of personal gain. Thus, Christian maturity requires that we ask whether we are more motivated by gratitude for God's mercy or by a futile attempt to earn it. God's unconditional pardon does not change the rules of Christian service, but it does change our motivations. The rules do not change; our reasons do.

Does God's great mercy toward his children mean that we can sin without consequence? May we indulge our worst inclinations without any concern because God promises to love us anyway? No, of course not. Sin will hurt us. Satan will damage us as much as he can through the allure of temptations. If we work without integrity, then we will destroy our reputation and self-estimation. If we yield our body to immorality, then our family will suffer. We should fear the consequences of our sin. The avoidance of consequences (of which a loving God warns) is a legitimate motive for turning from wrongdoing. Still, we must be even more overwhelmed by the love of our God, or we cannot be holy.

Will affirming the vastness of God's mercy lead people to sin by tempting them to take advantage of grace? It could, were there not at least two scriptural principles that caution Christians about abusing God's mercy: the nature of God's discipline, and the assurance denied to abusers of grace.

First, God will administer loving discipline for wrongdoing in order to keep his children from experiencing even more extreme consequences of sin. This discipline can be quite rigorous, because while the damage of sin unchecked can be so devastating, our wayward impulses can be so strong. There is an appropriate dread of divine discipline that motivates us to avoid sin. Still, in order for discipline to operate properly in the Christian life, we must remember that God's discipline for his children is never punitive or damaging (see the discussion of this point in chapter 7).

God does not penalize his children for their sin, in the sense of imposing a penalty or requiring suffering to compensate for sin. Jesus took the penalty of all our sin—past, present, and future—on the cross. God's punishing wrath is still poured out on unbelievers, but not on his children. God's discipline will never spiritually damage his children. However, by its discomforts, disadvantages, and real pain God's loving discipline will help us grieve for our wrong, turn us from harm, and strengthen us for future trial.[10]

Divine discipline is God's merciful expression of his love for children who deserve his wrath but will never receive it. In a classic illustration, Samuel Bolton contrasts God's attitude toward evil in the lives of believers with his attitude toward evil in the lives of those who trust in their own goodness:

> Under the Gospel He [God] looks not upon the weakness of saints as their wickedness, and therefore he pities them. Sin makes those who are under the law the objects of God's hatred. Sin in a believer makes him the object of God's pity. Men, you know, hate poison in a toad, but pity it in a man. In the one it is their nature, in the other it is their disease. Sin in a wicked man is as poison to a toad. God hates it and him; it is the man's nature. But sin in a child of God is like poison in the man; God pities him. He pities the saints for sins

and infirmities, but hates the wicked. It is the nature of one, the disease of the other.[11]

God pities rather than scorns believers for the wrong in our lives. Thus, his treatment of our failures is motivated by mercy rather than by cruelty or contempt. The anger God expresses over his children's wrongdoing is more concern for the damage we do to ourselves than for our crossing him.

Even when we are in the throes of the worst discipline that God may bring, he loves us no less. He still delights to call us his own children and grieves for the ravages of sin in our lives. God's design for his discipline is like chemotherapy for cancer. He purposes to remove the far greater malignancy of spiritual corruption by means that may shock our system and deny us past comforts. But the pain we experience is "medicinal," and the heart that administers it is full of mercy.

Should even this mercy become for us an excuse to sin, God's Word cautions us that those who abuse his grace have no assurance of his mercy. God works all things together for good to those who love him (Rom. 8:28). Love in Scripture is never defined as taking advantage of another's care, abusing their trust, or imposing on their generosity. If we knowingly continue in flagrant wrong under the presumption that "It won't matter, because God always forgives his children," we must question our commitment to him.

While it is certainly true that the wells of God's forgiveness are inexhaustible, and that he who commands us to forgive seventy times seven (Matt. 18:22) will do the same, there is no human assurance that his love covers us when there is no evidence of our love for him. God's mercy is not subject to the variableness that characterizes human actions and attitudes (James 1:17), but our assurance that we are living under his mercy can wane when we wander. Conversely the heart that truly longs for God can be assured even by these longings that God's mercy will apply despite much human failing (Rom. 8:5-7).[12]

Challenging others and ourselves toward holiness on the basis of the relational certainties of God's love, while honestly warning of the personal consequences of our sin, can prove quite difficult. The conditional nature of many human relationships accustoms us to thinking of God's love as being subject to the vagaries and degrees of our obedience. The consequences of sin reinforce this misconception. It is wrong to think, however, that because there is a divine discipline or temporal consequence resulting from personal sin, God's love is altered. Considering what actually can change in our relationship with God because of our personal wrong, and what cannot change because of his abiding care, will help clarify the Bible's message and our motivations:

OUR RELATIONSHIP WITH GOD

WHAT CAN CHANGE	WHAT CANNOT CHANGE
Our fellowship[13]	Our sonship
Our experience of his blessing[14]	His desire for our welfare
Our assurance of his love[15]	His actual affection for us
His delight in our actions[16]	His love for us
His discipline	Our destiny[17]
Our sense of guilt	Our security[18]

We reveal much of our theology to others when we complete the sentence, "Stop doing that, or God will . . ." The words that finish such a sentence will reveal whether we believe that divine love is changeless or that it is conditional. And what we believe in this regard will determine whether we live in joy or in fear, and whether our service is willing or grudging.

Our children understand the difference between unconditional love and merited affection, and so do God's children. Only when our heart's loving response to God's mercy becomes our primary motivator do we delight to serve him. Without this delight neither true worship nor sacrificial service are possible. Writes Horatius Bonar,

> The love of God to us, and our love to him, work together for producing holiness. Terror accomplishes no real obedience. Suspense brings forth no fruit unto holiness. No gloomy uncertainty as to God's favor can subdue one lust, or correct our crookedness of will. But the free pardon of the cross uproots sin, and withers all its branches. Only the certainty of love, forgiving love, can do this.[19]

In the depths of God's constant love we find an appreciation of grace that makes our service rich, sweet, and honoring of him.

Before we lift the first gospel hammer or drive the first spiritual nail in kingdom service, the apostle Paul makes us pause to ask ourselves this question: "Why do I do what I do?" Our fallen minds and twisted consciences might supply a variety of answers to that question—guilt, fear, pride, self-protection, or personal gain. So, lest we damage the kingdom or ourselves with ill-conceived notions, Paul supplies our motivation. He says to build "in view of God's mercy." If we serve him primarily so that we will not feel bad, guilt motivates us and self-justification becomes our perspective. If we serve him principally so that we will gain his affection or avoid his punishment, self-interests fill our vision. When we keep his mercy in view, the grace of God motivates us and his purposes remain our priority.

THE POWER OF MERCY

Mercy does not merely affect our *attitudes;* mercy also energizes our *abilities.* The grace of God evident in his mercy provides motivation *and* enablement for the tasks God sets before us. These features of grace become especially important when we feel overwhelmed by all that God requires of us in the building of his kingdom. God's requirements can cause us to fall into a mental conversation that sounds something like this: "I would like to help, but I'm not sure I can. I'm not sure that I'm able. I don't think I'm strong enough or good enough to do kingdom work for God."

Such thinking is not necessarily ill-considered. We are wise not to attempt tasks that we do not have the ability to complete (see Luke 14:28-33). We need more than desire to do a good job for God. We need the energy to see the task through, and we need resources to accomplish it. Paul tells us where we can get both. Mercy holds the power we need. In mercy we find the encouragement needed for our drive and the enablement needed for our service.

A generation ago young people recited Romans 12:1 from the *King James Version* of the Bible this way: "I beseech you therefore, brethren, *by the mercies of God,* that ye present your bodies a living sacrifice . . ." The phrasing "*by* the mercies" captures a rich dimension of Paul's original intent. In the following verses Paul indicates the magnitude and specifics of what God requires of us in his kingdom work. But before he describes the tasks before us, Paul gives us the tool we need to do the job. Mercy is the instrument—the leverage—that gets the job done. *By* God's mercy we accomplish what God requires. We are not only to keep mercy in view, we are also to keep it in use.

ENCOURAGEMENT POWER

Mercy becomes our power when we recognize the freedom it provides. As has already been discussed, we cannot expect to serve God very effectively when we are carrying a load of guilt on our back. Our service becomes powerful as we recognize that Christ has released us from the burden of sin. By God's grace we stand tall, ready, and able to do God's will. God's work in our behalf provides the encouragement that makes us strong.

Mercy is the good news that God is for us (Rom. 8:31). He is on our side. He is in our corner. The mercy of God's continuous support is a powerful source of the believer's strength in the face of our own faults and frailties. Think of the strength that another's support can provide in the context of Olympic competition. Our town has become a magnet for young boxers, and we follow the Olympic boxing competition closely. Despite their great talents, the youthfulness of most of the fighters makes them particularly prone to mistakes. Yet, even when an immature boxer's own "showboating" sets him up for a sucker punch, I have never seen a coach walk out on his athlete. No matter what the fault, the coaches stay in their fighter's corner. God's grace reminds us that he always remains in our corner, too.

Even when we, like some of the young Olympians, have taken a blow to the chin due to our own mistakes and pride, God never turns his back on us. When we have boxed with sin, failed, and fallen, God is still for us. He does not wait for us to lift ourselves off the mat before encouraging us. God shouts from our corner, "Get up, child. Yes, you forgot what I told you, but I'm still here for you." Were God to walk away when we go down, leaving us alone and ashamed, then we would have no reason to get up again. But our God promises never to leave or forsake us (Heb. 13:5). His encouragement lifts us from the paralysis that our own guilt would impose and makes us the vital warriors he desires for the kingdom's battles.

In Old Testament worship, innocent animals were killed in sacrifice to atone for sins. But dead animals could neither please God nor ultimately atone for sin. So God sent his own Son as an atoning sacrifice to completely take the guilt of sin from his people once and for all (Rom. 6:10; Heb. 10:10; 1 John 4:10). No longer desiring dead sacrifices, our God now calls us to offer our bodies as living sacrifices to carry out his will (Rom. 12:1). He wants people who are strong, able, and willing to fight for his causes. Therefore, God tells us to keep in view the mercy that will keep us vital and valiant in his fight.

Our God's support grants us power. As we rejoice in his mercy we find the resolve to get up and fight again. Horatius Bonar writes, "There is no spring of holiness so powerful as that which our Lord assumes: 'Neither do I condemn thee; go and sin no more' (John 8:11)."[20] There is power in love that guilt cannot imitate. There is capability in mercy that intimidation cannot begin to tap.

Knowledge of unconditional support unleashes human power. Missionary leader Paul Kooistra tells of a study that one state's department of education conducted some years ago. Educators wanted to know why remedial studies programs throughout the state were failing. The programs were supposed to supply extra help for students who were struggling academically in order to bring them up to the performance levels of their peers. Unfortunately, whenever children entered the program, they were stigmatized in their schools and in their own minds as problem students. Because they were put in a program for slow students, the children labeled themselves as failures. Children simply gave up once the school assigned them to the special classes. The program that was intended to promote their learning instead became an academic whirlpool. No student who entered the remedial studies ever got out of the program . . . with one exception. Her name was Edy.

Edy was a track star, and everyone called her "Speedy Edy." Everything about her was fast except her academic progress. She was put in the program for slow learners, but somehow she broke free of its whirlpool effects. When Edy's scores indicated she was back on peer level academically, the state officials concentrated their research on her. Everyone wanted to know what was different about the instruction that made her succeed in the remedial program that kept so many others failing. What made Edy tick?

The researchers talked to Edy's teacher to get details:

"What did you do with Edy that was different than what you did with the other children?"

"Nothing," the teacher replied.

The researchers pressed, "Did you use different books or vary the assigned curriculum?"

"No," said the teacher. "We all used the same materials."

"You must have done something different with Edy," said the researchers. "Think what was different about the way you interacted with her."

The teacher thought, and then almost as a question offered an answer. "Do you know that Edy runs track?" asked the teacher.

"Yes," said the researchers. "We've heard all about Speedy Edy."

"Well," said the teacher, "when Edy runs, I go to her meets and cheer for her."

That was the difference. When her world gave her a failure label, Edy found a teacher who supported her anyway. The encouragement empowered her. The undeniable care of her teacher gave her an ability to break free of her mental bonds. As the compassion of a teacher granted Edy strength, so the mercy of our God supplies ours. Our God does not merely cheer for us. He died for us. He came to where we race against our own weaknesses in order to free us from our spiritual bondage, and now he sits at the right hand of the Father interceding for us even when we fail (Rom. 8:34). Intercession is not quite like cheering, but it just as clearly shows that we have an unfaltering Advocate.

Christians gain spiritual power from the certainty of God's support. Self-preserving, human efforts may result from fear of a God who will get you if you get out of line, but such works mistake outer conformity to God's standards with holiness from the heart.[21] "Spiritual worship" (see Rom. 12:1)—the selfless actions and inner desire to honor God—cannot result from threats. Proper fear of God in his people is not a concern for his wrath but a reverence for his holiness.[22] We must reverentially fear his nature, but should not doubt his nurture. He will not harm those who are covered in the righteousness of his own Son and who, thus, are divinely loved as dearly as he. Spiritually vital and enduringly vibrant service flow from a heart that sings, "I am his and he is mine forever and forever. I cannot be taken from the palm of his hand. He is for me. Mercy claimed me and, though I may lose my grasp on him, my God will not let me go."

ENABLEMENT POWER

We must confess that sometimes, in view of this divine mercy, we feel pain rather than hope. If we have been guilty of serious, long-term, or repetitive sin, then we feel worse because we have not done better. Our consciences may cry out, "Lord, I would love to serve you better in view of your mercy, but you know me. You know how weak I am. You know how I keep on failing. You know my temper, and my tongue, and how temptation seems to get the best of me. Lord, I wish I could honor you with my life. I wish I could serve you, but I can't. I just can't."

Yes, we can. By God's grace the power is already ours, and we need only understand how to plug into it. The resources for accomplishing God's purposes come in two forms: provision and assurance.

Provision

Most of my life I read key phrases of this passage (Rom. 12:1-2) the wrong way. I read the passage as if it said, "In view of God's mercy, present your bodies as living sacrifices, *and then you will be* holy and pleasing to God." Probably many others have read this verse the same way. We think that by presenting our bodies as sacrifices to God we will please him. But the verse does not talk merely about our pleasing God; it also talks about being holy. That word "holy" should give us a clue that my former reading was wrong.

No matter how much we sacrifice, we cannot make ourselves holy to God. God's standard of holiness is as high as the heavens. Our best efforts will not make us "holy." If we are to be holy it will only be by God's provision. That's the point! The words "holy" and "pleasing" are not conditions of God's acceptance; rather, they are fruits of his mercy. These key words are not descriptions of what we *will be;* they are declarations of what we *are* in Christ: holy and pleasing to God.

By Jesus' cleansing work on the cross God declares us to be holy and pleasing to him. The offering of our bodies as living sacrifices does not make us holy and pleasing to God. He has made us holy and pleasing to himself. This is the fundamental truth that enables us not to be conformed to this world nor to succumb to its temptations (v. 2). So powerful is the nature of God's provision for us that Paul says if our minds truly grasp this new thought, then our lives will be "transformed" by it (v. 2).

Paul begins developing this thought of transformation "by the renewing of your minds" much earlier. Two full chapters before writing these words, Paul says that the ancient Jews did not understand God's provision. Their minds were gripped with a view of God that made them read their Scriptures the way that I formerly read this passage. They thought that their actions would make them acceptable to God. Paul writes:

> Brothers, my heart's desire and prayer to God for the Israelites is that they may be saved. For I can testify about them that they are zealous for God, but their zeal is not based on knowledge. Since they did not know the righteousness that comes from God and sought to establish their own, they did not submit to God's righteousness (Rom. 10:1-3).

By trying to make themselves acceptable to God, the Israelites minimized the holiness God requires and, thus, dishonored him. Their zeal was not based on proper knowledge. Paul says that we should not get trapped in their way of thinking. We should be transformed by the renewing of our minds with the understanding that holiness comes from God and not from us.

Renewing our minds by focusing on God's provision of mercy rather than on our acquisition of acceptance provides various means of transforming power. First, we do not minimize God's holiness by assuming it is such a slight thing that we, mere humans, could gain it. We are forced to a "healthy despair" of our efforts that leads us to drop all pretense of our sufficiency and goodness, and by necessity put our faith in him.[23] Second, because we trust his provision for our righteousness, we need not succumb to the anxiety that our actions will never be sufficient to earn his satisfaction. We are free to serve him without paralyzing fear.

The early church robed adult believers in white after their baptisms. The garments did not indicate believers would never again sin. They signified the holiness God provides despite our impurities. The robes covered an imperfect person. The implications remain vital for us today. We do *not* have to despair of ever attaining the perfection that would warrant God's acceptance. By recognizing the richness of his provision, we have the resources necessary to move forward in his service. We need never say, "I can't do anything right. I always mess up. I have tried time and time again to live right and I always fail. If I try anything I will only look bad and get God mad, so why try?"

Some Christians are so afraid of stepping out of line that they never get in step with God. Fear of the loss of what little holiness they think they have managed to scratch out in life has led to paralysis. They are not serving God with vigor and energy because they do not want to risk losing what little mercy they think they have managed to corner. Such believers will not serve God well until they realize how rich are the resources of his mercy.

My father has worked with Third World farmers as an agricultural adviser. He says it is nearly impossible to get some of these farmers to use advanced farm technologies, because they live so close to the edge of their existence. If some new farming technique fails, they will starve. For them it is better to keep struggling along with what little they have, rather than risk everything on something untried. Abundance that would revolutionize their lives is within their reach, but they are paralyzed because they are so conscious of their poverty.

God does not want us to be caught in the paralysis of spiritual poverty. Through the doxology that Paul uses to prepare us for the requirements of this passage, God tells us of the richness of his provision so that we will serve him with courage and vigor:

> Oh, the depth of the riches of the wisdom and knowledge of God!
> How unsearchable his judgments,
>   and his paths beyond tracing out!
> "Who has known the mind of the Lord?
>   Or who has been his counselor?"
> "Who has ever given to God,
>   that God should repay him?"
> For from him and through him and to him are all things.
>   To him be the glory forever! Amen (Rom. 11:33-36).

God says in essence, "I have already declared to you that by the work of Jesus Christ you are rich in mercy. Now build my kingdom with the energy and effort that befits those with unlimited resources. Be done with the self-doubt and fear of loss that cripples those poor in faith. I have declared you holy. Be about the business of building my kingdom. Stop saying that because you are not a Moses, or were not raised in the right environment, or wandered to other priorities, or made some mistakes, you cannot serve God. Yes, you can."

We who are rich in mercy have God's business to do, and no one can say that we are underfinanced. God's gracious provision empowers us for his service.

Assurance

We may still find ourselves saying: "Lord, thanks for the wealth of mercy. You sure know I need it, and I would like to serve you better. I wish I could, but you know me. You know I can't please you. I am trapped in this sin . . . or in this job . . . or in this relationship. Lord, you might as well give up on me. I have. You know I can't change. You know I'll never be able to please you."

"I have already made you pleasing to me," the Lord replies.

"Me? With all my sin and shame?"

"Yes, you are able to please me," says the Lord.

It sounds amazing, but God says that sinful people please him. He has made us living sacrifices, holy and "pleasing" to him (12:1). Because we are holy through the work of his Son, God declares that we already please him despite our imperfections. This is a wonderful assurance, and again the result is power.

In the 1980 Olympic games, Soviet coaches tricked one of their weightlifters. They *told* him the weight that he was lifting on his final lift was 499 pounds, a weight he had lifted before in practice and knew he could handle. However, in fact, the coaches had instructed Olympic officials to put 500.5 pounds on the bar. This was a world-record weight the athlete had never been able to hoist before. He stepped to the bar . . . and lifted it. Believing that he could do the task, he did it.

There is power in believing that we are able, and we know that we are able to please God because his Word says so. We do not gain this ability to please God by some trick, but by the work of his Spirit in us. Satan would love for us to believe that we can do nothing. He wants to paralyze us with self-doubt and past shame. In contrast, God has filled us with his Spirit of power, and cleansed us with the blood of his Son. He tells us in his Word that we *are* able to please him. We are able to serve him. Our lives can be a joy to him. Our service can build his kingdom. He says so. We can go about the business of God with confidence because his mercy makes our work pleasing to him.

───── MERCY RESTORED ─────

By his mercy God claims us. By his mercy he encourages us. By his mercy he empowers us. So echoes the grace that makes our service sweet and our hearts strong. When these echoes resonate in our hearts as well as our ears, we discover the renewing power of the gospel that makes our faith and zeal fresh and dear.

The young mother introduced at the beginning of this chapter still needed to discover this refreshing grace of God. The day after her experience in the park she again sought some relief from the summer monotony. She took her children to Vacation Bible School. She soon was to discover how much her heart was still aching from the revelations of the previous day.

When she went to pick up her children at noon, the program was running a little late, so she sat in her car listening to the voices of the children waft out the church windows. Their singing and laughter did *not* lift her spirits. Instead, it made her remember the joylessness of her own walk of faith, and again melancholy gripped her.

She remembered when Jesus was just another word for joy; when folding your hands to pray meant you were talking to God; and, when you said,

"Lord, I'm sorry," you really felt forgiven. Recognition of the things that once filled her heart now only made her feel more empty. Her head fell to the steering wheel, and the tears came again with a silent sigh of spiritual longing. So quiet was her grief that she could still hear the children's songs. The closing exercises of the Bible School were ending, so the children were singing their marching song—the song that was supposed to take them into the world with zeal for the Lord. When the words penetrated her consciousness, the mother drew in her breath with a startled gasp.

The children sang, "I will sing of the mercies of the Lord forever, I will sing, I will sing; I will sing of the mercies of the Lord forever . . ." Sudden realization flooded over the mother like a shock wave from heaven. The words of mercy lifted her head from the wheel. "That's it," she thought. "That's what I have forgotten."

Once she had sung that song with the joy the children now echoed. But somewhere, somehow life with its busyness, along with the guilt of a thousand failures, the negligence of ten thousand duties, and the pursuit of a million priorities other than God's, had taken the words from her lips and the truths from her heart. More and more she had performed the duties she could manage for divine favors and out of human dread. Now in the song of the children she saw a way back to the warmth she had known. Affirmation of God's mercy was the way back into his arms and all the joy that was there.

She sang with the children as new joy flooded into her heart: "I will sing of the mercies of the Lord forever." Now there was cause for loving zeal again—here was new strength. She knew that, in view of this mercy, she could seek him again, serve him afresh, and love him anew. By mercy God clasped her heart, captured her commitment, and reclaimed her joy.

By mercy God again made this woman's service sweet and her heart strong. Such grace God will grant us, too, as each of us asks, "Why do I do what I do?" and as we each answer, "Because of God's mercy."

Works That Really Matter

In an article titled "My Father's Legacy," Roy Atwood describes his father's passing away:

> The days of my father's life were, by reason of strength and God's grace, 80 years (Ps. 90:10). He died a year ago. We still grieve his death, of course, but as the pain of his passing fades, we struggle with new pain: the realization of how swiftly the memory of someone as close as a husband, a father, and a friend can fly away. If each day dims the memory of the contours of his face and the sound of his voice, what will we remember of him ten or twenty years distant? What will his children's children know of him, his life, his hopes and fears, his failures and successes, or his view of God's world? What will be the legacy of his life?
>
> Over time, we will forget the things he enjoyed. He loved the company of his well-oiled tools and rifles. He loved the rhythmic pulse of waves against the hull of his sail-boat running ahead of a fresh breeze. . . . However, over time, the waves will not reflect his image, and his precious tools and guns will be recycled into someone else's rusty barbecue or dented wheel barrow.
>
> We'll forget the work of his hands. . . .
>
> We'll forget his strengths and weaknesses. . . .
>
> We'll even forget how his illusions of independence and self-sufficiency were shattered in 1988, when he fell off the roof of his home while cleaning the gutters in the rain, landed on the corner of a concrete sidewalk, and broke his spine between his shoulder blades. The fall almost killed him. In a split second, his pride and dreams and many of the things he loved most were gone. He never walked or worked in his shop or sailed again. He struggled with depression

and suicide many times. He never wanted to be a burden to his wife or his children, but his self-sufficiency was—in an instant—gone forever.[1]

This loving account candidly exposes a truth hard to face. All that we build, love, and live for will fade. The fading may take a minute or it may take millennia, but time and erosion will ultimately erase all our accomplishments from human memory. We, too, will be forgotten. Inevitably, time will erode our significance. We want to be remembered. We want our work to have lasting meaning. Yet we forget and will be forgotten.

Not only do the ravages of time seem to render our accomplishments insignificant, so also do the realities of grace. If God does not measure our worth by what we do, then why should we bother to serve him? Those who have experienced failure and have participated in serious sin may be encouraged by the good news that God does not value us according to our religious performance. However, there is a less attractive flip side to unconditional love: the apparent devaluing of obedience.

If our righteousness really makes no difference to God, then sacrifice is for fools and holiness can cost everything for nothing. Grace that entirely denies the worth of our works cheapens the deaths of martyrs and makes superfluous the devotion that causes our pain.

To properly evaluate the place of good works in the Christian life, we must understand that grace maintains the value of God's children apart from any merit of their own; but we must *also* understand that God uses our obedience to promote our good and his glory. By our accomplishments, God works his holy purposes in our lives, provides us with many temporal blessings and, most of all, fulfills our Spirit-instilled longing to honor God with all our heart, soul, mind, and might (cf. Deut. 6:5; Matt. 22:37). While we must be careful not to define blessing only in terms of material possessions or earthly ease, we must also embrace the promise that God "rewards those who earnestly seek him" (Heb. 11:6).

We know much of God's goodness, justice, mercy, and truth by the way he responds to our efforts to serve him. God's honoring of our righteousness does not change the degree of his love for us or imply that we can earn his affection. Still, his recognition and reward of righteousness does indicate that he values efforts that conform us more to his image. In so honoring our works, God demonstrates his regard for his own glory and cultivates in us an appreciation for the beauty of his holiness. The righteousness in us that God motivates and enables by his grace, he also graciously blesses.

The Bible confirms the value to God of our good works by underscoring his promise not only to bless them but also to make them endure. The psalmist writes:

PSALM 112

[1]Praise the LORD.

Blessed is the man who fears the LORD,
*   who finds great delight in his commands.*

[2]His children will be mighty in the land;
*   the generation of the upright will be blessed.*
[3]Wealth and riches are in his house,
*   and his righteousness endures forever.*
[4]Even in darkness light dawns for the upright,
*   for the gracious and compassionate and righteous man.*
[5]Good will come to him who is generous and lends freely,
*   who conducts his affairs with justice.*
[6]Surely he will never be shaken;
*   a righteous man will be remembered forever.*
[7]He will have no fear of bad news;
*   his heart is steadfast, trusting in the LORD.*
[8]His heart is secure, he will have no fear;
*   in the end he will look in triumph on his foes.*
[9]He has scattered abroad his gifts to the poor,
*   his righteousness endures forever;*
*   his horn will be lifted high in honor.*

[10]The wicked man will see and be vexed,
*   he will gnash his teeth and waste away;*
*   the longings of the wicked will come to nothing.*

Three times this Psalm tells us what will endure forever (vv. 3, 6, 9): righteous actions, righteous persons, and God's righteous care. Knowing that our accomplishments have enduring significance and are part of heaven's plan for our lasting security encourages us to serve God not primarily for rewards that will fade but for eternal purposes.[2] This perspective does not deny that God ordinarily blesses obedience with earthly benefits, but it does keep us from considering those benefits only in terms of material prosperity and personal comfort.

Those whose affections have been renewed and reshaped by the Spirit of God desire above all things the fulfillment of God's purposes even at the cost of their own pleasures, advantages—and life, if need be. For such reasons the writer of Hebrews not only commends those whose faith delivered them from lions, flames, and sword, but also those who in faith suffered torture, jeers, flogging, prison, stoning, being sawn in two, death by sword, deprivation, destitution, and persecution (Heb. 11:33-40).

Because God's eternal purposes may require the forfeiture of earthly benefits, we cannot make temporal rewards the chief motive of our obedience. Such rewards are not absolutely promised in Scripture and would be unsuitable as the chief aim of our lives.[3] If Christians always received material blessing as a recompense for obedience, then it would be impossible to separate personal duty from divine bribery. Christianity would become merely a bartering system for personal gain. God's ends are not so shortsighted or earthbound. Understanding God's enduring purposes, so that we can appreciate the significance and blessing of our good works, requires an in-depth understanding of the three things God promises will never fade away: righteous actions, righteous persons, and his own righteous care for us.

—— OUR RIGHTEOUS ACTIONS ——

At the end of the psalmist's description of the righteous man, one of Scripture's most amazing statements appears. Speaking of the righteous person, the Bible says, "[H]is righteousness endures forever." This is an extraordinary promise. What can we do in this life that will last forever? Were we to amass the fortune of Bill Gates, write a novel equal to Hemingway, achieve the recognition of Elvis, or build an empire to rival Alexander the Great—none of these would last forever. Yet people expend their life's wealth, wisdom, and work striving for something that will make their mark.

The poet Percy Bysshe Shelley's fabled Ozymandias rises from desert sands to mock all who think that their works will last. Shelley writes of meeting a traveler from an "antique land" who tells of discovering the remnant of a huge statue. In the traveler's account, the massive head of the statue lies on the ground, and its trunk has disappeared. Only legs of stone remain standing on a pedestal with these words:

"My name is Ozymandias, king of kings:
Look on my works, ye Mighty, and despair!"

Apart from that boast of great achievement, no other sign of Ozymandias' empire can be seen. Shelley concludes simply,

Nothing beside remains. Round the decay
Of that colossal wreck, boundless and bare
The lone and level sands stretch far away.

The message is clear: despite its apparent greatness, no human achievement really distinguishes anyone for long.

No matter what we achieve or amass, someone else has done or will do more, or better, or younger, or faster, or against greater odds. Those who do make some significant mark still discover that time and circumstances eventually level every achievement. And even if that leveling does not occur immediately, one's own ability to appreciate the significance of an achievement has a finite limit. Yet against the backdrop of the temporary nature of all human accomplishment, Scripture declares that something will endure: our righteousness. How can this be?

BY RIGHTEOUS INFLUENCE

The mystery of the enduring nature of our righteousness is partially solved by recognizing that preceding the promise of lasting righteousness are God's promises of generational influence and home establishment. The psalmist says that the children of the righteous will be mighty (Ps. 112:2), and that his house will be known for its prosperity (v. 3). We should recognize that these are idiomatic Hebrew expressions of general blessing. They are not unqualified promises of a life without problems. This is evident in the following verses, which indicate that even the righteous must face times of darkness (v. 4), temptations of greed and selfishness (v. 5), matters that threaten one's equilibrium (v. 6), bad news (v. 7), and foes (v. 8).

God does not absolutely promise that all godly people will have families without problems and homes without leaks. Nevertheless, the psalmist wants us to understand that one of the ways God blesses is by the effects of personal righteousness rippling through one's family and home. Godliness establishes homes on foundations more secure than the world can provide.

Recently the Rev. Stuart Perrin, one of the long-term leaders of our church, died. Stuart's two sons—both pastors—shared the preaching of the funeral message. They told of their father's spiritual heritage. Weakened by cancer complications, their father's mother contracted influenza in their northern Minnesota home and died when he was only four. The family had been made destitute by paying for multiple illnesses. There was nothing material the faithful mother could pass along to her four-year-old child. Still, as she lay dying, she called the boy to her bedside. She told him that though she had no earthly goods to give him, she was leaving him a heavenly inheritance. Then she shared with the young boy these words of Scripture that he held dear the rest of his life:

> Do not fear, for I am with you; do not be dismayed, for I am your God. I will strengthen you and help you; I will uphold you with my righteous right hand (Isa. 41:10).

When Stuart's son, the Rev. Dan Perrin, told that account, his wife and children all nodded their heads, as did the wife and children of Dan's brother, Ric. They had all heard the story many times. But the story was more than sentiment. As each of the grandchildren and great-grandchildren of that dying mother nodded acknowledgment of the account, there was evidence that her righteousness was enduring to the third and fourth generations of those who loved the Lord. Her righteous influence endured for multiple generations though her life was cut short.

This godly family demonstrates how our righteous influence can have enduring effects. Very few things that we do in life have more than a passing significance. Fewer have a lifetime of impact. For God to promise that our righteousness can have an impact for three or four generations is a great treasure for every parent, grandparent, teacher, or leader who wants to pass on a legacy of faithfulness to succeeding generations.

But what is truly astounding is that God does not promise that such a legacy will last for only a few generations; he promises that the influence of our righteousness will endure forever—a thousand thousand generations. This is a great grace—a provision of heavenly proportions not achievable by human effort—that should motivate holiness in us even when times are hard and blessings are not presently evident.

By promising to use our righteousness to influence generations and secure our homes, God helps us order our priorities. Though there are times when we must give our families less attention due to the press of circumstances or competing responsibilities, hearts that are conscious of eternal implications guard home life. None should ignore the incentive that the grace of enduring righteousness provides. I, too, must honor God as I balance my work and travel schedule against my family obligations.

All who are in responsible positions know how work priorities cry for attention and urgency. Still, God intends for us to weigh eternal consequences when we consider spending a few minutes with a child in the sandbox against seeking a few more ways to impress a client, or when we weigh time at home against spending a few more days away to earn more corporate recognition or a bonus check. The grace that provides for our righteousness to influence eternity calls most of us to serious reflection and repentance as we consider our family priorities against the personal compulsions of fame and gain.

BY RIGHTEOUSNESS ITSELF (V. 3B)

As impressive as are the promises of the enduring influence of our righteousness, they are not the most impressive nor mysterious aspect of the psalmist's message. The psalm does not only suggest that the *influence* of our righteousness will endure forever; it specifically says that our righteousness *itself* will endure (v. 3b).

This promise of enduring righteousness is difficult for me to grasp. I can imagine how righteous influences could endure. Cascade theories in science speculate that, as a result of multiple cause-and-effect sequences, a butterfly flapping its wings in Hong Kong can result in a thunderstorm in New York weeks later. I can similarly theorize how one's faithfulness can reverberate with enduring effects that God controls. Still, it is hard for me to fathom how the original righteousness itself endures. Still the Bible says, "righteousness endures forever."

The eternal nature of our righteousness echoes in the apostle Paul's familiar words, "For we are God's workmanship, created in Christ Jesus to do good works, which God prepared in advance for us to do" (Eph. 2:10). Each good work that we accomplish God prepared for us to do before the foundations of the world were laid. Each word of encouragement, gesture of charity, or act of courage and compassion is a vital link in an eternal chain of God's purpose. The significance of each action is marked not merely by its passing place in time but by its permanent position in God's eternal plan for establishing his everlasting kingdom. Knowing that the righteousness itself, however insignificant to us, is actually part of an eternal plan changes our perception of the importance of our lives, and should revolutionize what we view as worthwhile for our efforts.

I have always felt that one of the purest acts of ministry is visiting Alzheimer's patients. Ordinarily, when I visit hospitals, nursing homes, and prisons, part of me—the noble part—is motivated by selfless care and a desire to take the hope of the gospel where it is most needed, but there is another part of me that visits more out of self-protection than compassion. Sometimes, I must confess, I go to those hurting because I fear that if I don't visit frequently or long enough, people will attack me for not fulfilling my pastoral duties. I do not have to worry about such mixed motives, however, when visiting an Alzheimer's patient in the later stages of the disease. Thirty seconds after I leave the room of such a patient there will be no remembrance of my visit. There may not even be any awareness of my presence while I am at the bedside. I get no "credit" for the visit.

The effort to bring a few seconds of human warmth to one of such fleeting awareness would seem of no lasting significance. But God says that righteousness endures forever. As unnoticed and inconsequential as such a small act of compassion may seem, it is eternal. How? I cannot fully explain. Perhaps the eternal significance lies in the difference such an expression of compassion causes in me as much as the effect it has on another. Still, where my explanation falls short, God's promise to preserve my righteousness endures.

This side of heaven we will not see how most of our small acts of kindness, or even our great acts of courage that are unnoticed or misunderstood, fit into God's eternal plan. But we walk and act in the faith that such actions are eternal, because God promises this is so. The grace that makes our righteousness more significant than we can imagine or arrange should inspire a willingness to serve where the world will not notice and to give of ourselves when no one else will bother.

Knowing the eternal implications of our actions enables us more and more to live for heaven's effects rather than for earth's approval. A gentle touch offered to a crying child on the street, an angry word withheld, the willingness to lose a business deal for integrity's sake, uncomplaining participation in the dreary routine of dishes and diapers, a smile offered to a harried clerk who has rung up the wrong bill—each unnoticed act of righteousness remains eternal and, as a result, is worthy of our efforts.

The Christian walks through the world with a hidden smile, knowing that by God's grace each act of love and sacrifice is eternal though the world cannot see it. As we see our world through the eyes of Scripture we know that each day and every moment is lived for eternity and, thus, that no righteous act is fruitless and no sacrifice is vain (1 Cor. 15:58). The life of faith embraces God's promise of enduring righteousness, allowing us to walk in the constant joy of knowing that our efforts and sacrifices do not escape his notice.

When we do not respond in kind to the angry driver who cut us off in traffic, we can grin with the awareness that our restraint of the moment produces long-lasting righteousness. We can laugh with the delight of thinking to ourselves, "That driver got an instant's satisfaction out of taking advantage of me, but I did something eternal in not reacting to him." Then the joy of the Lord again becomes our strength for continued and reinvigorated obedience. This is the strength we need not only for moments in traffic but for months in abusive homes, for careers in thankless professions, and for lifetimes of chronic disease and inexplicable difficulty that make no sense apart from the promises of eternity.

A RIGHTEOUS PERSON

Our scriptural spectacles not only help us to see the difference between temporal and eternal endeavors, they also enable us to discern what (or whom) God eternally treasures. A key shift of wording occurs the second time that the psalmist identifies what endures forever. He says that a righteous person himself will be remembered forever (Ps. 112:6).

As comforting as is the promise that we personally will be remembered forever, it seems as improbable as the assurance that our righteousness will be so remembered. When my family last moved, I had the opportunity and obligation to rummage through the various boxes stored in our attic to decide which accumulated "treasures" we really needed to load into the moving van. Leafing through old papers in one box, I discovered my final college report card.

Surely I saved this record because the grades were once very important to me (twenty-five years ago). I opened the envelope to revel in what I recalled as academic excellence, but no such joy awaited me. Years of modulating heat and humidity in the attic had caused the ink to fade from the grade card. No grades were visible. Time had even erased the list of courses I had taken. Without the written record of my work I could not remember my grades, what classes I had taken, or even who my professors had been.

As an educator, the failure to remember my own academic endeavors is quite distressing. If I can forget grades, courses, and instructors, then this may be true of other people. It may even be true of my students. My students, too, are likely to forget their grades, the contents of the course I taught them, and me!

Still, my God promises that he will not forget me. He will not forget me even though my classes are forgettable. Though he knows better than anyone that there are only occasional flashes of eloquence amid the jumble of supposedly sophisticated words; that there are shameful bursts of impatience despite infrequent thoughts beyond the obvious; that there are long stretches of mediocre repetitions of stale lectures punctuated by too-frequent expressions of personal arrogance . . . 'though he knows and endures all of this, my God promises to treasure his memory of me forever.

The best time to be reminded of God's enduring memory of us is probably when we have lost what we thought would make us significant, or when we have achieved it only to discover the hollowness of what this world says is glorious. So many spend their lives in frenetic pursuit of what will set them apart, only to discover that achievement gained or lost is more a matter of circumstances and timing outside of our control than of personal giftedness and character.

Joseph Conrad's antihero in the film version of *Lord Jim* speaks with biblical poignancy of the unreality of human assessments of our achievements. He recounts the things that have formed his own reputation and says, "I have been a so-called coward, and I have been a so-called hero, but I tell you now there is not the breadth of a piece of paper between the two." For such reasons the Bible graciously points away from our achievements as the primary basis for our remembrance and says, instead, that God remembers *us*.

Against the backdrop of life's futility and peril, the psalmist promises that the memory of the righteous will endure. Though this world holds no guarantees of respect, recognition, or remembrance, God promises his own people this surpassingly royal treatment: an eternal record. "The righteous will be for a memorial forever," the psalm literally says. God will make a righteous person a memorial of divine blessing for all of heaven and earth to honor.

But surely this cannot be. Millions of faithful have died unnoticed and unremembered. Common sense tells us this. Who among us really expects to be remembered by history? A little more that a half century after the end of a world war we struggle to remember those who fought and the significance of their cause. The memorials of those who died in the defense of our liberty decay without adequate funding from the very nation they defended. How, then, can God promise eternal remembrance to the righteous?

The answer is that the names of the righteous are memorialized not in the records of earth but in the annals of heaven. The prophet Malachi writes of the Day of Judgment:

> Then those who feared the LORD talked with each other, and the LORD listened and heard. A scroll of remembrance was written in his presence concerning those who feared the LORD and honored his name (Mal. 3:16).

For the righteous this is enough—God will remember us. Though friends and family forget us, and though our name becomes tarnished and belittled, yet our God holds us forever in his heart as a precious treasure.

We may work for a company for thirty years and, three weeks after departing, be treated as though we were never there, but God will continue to rejoice over us forever. The aging invalid in a nursing home whose children never visit, and whose friends have all departed, is not forgotten. God maintains an eternal record of the righteous and from heaven offers this assurance: "I remember you. I will never forget you."

Confidence in heaven's memory grants earthly courage for divine purposes. Because God will maintain our name in his records, we do not need to fear that a failure properly to calculate what will bring us the most recognition, respect, or significance will disqualify us from heavenly glory. We can afford the vulnerability with others that compassion and grace require—loving the unlovely (v. 4), lending freely (v. 5a), acting justly (v. 5b).

My father once turned down a promotion that would have required a move to another city at a time when he felt it was more important that we have family stability. Though I write of the selflessness and nobility of that decision, his company has already forgotten, and one day I will forget what my father did. The earthly record of his sacrifice will fade with the ink of these pages. But heaven will not forget. What my father did in faithfulness to his family and to his God will be memorialized with my father's name in heaven.

As I write these words I must continually preach them to myself. Each year our seminary must raise millions of dollars to continue to support the ministries God has committed to our care. If we do not raise the money, it will not matter how nice is the title and prestige of my position; the year will be counted as a financial failure. And if there are repeated years of financial shortfall, then I will be judged to have failed in this position no matter what quality of books I have written, or how wisely I have taught, or how carefully I have administered.

The financial responsibilities of my position sometimes weigh heavily on me, and I can become paralyzed by their pressures. In those moments I also must hold precious the promise that God does not measure my worth by earth's accomplishments. As I am faithful to him, regardless of outcomes, he remembers and treasures me forever. My name is written in heaven, and nothing done here will erase it there.

Whether our calling is to professional ministry, business, homemaking, the arts, or politics, all of God's people need these truths of heavenly remembrance. God will call some of us to endeavors that do not flourish. Some of us will assume positions where we will not experience success as the world measures it. Many of us will serve people who do not appreciate us. A sad number of us will have marriages that come unglued. All will face challenges to our sense of significance. In each of these areas, the degree of our continued faithfulness will in large measure be determined by how real and deep is our perception that God remembers and values us even when others do not.

We must rest in the faith that regardless of what pressures or failures come upon us, we need never fear any loss of real significance. God has promised never to forget us. We are precious to the eternal King of the universe. Our name is written in his book of remembrance, and nothing in this world can ever erase it!

——— GOD'S RIGHTEOUS PROVISION ———

This promise of divine remembrance goes against the logic of our world and perhaps against our own consciences. We may like the words of assurance but still doubt their truth because we know that there is nothing in us or our accomplishments that warrants this eternal record. In fact, we may know that our weaknesses and failings have sufficiently eroded our stature before God to justify his forgetting his grace to us. Candid assessment of our lack of warrant to claim a heavenly memorial indicates why we need this psalm's final explanation of why we will not be forgotten.

The third time the psalmist mentions righteousness enduring forever he adds the ultimate reason that God will not forget his people. God promises their remembrance not on the basis of their accomplishments or inherent worth, but on the basis of his own action in their behalf. Heaven's remembrance is not because of our having done righteous deeds or our having been righteous people, but because of God's having made righteous provision that he will not forget.

A HOLY RESCUE

The psalmist repeats the assurance that a person's "righteousness will endure forever" in order to make a key addition in the final refrain (v. 9). To the repeated assurance of enduring righteousness the psalmist adds the promise that a person's "horn will be lifted high in honor." This is an unfamiliar expression for our modern ears, but the Hebrews understood. The divine promise to lift the "horn" (a word symbolizing dignity or strength) of a righteous person meant that God would maintain or provide an individual's honor. The individual does not provide his own regard. The verb is made passive to indicate that the person's dignity is lifted up, or maintained, by another.

The emphasis on divine provision grows with the realization that six of the seven times the term "horn" is used in the Psalms, either it refers to God himself or it occurs in tandem with a description of what God will do for his people. Thus, the words of the psalmist are here meant to assure us that God himself acts in our behalf to provide the dignity and strength we need to justify a divine remembrance.

This promise of holy preservation continues the earlier assurance that a righteous person need not fear because "in the end he will look in triumph on all his foes" (v. 8). God's ultimate rescue of the righteous becomes the source of vexation of the wicked (v. 10), but it is the source of animation for us. Knowing that our weaknesses and the challenges we face will not ultimately destroy our heavenly status gives us courage for our earthly battles.

A pastor friend of mine is a Vietnam War veteran. Today he pastors in a very challenging setting that he will admit causes him occasionally to doubt his adequacy for the battles he must face. Still, he has faced major hurdles and setbacks without flinching, and has experienced God's blessing on stalwart efforts. As a military veteran my friend expresses his resiliency this way:

> A well-trained soldier is not afraid of his adequacy in battle. In fact, in some ways he looks forward to the challenge of using his skills and equipment. It is not the fighting that scares him. It is the realization that out there somewhere may be a bullet with his name on it. But the wonder of the Gospel is that God promised there is no such bullet for the believer. Though we are in for the fight of our lives and may experience great loss—even of our lives—we know that the enemy is ours. God has promised that our souls are secure, and that he will ultimately defeat all our spiritual foes.[4]

The Bible's assurance of our eternal security is meant to equip us to fight fearlessly in the righteous causes to which God calls us.

A HOLY TRANSFER

The same grace that offers us protection that we could not forge also provides honor we cannot earn. The very first verse of Psalm 112 marks a holy transfer. The preceding Psalm 111 (which was meant to be read in tandem with Psalm 112) is devoted to describing the Lord and his righteousness. Though Psalm 112 starts the same way, the focus soon shifts. Praise of God moves to descriptions of blessing on the one who "fears the Lord." Scripture identifies those who fear the Lord as those who in abject humility recognize that their present existence and future eternity are dependent on God's mercy (see Luke 1:50; Acts 9:31).[5] To such people God promises his blessing, but the source of that blessing is not in them.

An amazing expression of God's grace appears in the way that these two psalms interact with each other. Ten times the psalmist uses the Hebrew terms applied to God in Psalm 111 to describe the righteous man in Psalm 112. Psalm 111 says God's "righteousness endures forever," and that he is "compassionate," "generous," "just," and so forth; and these same concepts are used to describe the righteous man in Psalm 112. The Bible transfers the terms of God's own character and attributes to the person who fears the Lord. Those who depend upon God's mercy receive the dignity they do not deserve and the honor they could not earn. They are granted the glory of God's own righteousness.

Ultimately this transfer of divine attributes to human vessels explains why God can promise to remember the righteous forever (2 Cor. 4:6-7). Our eternal record is not based on what we accomplish but on God's work in our behalf. While we have the privilege of participating in eternal causes, the reason that the righteous and their works endure forever is that God sanctifies our feeble and faulty efforts by instilling his own righteousness in them.

Ultimately it is God's righteousness alone that is worthy of an eternal remembrance. In his grace he shares his holiness with us so that our works will have the status of his own. Our works are made worthy of eternity by virtue of the mercy in *him*, rather than on the basis of the merit in *them*.

The New Testament expression of this promise of imputed (or transferred) righteousness is the apostle Paul's often-repeated expression "in Christ."[6] Paul uses this phrase to refer to the continuing effect of our sin being covered by Christ's atoning blood. Not only did his blood wash away the guilt of our sin, it continues to cover us with his holiness so that we are always in union with him—enveloped by his mercy, clothed in his righteousness. His righteousness so permeates and encapsulates our works that, though they are always imperfect, yet our holy God can use them.

God allows us to express our love for him through our good works, which he uses in the world to accomplish his kingdom purposes. He also uses our works in us to conform us more to the likeness of Jesus. Still, the righteousness accomplished by our good works does not result from the purity of our actions and motives—for our actions and motives have too much of the mix of our fallen humanity in them. Our righteousness, rather, depends always on God's application of the sanctifying merit of Christ's blood to even our best works. A portion of the *Westminster Confession of Faith* cited earlier beautifully expresses how and why God uses our works even though they will never reach the standard of perfection his holiness requires:

> [B]elievers being accepted *through Christ,* their good works are accepted *in Him;* not as though they were in this life wholly unblameable and unreprovable in God's sight; but that He, looking upon them *in His Son,* is pleased to accept and reward that which is sincere, although accompanied with many weaknesses and imperfections [emphasis mine].[7]

God demonstrates his sovereign care by blessing what does not measure up to his standards—and would even warrant his judgment based on its own merit—by accepting our sincere obedience on the basis of Christ's work in our behalf. When Christians bring their bouquets of good works, our Savior shows his mercy as he "gathers out all the weeds from their duties and makes them acceptable to God."[8]

Francis Schaeffer referred to this grace, by which Christ purifies our works so that they glorify God and sanctify us despite their imperfections, as "the present value of the blood of Christ."[9] The phrase reminds us that our dependence on Christ's justifying work to forgive our sins does not cease when we become Christians. We do not come to God on the basis of Christ's shed blood and then maintain our holy status by personal grit and determination. Rather, every day and in every action we are dependent on our Savior's grace to wash our works in the purifying streams of his blood. Apart from him we can do nothing that pleases God. Through him and in him alone we are enabled to do those works that please God, sanctify us, and have eternal significance.

I began this chapter with Roy Atwood's account of the passing of his father, who had become an invalid after enjoying active pursuits most of his life. Atwood does not end the story, however, with the acknowledgment of his father's loss of strength and pride. Another source of significance eventually took over his father's broken body:

> In his state of almost complete physical and spiritual dependency, God turned him to Christ and his sufficiency. . . . We will not soon forget how dramatic and obvious was the change in his life: his anger was replaced by joy; his bitterness by tenderness; and his hardness by a gentleness of spirit. His final years as a faithful Christian man, husband, father and grandfather were his finest. But even these will fade with time.
>
> So if all that my father was and did in this life will vanish over the years, what will be his legacy? All that can endure is the work of someone else who does not forget or fade with time. Only the Atoning work of the Lord Jesus Christ—not my father's own good and bad deeds—will be his legacy to his family and friends. The only legacy he could leave us is the simple testimony that he has triumphed over death through Christ's gracious work of redemption—plus nothing.
>
> My father's legacy to his children's children will be that God's grace and covenant faithfulness were sufficient even for a man whose face and voice many will soon forget . . . because Christ's person and work endure.[10]

Atwood's father experienced the reality of the holy transfer that the psalmist extols. As God's own character and attributes took root in the soil of a human soul, anger was replaced by joy, and bitterness was transformed into a sweet spirit. Yet even this exchange of characteristics was not the ultimate miracle of the divine transformation God accomplished in the aging man's life.

More profound than the reformation of personality was the promise of eternity. For even when the joy and tenderness of character would fail, God's work in the man would not. When strength of body and will ultimately yielded to the realities of mortality and the ravages of time, God preserved and continues to maintain the legacy of righteousness that his Son alone provides. Neither death nor the passing of time will rob from God the memory, significance, and presence of one who has been granted the holiness of Christ forever. Because his righteousness is ours, his triumph over sin and death is ours. No act or life committed to him ever loses its eternal place in his kingdom. In the world revealed by the eyes of faith there are no little deeds and there are no little people.[11]

God's transfer of his righteousness to us grants us a beautifully fresh perspective on the service he allows us to do for him. Because God makes our works holy, not only are the great achievements of our lives pleasing to him and purposeful for his kingdom, but so are the unnoticed and insignificant actions we do in his name.

No cup of water shared, no load lifted, nor any life given in the cause of righteousness is ever insignificant regardless of the world's estimation. By bathing even small duties in the character of his righteousness God makes our actions holy, and as such they are as pleasing to him as the most majestic choral anthem on Easter morning and as precious as the prayer of a child in whom there is no doubt. The proof of the value of such acts is their enduring significance in the kingdom of the One who forgets neither the deeds done in his name nor those who do the deeds—for his glory.

——— OUR LEGACY ———

As we consider where God may be calling us—to the mission field, to a stand of courage in our present profession, to a testimony of faithfulness in a troubled family, or to a place of sacrifice in the cause of Christ—we must not forget what God will remember. Our Savior says that no act of divine commitment and no person who serves him will ever be forgotten, no matter what their significance from a worldly point of view. Such a biblical perspective will make us "content to fill a little space if thou be glorified"[12] and will assure us of the value of every duty done for Christ. If we think that the battle is not worth fighting because the odds against us are too great or the failures of the past are too overwhelming, then we must consider again the provisions of our God. He promises us an eternal rescue, and a reckoning to us of his own character, so that we can commit ourselves to the only purposes that are eternal.

Because of its everlasting significance, no work done for God is trite, and no person who serves God will be forgotten. To give this encouragement to those who may serve in places insignificant by the world's estimation, church history professor David Calhoun likes to tell graduating seniors at Covenant Seminary this story of the missionary statesman Charles Simeon:

> Simeon kept a portrait of the deceased missionary Henry Martyn over the mantel of his fireplace. Simeon had served as a spiritual father to Martyn at Cambridge, honing the young man's theology and inspiring him with missionary zeal. It was Simeon who saw Martyn off as he left Portsmouth and sailed for Asia.
>
> They never saw one another again. But for seven years Simeon constantly kept the novice missionary in his prayers through the young man's amazingly successful ministries in both India and Persia. Then came the terrible message. After only those few, fervent years word came to England that Martyn had contracted a disease and died on the mission field.
>
> A portrait of Henry Martyn, painted in India, was sent back to Simeon. He hung it in the honored place over his mantel so he could tell others the testimony of his young friend. Years later looking at that picture he would say to guests, "See that blessed man. No one looks at me the way he does—he never takes his eyes off me; and seems always to be saying, 'The years are short. Be serious. Be in earnest. Don't trifle—don't trifle.'"[13]

Someone else never takes his eyes off of us. He holds us in his precious regard forever. Our God has given us this wonderful blessing of his grace. He will preserve our righteousness forever. Out of love for him and in appreciation of the significance of what he allows us to do, we should make the most of his provision and believe that what is done for him is never a trifle. For whatever is done for man will pass, yet all that is done for God will last.

That's Not Fair

"That's not fair!" said my son.

He had just purchased a hat on a first-time-ever visit to France and the storekeeper gave him change in Belgian francs. Said the French clerk, "I have run out of French francs. You don't mind if I give you change in Belgian francs instead of French francs, do you?"

My son thought, *A franc is a franc. So, sure, that will be all right.*

Only later did my son's cousins who live in Belgium tell him the sad truth: about five French francs equal the value of a United States dollar, but it takes about forty Belgian francs to do the same. My son had gotten francs as he had expected, but they were worth only about an eighth of what he should have received in change. The accounting of the clerk left something to be desired. My son was rightly offended by not receiving what he was due.

We should feel some of my son's offense when we read Jesus' parable of the workers in the vineyard. Everyone receives a certain amount of money—a day's wage—for their work, but some have worked only a fraction of the time of others. That's not fair. Even though Jesus tells the account, what the master pays his workers is still not fair. If I were to hire one of my children to clean out the garage for a few bucks, and he worked from seven until noon, then I would not even consider paying the same amount to another child who joined him in the task for the last twenty minutes. Yet Jesus says that such is the accounting system of the kingdom of heaven. Here is how Jesus explains heaven's economy:

MATTHEW 20:1-16

[1]*"For the kingdom of heaven is like a landowner who went out early in the morning to hire men to work in his vineyard.* [2]*He agreed to pay them a denarius for the day and sent them into his vineyard.*

[3]*"About the third hour he went out and saw others standing in the marketplace doing nothing.* [4]*He told them, 'You also go and work in my vineyard, and I will pay you whatever is right.'* [5]*So they went.*

"He went out again about the sixth hour and the ninth hour and did the same thing. [6]*About the eleventh hour he went out and found still others standing around. He asked them, 'Why have you been standing here all day long doing nothing?'*

[7]*"'Because no one has hired us,' they answered.*

"He said to them, 'You also go and work in my vineyard.'

[8]*"When evening came, the owner of the vineyard said to his foreman, 'Call the workers and pay them their wages, beginning with the last ones hired and going on to the first.'*

[9]*"The workers who were hired about the eleventh hour came and each received a denarius.* [10]*So when those came who were hired first, they expected to receive more. But each one of them also received a denarius.* [11]*When they received it, they began to grumble against the landowner.* [12]*'These men who were hired last worked only one hour,' they said, 'and you have made them equal to us who have borne the burden of the work and the heat of the day.'*

[13]*"But he answered one of them, 'Friend, I am not being unfair to you. Didn't you agree to work for a denarius?* [14]*Take your pay and go. I want to give the man who was hired last the same as I gave you.* [15]*Don't I have the right to do what I want with my own money? Or are you envious because I am generous?'*

[16]*"So the last will be first, and the first will be last."*

Dust from the departure of the rich young man, who wants to know what he must *do* to inherit eternal life, is still in the air (Matt. 19:16-30; see chapter 3 of this book). Having learned that to claim eternal life he must be willing to give up everything and turn from self, the young man turns from Jesus instead. The apostle Peter misses the point. He asks, "What do those of us get who have given up everything to follow you?" (see 19:27).

Peter seems to think that because he has given up his previous ambitions, home, respectability, and steady income, he has earned some recompense from God. He wants to know the payoff for his good works. We can understand Peter's logic. We expect God to be fair and for his kingdom to operate according to just principles. Since his Word assures us that he uses our righteousness for his good purposes, we expect him to compensate us according to the degree and duration of our labor in his behalf. Yet in this parable Jesus clearly teaches that an exact accounting based on our work is the last thing we should want from God.

Such righteousness as we have is the result of Christ's work rather than our own (see chapters 2 and 9 of this book). Those who desire just recompense from God on the basis of their own great labors have not yet faced their greater need of his generosity. To claim God's blessings, we must appeal to grace rather than to justice. God responds to such appeals because of what this parable teaches us about the nature of his heart.

———— GOD VALUES ALL OUR LABOR ————

In Jesus' parable, the master of the vineyard employs some who will work all day (Matt. 20:1-2). There is much to do, and those who labor from the day's beginning to its end receive a full day's wage just as the master has promised (v. 10). Because Jesus tells the parable in the context of explaining God's regard for sacrificial service, we quickly and correctly conclude that God values prolonged dedication. This is made abundantly clear by Jesus' promise, preceding the parable, that the apostles will rule with him in heaven. Jesus even expands that promise by adding, " . . . [E]veryone who has left houses or brothers or sisters or father or mother or children or fields for my sake will receive a hundred times as much and will inherit eternal life" (19:29).

THE LABOR THAT STARTS EARLY

Christ's expressions of appreciation for those who have sacrificed to serve him endorse our own commendation of those who have influenced us by their early and long service for God. The student body of our seminary recently rose spontaneously to give a standing ovation to those senior professors and board members who have given their lives in sacrificial service to God's work. I have also recently had the privilege of participating in ceremonies to honor pastors who have served churches for twenty-five, thirty, and fifty years. And I have shared in the joy of honoring couples whose many decades of marriage provide hope and inspiration for us all.

In each of these cases the honor we give for service that began early in life reflects the joy God himself expresses in saying, "Well done, good and faithful servant" (Matt. 25:21-23). God's purposes may require those who will give a lifetime of service to him, and he rewards us with the knowledge that he greatly values such labor.

THE LABOR THAT STARTS LATE

Still, while we rejoice in knowing that God recognizes the labor that has born much fruit, what troubles us about this parable—and what Christ *means* to trouble us—is that God equally compensates those whose work starts late. We can imagine the situation Jesus describes. At six in the morning the master comes to the marketplace looking for laborers. He hires those who are available. Then, he comes again at nine, and at twelve, and at three, and at five (vv. 3-6). By six in the evening darkness forces the work to conclude, so he begins to pay the day's wages.

The master starts the wage distribution with the ones who came to the vineyard last, those who worked only an hour (v. 8). To the surprise of all, he gives them a whole "denarius," a full day's wage (v. 9). We can easily imagine the eyes of those who have worked all day opening wide. They are thinking, *If these latecomers who have worked only an hour get a full day's wage, then we who have worked all day are sure to get much more.* We can sense the early workers' anticipation. And we can sense their disappointment when those who came early not only are paid last, but also get no more pay than those who started so late (v. 10).

Jesus uses the master's equal compensation of the latecomers to help us rightly value his purposes and his people. Ultimately, we do not know why the master of the vineyard treats those who start late as the equals of those who begin early. Some commentators have tried to make sense of the master's decision by speculating that a weather system could have been approaching that threatened the crop. If damaging wind, hail, or cold were coming, then it would make sense that the late harvesters became as important to the master as those who had come early.

Other experts have identified varieties of grapes whose optimum sugar content requires that they be picked in a very narrow window of time. Having workers arrive for such a time frame would also have been very important and could have accounted for the master's extra degree of appreciation.

Each of these possible explanations is mere speculation. All we really know is that the master believed the later labor was as valuable to his purposes as the early labor. The message for us that will bring unity to our churches and peace to our hearts is that God has purposes for both early and late work, and they are of equal value to him. Our labors are no less valuable to God because they come later in our life, or in the life of our family, business, church, or community.

A few years ago I participated in a study tour of Germany. Our professor was the New Testament scholar Dr. Hans Bayer. Throughout the journey he told us the significance of various sites in church history, provided translation when needed, gave us a wonderful spiritual lesson each day, and accompanied our singing on the bus with his violin. The whole trip was extremely memorable, but one event stands out above all others. We had virtually finished our tour of historical sites. After a long day of travel, we arrived at a hotel in Berlin where we would spend the night before flying home. While we were waiting for our room assignments, a number of us drifted into the lobby adjoining the reception desk.

In the center of the lobby a little jazz combo of Turkish immigrants was doing their imitation of Frank Sinatra singing, "I Did It My Way." Bayer took out his violin and asked the musicians if he could join them. Then, with hotel guests from many countries gathered around, Bayer led the jazz combo in playing "Amazing Grace" and "A Mighty Fortress Is Our God."

Bayer had not formally prepared for this moment of Christian witness that came so late on our tour. The earlier days of study and lecturing had taxed him far more in terms of his labor and energies. Yet many on our tour said afterwards that Bayer's willingness to use his talents to touch that secular, urbane setting with the beauty of the gospel was the most spiritually impacting moment of the whole tour. Though the labor that provided for the moment was late, unplanned, unrehearsed, and brief, God used it as powerfully as all the previous labors.

Knowing that God's purposes can be fulfilled equally by the labor that comes early and that which comes late is important for us all. For while we rejoice in honoring those who have made long-term contributions to the work of God's kingdom, such commendation can create discouragement for others. By honoring the early laborers, those who have come to faith more recently, or who only recently have begun to apply themselves to laboring for God, may think that all the important work has already been done.

Workers who come late may wonder if they have "missed the boat" of doing something significant for God. But had Martin Luther felt that all the important work had been done a century earlier by John Hus, then the magnificent work that God did in the German Reformer's life would not have flourished. Had Francis Schaeffer believed that the philosophical defense of Christianity had already been completed by preceding theologians, then a generation of young people who needed honest answers to honest questions would not have known how its angst and fears about modern culture really are addressed by the gospel. And Billy Graham's mother was not doing lesser work because other mothers had already raised great evangelists.

We can easily be disheartened by measuring ourselves against others who have known Christ longer, begun their studies earlier, or are further down the knowledge, faith, and Christian career path than we. If we begin to think that we will never catch up, or will never have anything valuable to offer because we have started so late, then we need to review Christ's words in this parable.

God honors the work that starts early, but he also has a purpose for the work that starts late, as long as it is devoted to his purposes. It is never too late to begin to serve our Master. Though we may have spent a lifetime walking down wayward paths, it is not too late to turn around. If our family devotionals have dropped from our routine, it is not too late to begin again. It is not too late for us to start to live a consistent testimony of speech, conduct, and witness at our place of work, even if we have spent years fitting in with the crowd.

Knowing that God can use the labor of any time in our lives, we should be encouraged to serve him early or late—for purposes that may well be hidden to us. It is best that we do not know why the master in Jesus' parable believed that the latecomers were as important for his purposes as those who arrived early. We rarely have full insight into God's reasons for when and how he calls us into his service. We should resist the natural conclusion that only long service is valuable to God. Such prejudice tends to minimize the value of not only our labor but also that of others who do not fit our arbitrary measurements of importance.

——— GOD VALUES ALL HIS LABORERS ———

When we assign worth only to those whose labor is obviously valuable, then we devalue the people God calls for special times and purposes. Christ will not allow us to second-guess his designs or depreciate his people.

Ultimately his parable not only confirms the value God places on all our labors, but also affirms the preciousness of all his laborers.

THOSE WHO ADD MUCH

The care of the master for those who come early and offer much is communicated in two ways: by his reward and by his rescue of them. The early laborers obviously are rewarded for a day's work by being paid a day's wage. While we cannot tie such compensation to definite material blessing for spiritual service, the Bible does promise that God will abundantly bless our work as he knows is best for our eternal good (see also chapter 9). Jesus' parable confirms this principle of blessing for service as the master rewards the workers for their labor.

Still, there is a subtler feature of the master's care. Twice the parable indicates that there is a kind of rescue involved in the actions of the master when he hires the workers from the marketplace. Jesus characterizes those standing around in the marketplace when the master returns at the third hour as "doing nothing" (v. 3).[1] Then the master asks those in the market at the eleventh hour why they are also "doing nothing" (v. 6). Thus, the master gives the workers livelihood (they get paid), but they also gain purpose. They are rescued from "doing nothing." This reminds us of when the apostle Peter tells us that Christ has rescued us from an "empty way of life" (1 Pet. 1:18). By laboring for our Master we are released from meaningless endeavors and pointless living.

This understanding of the purposeful living that comes only from serving God cautions us against any resentment we might feel toward those who receive the blessings of heaven by a commitment to Christ on their deathbeds. Some Christians mistakenly protest, "It's not fair that I have worked and slaved for the Lord all of my life, have missed all the fun of sinning, and a guy who accepts Jesus on his deathbed gets to go to heaven just like me." Such an attitude demonstrates a basic misunderstanding: the ones who "missed out" are not those who walked with Jesus daily, knew the assurance of divine care in personal difficulty, could entrust their family to God's hands, rested in the assurance of personal purpose regardless of earthly recognition, and claimed eternal purpose and salvation throughout life. The ones who lived so long without these treasures in order to pursue the vain pleasures and empty pursuits of the world are those who really missed the best that this life can offer.

Each Christian has a part in God's grand purpose. Whether we work in professional careers, hourly-wage positions, business, politics, education, homemaking, church service, or outer-space technology, our lives fit into God's divine purpose. Through us God is countering the assault of Satan on the people of this world. By our words and witness in both good times and bad, the Lord spreads the truths of Christ's love that will save souls eternally. We are part of God's mission to his church, this world, and countless loved ones of our own, including those whom we do not yet know but will someday meet as members of our heavenly family. This is a glorious task, and God fixes his regard for us based on the special part he has chosen for each of us in this grand mission, even when the role may be obscure to us.

THOSE WHO ADD LITTLE

Because of our frequent inability to discern how special are our roles in God's grand plan, Jesus' parable also affirms the value of those whose work apparently adds little to his purposes. Some worked only an hour in the vineyard, but the master honored them not only with equal payment but also with first payment. Such recompense dismantles our human economies.

We may be tempted to say that the master's accounting is not fair, but the parable dramatically demonstrates the principles of God's grace. He values us apart from the degree or extent of our work. This does not mean that God considers our work unimportant (see chapter 9). He simply refuses to measure our worth by our work. We are not precious to him because of the way we compare to others. Every gift, every effort, and every life offered for God is precious to him regardless of our human inability to see its eternal worth (see Rom. 12:6; 1 Cor. 12:4-25; Eph. 4:7-16).

Assessing our contributions

God's cherishing of us apart from human estimations of our worth should keep us from disparaging our own contributions to his work. Among those who tend to minimize their worth to God are those who make a commitment to him late in life. These Christians often carry a deep sense of guilt for not having worked more for the Lord earlier, not having led their children in the ways of the Lord, or not knowing as much of the Lord as do others of their age or station in life. These concerns are painful and legitimate. Still, such Christians need to know how precious is their conversion to Christ and how powerful a role it can play in his purposes.

Those who turn to Christ late in life have traveled a more difficult road than I have with my Christian family upbringing. The significance of a decision to follow Christ is immense when it requires turning from a lifetime of other practices and pursuits. People who make such dramatic and courageous decisions at a time of life when most are "set in their ways" provide a bright beacon of hope that change is possible and that a lifetime of emptiness does not have to be prelude to an eternity of the same.

These brightly shining testimonies of personal change powerfully serve God's eternal purposes. One who speaks from the perspective of changed commitments late in life will often have more credibility than I do in contrasting the rewards of the Christian life with those of the world. Such a testimony is different than mine, but it is no less essential for the spread of the gospel. Those who have little time to serve God are as important as those have been chosen for longer—but not more important—purposes.

Assessing others' contributions

God's desire to enlist the service of those who seem to have little to offer should not only comfort us, it should also caution us against disparaging the contributions of others. In Christ's parable, those who have worked more grumble against the landowner when he gives equal pay to those who have worked less (Matt. 20:11-12). We often see this kind of resentment in Scripture. The grumblers' attitude reflects that of the Pharisees who begrudged Jesus' compassion for the tax collectors and prostitutes (Mark 2), the elder son who resented the welcome of his prodigal brother (Luke 15), and the religious leader who despised the honor given to a sinner whose only claim on heaven was that she loved Jesus much (Luke 7).

Without an appreciation of the nature of grace, we too can grow resentful of those whom God blesses who do not know as much as we, are not as orthodox as we, are not as good as we, or have not worked as long and suffered as much as we. When those not as apparently talented or deserving as we receive prominence or position, Christ's parable reminds us that his grace does not depend upon our merit but purely upon the purposes in which he delights. On the days when we are tempted to "tally up" our accomplishments, this is not a truth we want to embrace; but on other days, when a truer accounting of our weaknesses and failures threatens to crush us, this message is our only hope. Because God delights to work through the weak and despised things of this world, so that all glory is his own, we need never fear that our failings destroy our usefulness to him (1 Cor. 1:27-31).

I needed to consider these truths of equal contribution despite human appearances when a wonderful young family in our church recently invited my family to dinner. During the meal, our hosts confessed that they had invited us with much trepidation. "We know that the Chapell family is spiritually high above us," said the father.

I must confess that a shameful part of me likes that assessment. However, the reality of what this young father faces every day sobers and corrects me. He lives out his faith under financial pressure in a family struggling with health problems, while working in a secular business where there is little support for his Christian principles. Daily he fights spiritual battles that I do not.

As flattering as it may be to think that my family is high on some imagined spiritual hierarchy, such assessments are impossible and improper. For how, then, should we evaluate the precious and unshakable faith of a seven-year-old in our church whose father died of an incurable congenital condition that the child also has? God will not be bound by our accounting systems when he determines the rewards of his kingdom. This may not be fair, but it is gracious beyond our ability to estimate.

THOSE WHO ADD NOTHING

The inappropriateness of using our various degrees and kinds of service to determine the recompense we deserve from God is apparent from the truths already explored in this book. We can offer no boast to God, when: his heart only responds to our spiritual desperation (chapter 1); he alone provides and seals the union with Christ that enfolds us into his family and purpose (chapter 2); his Spirit renews our hearts with the desire to honor him (chapters 2 and 3); his blood sanctifies even our best works to make them acceptable to him (chapter 3); his love and providence defeat the power of temptation (chapter 4); his Word tells us how to love and serve him (chapter 5); he equips us with faith and resurrection power to defeat sin (chapter 6); his discipline turns us from the dangers of sin (chapter 7); his mercy provides our motive to honor him (chapter 8); and, he alone grants our works eternal significance, based on his character rather than our own (chapter 9).

All that we require for growing in godliness, our God provides. In themselves our works provide no basis for boasting, no foundation for comparison to others, and no claim on heaven's blessing. Though it flows through us, the righteousness that sanctifies us before God originates in him. We strive in the strength that he generates, reach for him with the love that he instills, and trust him with the faith that he provides. We are engaged in the battle against sin and Satan, but the victory is the Lord's.

While God uses what we do to conform us to the likeness of his Son and progressively to sanctify our character, the work that pleases him is of his Spirit and, thus, cannot contribute to our spiritual merit. Our will and work are the instruments of God's transformation of our life, but he is the agent who employs them for his purposes.[2] Our human psyche and perceptions may make us feel as though the goodness we perform originates in our resolution, but Scripture reveals the divine impulse behind all our righteousness.

The more we wrestle to be free of besetting sin, the more obvious it becomes to us that God is our Rescuer. Anthony Hoekema astutely writes, "The more active we are in sanctification, the more sure we may be that the energizing power that enables us to be active is God's power."[3]

Some have suggested that the way to summarize these dynamics is to say that the cause of our sanctification is 100 percent of God and 100 percent of us. If what is meant by this statement is that God's working in us requires all of the engagement of our heart, mind, soul, and strength, then the summary is accurate. However, if what is meant by the dual 100 percents is that God simply supplies all the help we need to do what he requires and subsequently credits us for the righteousness we choose to do, then we should not agree.

In addition to the logical incomprehensibility of an earthly and a heavenly party each having total responsibility for one's holiness, we must also face the theological impossibility of the work of a finite, fallen creature providing the holiness that God requires. In gratitude we strive with all our might to please God, but we recognize that all we do that pleases God is of him (Phil. 2:12-13). Adolf Köberle writes,

> When the will of God is done out of thankfulness the whole idea of becoming good through doing good is excluded. Then I no longer claim any reward for my works because God has already given me everything. Then the reckoning of merits, according to St. Augustine's splendid phrase, is nothing but "a reckoning of God's gifts." The good works of Christians are no "accomplishments" that deserve meritorious distinction but they are "fruits" that have grown out of the creative power of the Word, out of a living union with Christ. . . . The one sanctifying himself because of

thankfulness does not claim for himself any honor for the renewal of his life. He who gives thanks remains humble for he gives the glory to God alone.[4]

While the responsibility for obedience is ours, the credit for righteousness is God's. This may seem inequitable, but it is no less unfair than *our* transgression being satisfied by *Christ's* death. There the fault was ours but the penalty was his.[5] Knowing that God supplies the holiness for which we are responsible gives us further reason to honor him, even when the process baffles us. And, lest our consternation lead us to frustration, God assures us that his grace is so magnanimous that, in the final judgment, he will praise *us* for the righteousness that he has enabled us to do! (1 Cor. 4:5b). This is not a sham, but rather is as understandable and dear as a father praising his child for writing her first letters, even though the parent supplied the pencil, paper, and instruction—and guided her hand.

God's grace is not easily reconciled to our math, but that does not diminish its beauty or scope. When we serve our Lord out of true and full thanksgiving for his defeat of the guilt and power of our sin, we are grateful not merely for his benevolently receiving our works but for his enabling of us to do what he will ultimately reward.

This side of heaven, we will never logically resolve the tension between human responsibility and divine provision in sanctification. But as we learn to acknowledge that God must provide what we need to please him, the result will be our full dependence upon his grace. While our logic may not be satisfied in this dependence, it is the only place where the heart conscious of its humanity can find rest. Any other alternative bases our acceptance with God to some degree on a righteousness that we cannot attain by our own doing or reasoning.[6]

The humility generated as we reach the limits of our reasoning in exploring such issues suggests why God does not fully expose heaven's operations to our minds. The fundamental temptation of humanity was a desire to know as God knows and thus become his equal (Gen. 3:5). Facing the finitude of our thoughts and actions forces us to look beyond ourselves for the spiritual deliverance we require. Thus while Scripture provides answers to the questions of our deepest needs, it does not answer all the questions that may arise in our minds. In fact, true humility before God causes us to acknowledge that Scripture does not merely provide answers to some questions we may have; it also provides the very questions we should ask.

Not all the questions that come to mind are those most critical to the heart that seeks God. While God does not forbid our consideration of any question, he designs his Word to lead our thoughts in paths of discovery that are most beneficial to our spiritual health. As water flows in a furrow to make a garden grow, so our thoughts are to flow in the courses laid by Scripture. Only in those lines does the Spirit produce in us the fruit that will most nourish our souls. Scripture asks and answers questions according to God's priorities and design. Thus, while all we need for life and godliness will be addressed in the Bible, some matters will remain hidden from our perceptions because God has deigned neither to ask nor to answer such questions in his Word (cf. Rom. 11:33; 2 Pet. 1:3).

Scripture asks the question, "Must we obey God in order to grow in godliness and please him?" Scripture's answer is a definite yes. Scripture also asks for us, "Where do we get the desire, ability, and faith to obey?" The answer is, we get each of these things from God. The Bible also dares to address the difficult issues raised by considering these two previous questions together. It asks, "Then, is God responsible if I do not obey?" The answer is no. There is no boasting before God, because of him, through him, and to him are all things (cf. Rom. 11:36); but neither can any say that God is to blame because we disobey (cf. Rom. 9:19-23; James 1:13-14; 1 John 1:5).[7]

Scripture does not resolve the tensions involved in these questions, but it does give us the answers necessary for us to serve God and to know how to seek his aid in doing so. That may not sound fair, but were God to act only mathematically with regard to our sin, then absolute fairness would condemn us all (Rom. 3:10, 23; 6:23). By his will alone God has made us spiritually alive and able to obey his Word. With this new spiritual life, God has granted us release us from the dominion of sin so that our will is free to honor him.[8] Still, we cannot exercise this freedom rightly without the aid of the Holy Spirit. This makes us responsible for our sin, but dependent on God for our righteousness.[9]

The questions regarding human responsibility and divine sovereignty in sanctification parallel questions regarding these same issues in justification.[10] Are we responsible for acknowledging our sin and confessing our need of the Savior? The biblical answer is yes (Rom. 10:9-13; 1 John 1:9). Who provides the ability for us to see our sin and in faith to seek salvation?

The Bible answers that God does, through the Holy Spirit (Rom. 8:6-11; 1 Cor. 2:10-12; Eph. 1:17-19). Do these truths make God unjust or unfair? The Bible answers no. God must act fairly, since justice is essential to his nature (Gen. 18:25; Deut. 32:4; Zeph. 3:5; Rom. 3:26). At the same time, Scripture acknowledges that these questions lead us to mysteries concerning the activity and operations of God that we cannot penetrate with finite minds in this life (Rom. 9:19-24).[11]

Because we cannot fully enter the mind of God, we should be cautious and charitable in seeking to answer all the questions raised by the issues of divine sovereignty and human responsibility. This is why the great theologian B. B. Warfield said that the essence of the gospel message is not predestination or free will, but grace—God's provision of mercy for his people.[12] This mercy tells us we must obey the standards of Scripture in order to please the God we love and to know his blessings. Divine grace also assures us that God will provide what we need in order to obey him, and that he will forgive us when we fail to do so.

Whether the issues concern justification or sanctification, we live in a clearing hewn by Scripture, with deep woods of mystery regarding divine sovereignty and human responsibility on either side. The Bible gives the answers we need to navigate the clearing, without giving us all the answers for negotiating the woods beyond.

In helping us travel through the clearing, Scripture tells us what direction to face for the answers to questions we must ask in order to progress in godliness. If the questions are, "Must I confess Christ as Savior?" and, "Must I obey him as Lord?" then Scripture turns us toward the horizon of the woods of human responsibility for our bearings. However, if the question is, "Where do I get the motivation and enablement to do what God requires?" then the Bible turns us toward the horizon of divine provision. Humility before God, then, becomes more than a matter of bowing before God in bewildered resignation to the impenetrable mysteries of divine sovereignty. True humility involves turning toward the horizon Scripture instructs us to face in answering the questions God encourages us to ask, so that we will be able to serve him with love and zeal.[13]

The effect of seeking holiness according to God's directions is that we will strive to please him. When our hearts ask, "Does God truly expect me to do as he commands?" then Scripture's answer will resonate with the Spirit's work in our hearts to insist that obedience is our responsibility. However, when we stand before God to give an accounting of what we have done, the Bible will provide the answer that our hearts will also confess: "God, all that I did for you, you enabled. I praise you for the grace that allowed me to know your blessings by working your will in me."

Whether we are standing before the final judgment seat of God, or are on our knees tonight petitioning his blessing, the truths of grace will keep us from saying, "Bless me, Lord, because of what I have done."

Our willingness to rely on God's mercy alone, rather than on our own accomplishments, ultimately hinges more upon our personal knowledge of his heart than upon our final explanations of his mysteries. No one has made this more clear to me than the noted theologian Robert Peterson, whom I asked to review this chapter for theological precision when my own mind began to tangle in the task of keeping all the strings of biblical thought unknotted. With wonderful pastoral wisdom Peterson gave this assessment:

> I have no corrections to offer, but one thing you might want to think about. Toward the end of the materials you asked me to review I jotted in my margin, "Knowing the person." The discussion had gone a few pages regarding questions, answers, the tensions, God's justice, etc., and the helpful illustration about the clearing in the woods. It was at the end of that material that I jotted the words above. It might be helpful to include somewhere in this section the important truth that knowing God (by his grace) permeates this discussion (and all of our discussions and more). It is easier to admit in humility that I don't have all the answers, indeed don't even know the right questions to ask, when I revel in the knowledge of God. He loves me and knows me and as a result, I know him. He is infinite and I'll never exhaustively know him or have all the answers that I might desire. But knowing him puts everything, even questions about the divine sovereignty/human responsibility tension in the Christian life, in a wonderful perspective. . . . Knowledge of the person enables us to trust and lovingly accept what we will not fully understand in this life. For instance, I will never perfectly understand my wife and the workings of her mind . . . but I can rest in her love for me and in doing so put myself in a much better position to try to understand the inscrutable. We are all little children climbing into our Father's lap and asking him our heartfelt but (from his perspective) childish questions.[14]

We trust God to do what is right and good even when we cannot explain all his ways *because we know him*. The love of a heavenly Father revealed in Christ's provision for us silences the cries and calms the fears of children who cannot fully explain his ways. Consistent exultation in the love made plain at the cross grants us insight into, and love for, the person of God, so that we trust in the rightness of his provision for us even when it remains mysterious. This is why the apostle Paul's meditations on God's mercy ultimately lead him to exclaim, "Oh, the depth of the riches of the wisdom and knowledge of God! How unsearchable his judgments, and his paths beyond tracing out!" (Rom. 11:33).

Paul both exults in God's mercy and humbly acknowledges that its depths are unfathomable to human understanding. The tension between Paul's adulation of divine love and his inability to exhaust the divine mind does not frustrate him. Instead, he grows more conscious of his dependence on grace and more confident of his heavenly Father's willingness to provide it. The same dynamics should occur in us as our growing awareness of God's person makes us both more confident of his love and more certain that we are entirely dependent on it.

The Bible's appraisal of the unholiness of our best works, and the Bible's assurance of the atoning provision of our loving God, will keep us from ever asking God merely to be fair. Whether we are seeking the pardon of justification, the furthering of our sanctification, or the ultimate rewards of our glorification, our appeal to God does not change. We always must say, "Bless me, Lord, because I believe Jesus met all the requirements of your justice that I could not meet. I do not ask your regard on the basis of my merit, but on the assurance of your mercy. Make your glory evident in me solely by your grace."

THOSE WHO SUBTRACT

Grace assures us that God does not account our worth according to the measure of our labors, even when we know we have worked counter to his will. Jesus' parable of the workers in the vineyard helps us see that God not only values laborers who apparently add little or nothing to his kingdom, but he even shows kindness to those who seem to subtract from it.

When the workers hired first complain about the master's generous payment to those hired later, how does the master respond? He says to one of the grumblers, "Friend, I am not being unfair to you. Didn't you agree to work for a denarius?" (Matt. 20:13). The fairness of the master is evident in his paying the worker what was promised at the beginning of the day. However, the generosity of the master is evident not only in his lavish payment of the late workers but also in his addressing his critic as "friend."

"Friend" conveys an attitude void of hostility. This affirmation of a merciful heart communicates an even more profound message. To sense how important is this simple address, we must consider the audience of this parable. The apostle Peter sparks the telling of the parable by following his claim, "We have left everything to follow you!" with the question, "What then will there be for us?" (19:27). In Jesus' parable, Peter's attitude is reflected in the words of the grumbler who wants extra compensation for all his efforts (20:12).

We should consider how Peter, then, must view this parable. He is among the servants who have been called to work early by his Master. He has already been on the road working and suffering for Jesus for a long time. Yet now Jesus says, " . . . [T]he last will be first, and the first will be last" (v. 16).

The natural human response to such a statement is, "That's not fair!" But as we have seen, the parable should have made it plain to Peter that fairness is the last thing that he should want from God.

The timeliness of this lesson for Peter is revealed in the events that soon follow. In the next chapter of the book of Matthew, Christ will enter Jerusalem. As events unfold there, Peter is called upon for his most challenging service to his Master. The work does not go well. The early-chosen, long-serving apostle denies his Lord three times.

Despite all the privileges of his early choosing, Peter does immense damage to his Master's cause. Christ well chooses the moment to tell Peter of the master who says to an offending servant, "Friend, do not be offended that I am generous."

The message of unfair but generous grace is for us also. Often we resolve to be more holy, to give of ourselves more freely, to give up more of the world, and to follow our Savior wherever he leads. All too soon most of us find ourselves to be betrayers of those resolutions and of our Lord. We become those who subtract from the work of his kingdom and, in the context of our privileges and desires to do so much better, the repugnance of our sin can so sicken us that we despair of ever being acceptable to our God. In those moments of self-reproach, Jesus' account of the generous heart of a master's grace must echo in our souls.

Despite our early longings for justice, we find our ultimate comfort in the God who says through his Son, "Friend, do not be offended by your Master's generosity that you, too, need."

On the trip to Germany that I described earlier, we passed the site of the Buchenwald concentration camp of World War II. Our German bus guide began to reflect on what became one of his consistent themes throughout that section of our journey: his own dismay at the evil of his father's generation. He asked, "How could they have turned their heads from the evil of the concentration camps? How could they have allowed the Holocaust?"

He spoke of the patterns of the German officers who oversaw the grisly work of the death camps. "Like good German engineers," he said, "they would destroy precisely one thousand people because that was in the work orders for the day. They would not murder one more or one less person. Then, having committed this monstrosity, they would go home to bratwurst and beer, play with their children, listen to a recording of Shubert and, then, return the next day to murder precisely one thousand more."

The guide gave this version of the account with palpable anger in his voice and with the confession that, as a result of his deep disgust over these injustices of a previous generation, he had not spoken with his own father in years. Yet later on our journey, while observing the drug-pushers and promiscuous young people gathered outside our hotel in downtown Berlin, this same guide openly verbalized his wishes for a new government that would "get rid of the street riff-raff."

The sin of disregard for the sanctity of human life that he so hated in his father unconsciously resided in our guide himself. His resolve to do better and to be better than a previous generation could not eradicate the fissures of hatred and prejudice in his own heart.

Defects reside in every heart. Some are as hidden to our consciences as were our guide's to him, but others glare in our vision. When we see the dimensions of evil within each of us, and learn to suspect that there are others as yet unperceived, then we truly value our Savior's promise to be more than fair. We all need his assurance that he is rich in mercy. Such generosity in him secures our hope, creates our willingness to repent of our waywardness, inspires our desire to labor in his vineyard, and equips us to serve him with the joy that is our strength.

Our striving for good, longing for holiness, and resolving endlessly to do better than we are, while facing the daily reality of our lusts, our capacity for unbridled anger, our tendency to resent others for their abilities, and our inability to serve God without concern for our own interests, can tempt us to despair. However, when we remember that we serve the One who calls his betrayer "Friend" (Matt. 26:50), then we have new hope for bearing fruit in our lives and new incentive to labor for him.

The riches of God's mercy not only secure our way to him, they also provide our daily motivation and enablement to serve him. For this reason our Master promises that he will be much more than fair. Our God will lavish us with his grace:

> [H]e does not treat us as our sins deserve
> or repay us according to our iniquities.
> For as high as the heavens are above the earth,
> so great is his love for those who fear him;
> as far as the east is from the west,
> so far has he removed our transgressions from us.
> As a father has compassion on his children,
> so the LORD has compassion on those who fear him;
> for he knows how we are formed,
> he remembers that we are dust.
> (Ps. 103:10-14)

Discussion Questions

INTRODUCTION: MY SOUL'S DELIGHT

1. Does it encourage or discourage Christians to know that the Bible agrees that "nobody's perfect"?

2. What do we see in the mirror of our consciences when we confess our sins?

3. How does God see us when we confess our sins? How does God provide for us so that he can view us as holy even though "nobody's perfect"?

4. Is our holiness a consequence of what we achieve, or of what God chooses to see?

5. We are saved by grace, but what keeps God loving us after we become Christians?

6. What are the consequences of the Bible's contention that our best works are to God only "filthy rags"?

7. How does God provide the holiness that he requires?

8. How might the message of grace actually lead to a loss of commitment to holiness? Is this a legitimate concern? Why?

9. Why does resting in God's grace alone enable us to serve him in true holiness?

10. How does the assurance of God's love release us from endlessly striving to please him for our benefit?

11. How does grace keep us from trying to bribe God, and make our service to him our delight?

CHAPTER 1: THE POWER OF JOY

1. What does God require of us?

2. Why do our good works not make God love us more?

3. Why would the disciples be concerned that Jesus would say that, when we have done our duty, we are still unworthy servants?

4. What advantages do we think will come to us when we trophy our good works? Why can we not leverage God with our good works?

5. How are most people in the world using scales of deeds to weigh out their acceptability to God? What is wrong with this approach?

6. Does God always wait until heaven to reward good works? Does he always reward good works in this life in the way that we ask him to or think that he should? Explain why.

7. What ultimate purpose does God desire to fulfill in our lives through our obedience?

8. Why is God more moved by our desperation than by our claims of goodness? How does knowing that God listens to our cries of desperation encourage repentance?

9. How does acknowledging our degree of desperation affect our expressions of appreciation for God's grace?

10. Why are not self-promotion and self-protection adequate reasons for serving God? What good does it do us to know that our best works merit us nothing?

11. If our best works are only "filthy rags" and merit us nothing, then why should we do good works?

12. How does knowing that God cleanses lepers create grateful joy in us? How does this joy enable us to serve God with greater strength?

CHAPTER 2: UNITED FOR LIFE

1. How can good teaching and the testimony of other believers in the church lead some of us to despair?

2. What function do the rules of Scripture serve, if keeping them is not the basis of our relationship with God? *-See sin*

3. Is the faith that saves us a result of extraordinary human resolve? *No*

4. In what way are we united to Christ's death? *- we-flesh, old self died c̄ Him on the cross.*

5. How do we become dead to the Law of God? How does the Law teach us that our human performance of its standards will not make us right with God? *-impossible to achieve. Need One to meet the laws demands for us.*

6. What does God provide for us through our union with Christ's death? *New identity, forgiveness, reconciliation.*

7. How does our union with Christ result in the death of pride? *I didn't earn it. me is dead, only good they in me now is Jesus*

8. How does our union with Christ result in the death of despair? *I now have power of Christ in me.*

9. What does God provide for us through our union with Christ's life? How can I receive credit for what I did not do? *Credit of Christs R+ resist sin. God made Christ my life*

10. What is definitive sanctification, and how does it differ from progressive sanctification? *God declared me Holy because of my union to Christ. R+ now in christ. It has been completed. I still have sinful flesh*

11. How does faith in our union with Christ enable us to live for him? What confidences does our faith in this union provide? *I never have to doubt God's love for me. don't need to strive for God's love. He sees me as R+ -my performance does not affect christ's love for me*

12. If our union with Christ secures our relationship to God, what role do various Christian disciplines and means of grace serve in the Christian life?

CHAPTER 3: REPENTANCE THAT SINGS

1. How can the pursuit of self-perfection assault our souls? What do we instinctively feel will make us right with God, or return us to a close relationship with him?

2. How can even words of repentance become a religious ritual that we use to barter forgiveness and blessing with God? Why is this a problem?

3. How does the holiness of God cause us to view ourselves?

4. How does the holiness of God cause us to view our wrong words and actions? How does the holiness of God cause us to view our *good* words and actions? _sinful

5. In what way does a correct assessment of our right and wrong deeds lead to a desire to offer confession? Do only bad people long to confess? - No

6. In what way does knowing that God is holy and that our best works will not merit pardon for sin lead us to a longing for grace?
   only hope

7. In what way is repentance a resting?

8. Why is repentance not adequately defined as seeking to avoid God's punishment?

9. How is repentance like longing for a lost love?

10. How is our delight in the Savior related to proper repentance?
    turn away from sin to christ   Put on christ

11. How can the sorrow of repentance lead to a heart of singing? Why is this rejoicing important?
    gratefulness

CHAPTER 4: ESCAPE FROM TEMPTATION

1. Is it true that the heart that loves God longs to keep from sinning? In what ways do we still find sin appealing and alluring even after we become Christians?

2. How do the pervasiveness and power of sin affect Christians?

3. Why is it a precious promise that God provides an escape from the power, as well as the guilt, of sin?

4. How does the commonness of temptation rescue us from despair?

5. How does the commonness of temptation rescue us from pride?

6. How does the Bible reveal the horror of temptation? How does the Bible reveal the power of temptation?

7. What sovereign promise does God make regarding the strength of the temptations that we face?

8. What sovereign promise does God make regarding a way out of the temptations that we face? Why is it hard for us to believe this promise?

9. What role does human resistance have in defeating the power of temptation?

10. What role does prudential avoidance have in defeating the power of temptation?

11. What role does a clear perception of our Savior's love for us have in overcoming temptation?

CHAPTER 5: CONSTRAINED BY THE LAW OF FREEDOM

1. Does teaching about grace tempt people to think that God does not have standards that we should honor? How does this happen?

2. Is God concerned about our obedience? Why?

3. What is ego-nomianism? How are we freed from it?

4. What is neo-nomianism? How are we freed from it?

5. Why do we make new laws for ourselves and others that are not clearly established in God's Word? What are we saying about our importance and status when we make laws not found in God's Word?

6. What cultural examples of neo-nomianism are evident in your setting? How can criticism of others for their neo-nomianism become an excuse for ignoring others' needs and only doing what we want?

7. How is making prudential choices different than establishing extrabiblical rules? Are such prudential choices important? Are they biblical? Why?

8. What is antinomianism? How does the law of love free us from antinomianism?

9. What aspects of the law of love are in effect for believers today? How does having clear biblical standards free us from confusion in ourselves and control from others?

10. How can talk about duty be gracious? How can talk about duty be ungracious?

11. What does it mean that "the imperative rests on the indicative and [the] order is not reversible"? What difference can this principle make in your life and relationships?

CHAPTER 6: FIGHTING WITH ALL HIS MIGHT

1. Why does Paul tell us to put on the armor *of God* in spiritual warfare?

2. What are some common misconceptions about the armor of God, such as who provides it, how we use it, and whose strength enables its use?

3. Should we expect the armor of God to protect us if we are not following godly patterns of life and worship? Why?

4. How does confidence in Christ's embrace strengthen us for spiritual warfare?

5. What is the nature of the "mighty power" that God provides for spiritual warfare?

6. What are some differences that the resurrection power of Christ makes in us? How do these changes indicate that we are fundamentally different creatures as a result of Christ in us?

7. How does faith in God's making us new creatures enable us to fight our Adversary?

8. What is the nature of our Adversary?

9. Who provides the weaponry and armor needed for spiritual warfare? How do you know, and what difference does this knowledge make?

10. Is there any degree of human effort involved in resisting sin? If so, what is the nature and function of this effort?

11. Why does spiritual warfare involve praying in the Spirit? How does the Holy Spirit change us?

CHAPTER 7: WHAT'S DISCIPLINE GOT TO DO WITH IT?

1. Is God's discipline contrary to God's grace?

2. How does the absence of discipline indicate the absence of care?

3. Is all biblical discipline punitive? If not, what are other purposes of biblical discipline?

4. What are some ways that God's discipline makes us tender?

5. What are some ways that God's discipline makes us hard?

6. How do our trials enable us to know God? How do the trials of others enable us to know God?

7. How does discipline confirm God's fatherly care for us? What would the absence of discipline indicate about God's care for us?

8. What does the eventual termination of discipline confirm about God's care for us?

9. How does discipline reveal the heart and hand of God?

10. What amazing things about God's presence does his discipline indicate?

11. Is God's discipline consistent with his grace? Why?

CHAPTER 8: THE POWER OF MERCY

1. What difference does it make if our hearts are in our work for God?

2. What motives other than mercy could Paul have used to try to motivate us? Why did he choose mercy above all other motivations to inspire our service to God?

3. How is the abundance of mercy used to motivate us for Christian service?

4. How does mercy get eclipsed as a motivation for us? How can trials help us reconsider the mercy of Christ in our behalf?

5. Why is guilt an effective motivator? Why is guilt destructive as a motivation, even if it is temporarily effective?

6. If people begin to expect their behavior change to get rid of their guilt, then who are they trusting to take their guilt away?

7. What happens to a child who obeys out of fear of parental rejection? What happens to a Christian who obeys out of fear of the heavenly Father's rejection?

8. In what ways do Christians punish themselves to get rid of their guilt?

9. How does the kindness of God lead to repentance? What aspects of God's kindness never change?

10. Does God's mercy mean that we can sin without consequence? What is the goal of God's discipline for sin?

11. How does mercy encourage and enable our service to God?

CHAPTER 9: WORKS THAT REALLY MATTER

1. If God does not measure our worth by what we do, then why should we bother to serve him?

2. How does God use our obedience to promote our good and his glory?

3. In what way does our righteousness endure forever? How does righteous influence continue? How does righteousness itself endure?

4. How can a righteous person be remembered forever? Where will a righteous person be remembered forever?

5. Why is it important for us to know that God remembers us apart from our accomplishments and/or failures?

6. In what ways does God rescue us by providing righteousness for us?

7. What qualities of his own does God transfer to us to enable our righteousness to endure? How does God transfer these qualities to us?

8. Ultimately, why does God make the righteousness that he transfers and the persons whom he makes righteous endure?

9. If the good work that we do endures forever in order to glorify God, then how important are even the most trivial (to earthly eyes) duties that we do?

10. How should it make us feel that what the world does not notice or count as significant is eternal? How should this reality motivate us?

11. What does "the present value of the blood of Christ" mean for the work that you do today for God?

CHAPTER 10: THAT'S NOT FAIR

1. Does it seem fair that God would not compensate more those who do more work for him? What in the nature of God makes us think that he would not operate this way?

2. Why would the apostles be concerned with Jesus saying that "the last will be first, and the first will be last"? Would this seem fair to them? Why?

3. Why would God value the labor for him that starts early and lasts long?

4. Why would God value labor for him that starts late and is short in duration?

5. How can we estimate the value of different kinds and durations of work for God? Ultimately, who alone can estimate the value of the different kinds of work that God calls us to do?

6. Are those who are called to Christian service early in life treated unfairly because others "get to go to heaven" even though they made a commitment to Christ late in life?

7. Have those who are called to Christian service late in life, or after others, "missed the boat" of being able to do something significant for God? Explain why?

8. In what way does God "rescue" us by calling us to serve him?

9. Why is it important to know that God values those who add little or nothing to his service, and even cares for those who seem to subtract from his purposes?

10. How might God powerfully use the testimony of someone who makes a commitment late in life, in comparison to someone who makes such a commitment early in life?

11. Why is it important to know that, while the responsibility for our works is ours, the credit is God's? Is this fair? Why does God operate in this way?

Bibliography

Alexander, Archibald. *Thoughts on Religious Experience.* 1845. Reprint, Carlisle, Pa.: Banner of Truth, 1967.

Alexander, Donald, ed. *Christian Spirituality: Five Views of Sanctification.* Downers Grove, Ill.: InterVarsity, 1988.

Atwood, Roy. "A Father's Legacy." *Credenda Agenda* 8, no. 4 (1996).

Baker, Mark D. *Religious No More: Building Communities of Grace and Freedom.* Downers Grove, Ill.: InterVarsity, 1999.

Bergman, Susan. "In the Shadow of the Martyrs." *Christianity Today* (August 1996), 22f.

Berkhof, Louis. *Systematic Theology.* Grand Rapids, Mich.: Eerdmans, 1996.

Berkouwer, G. C. *Faith and Sanctification.* Translated by John Vriend. Grand Rapids, Mich.: Eerdmans, 1957.

Blankenhorn, David. *Fatherless America.* New York: Harper, 1996.

Bolton, Samuel. *The True Bounds of Christian Freedom.* 1645. Reprint, Carlisle, Pa.: Banner of Truth Trust, 1978.

Bonar, Horatius. "Horatius Bonar Talks about Holiness." *Free Grace Broadcaster* (October 1993), 32.

Bridges, Jerry. *The Discipline of Grace.* Colorado Springs: NavPress, 1994.

Buchanan, James. *The Office and Work of the Holy Spirit.* 1843. Reprint, Carlisle, Pa.: Banner of Truth, 1966.

Calvin, John. *Institutes of the Christian Religion.* Edited by John T. McNeil. Translated by Ford Lewis Battles. Philadelphia: Westminster, 1960.

Carson, D. A. *How Long, O Lord?* Grand Rapids, Mich.: Baker, 1990.

Chalmers, Thomas. *Sermons and Discourses.* New York: Carter, 1846.

Chapell, Bryan. *In the Grip of Grace.* Grand Rapids, Mich.: Baker, 1992.

——————-. *Christ-centered Preaching.* Grand Rapids, Mich.: Baker, 1994.

——————. "From Heaven's Perspective." *Decision* (May 1995), 32f.

——————. *Using Illustrations to Preach with Power.* Wheaton, Ill.: Crossway, 2001.

Clowney, Edmund. *The Unfolding Mystery.* Colorado Springs: NavPress, 1988.

Colquhoun, John. *Repentance.* 1826. Reprint, Carlisle, Pa.: Banner of Truth, 1965.

Dieter, Melvin E., et al. *Five Views on Sanctification.* Grand Rapids, Mich.: Zondervan, 1987.

Ferguson, Sinclair. *John Owen on the Christian Life.* 1987. Reprint, Carlisle, Pa.: Banner of Truth, 1995.

——————. *The Holy Spirit.* Downers Grove, Ill.: InterVarsity, 1996.

Gray, Rick. World Harvest Mission and Mission to the World prayer letter. Summer 1999.

Hughes, Kent. *Ephesians.* Preaching the Word. Edited by Kent Hughes. Wheaton, Ill.: Crossway, 1990.

Hunt, Susan. *The True Woman.* Wheaton, Ill.: Crossway, 1997.

Jones, David. *Biblical Christian Ethics.* Grand Rapids, Mich.: Baker, 1994.

Köberle, Adolf. *The Quest for Holiness.* Translated by John C. Mattes. Minneapolis: Augsburg, 1936.

Lehmann, Helmut, gen. ed. *Luther's Works.* Edited and translated by John Doberstein. Philadelphia: Fortress, 1966.

Liddell, Eric. *The Disciplines of the Christian Life.* Nashville: Abingdon, 1985.

Lovelace, Richard. *Dynamics of Spiritual Life.* Downers Grove, Ill.: InterVarsity, 1979.

Manton, Thomas. *A Treatise of the Life of Faith.* Ross-shire, Scotland: Christian Focus, 1997.

Marshall, Walter. *The Gospel Mystery of Sanctification.* 1692. Reprint, Grand Rapids, Mich.: Reformation Heritage, 1999.

Matzat, Don. *Truly Transformed.* Eugene, Ore.: Harvest House, 1992.

Miller, Rose Marie. *From Fear to Freedom*. Wheaton, Ill.: Harold Shaw, 1994.

Murray, John. *Collected Writings of John Murray*. 4 vols. Carlisle, Pa.: Banner of Truth, 1976.

—————. *The Covenant of Grace*. 1953. Reprint, Phillipsburg, N.J.: Presbyterian and Reformed, 1988.

—————. *Principles of Conduct*. Grand Rapids, Mich.: Eerdmans, 1957.

Olford, Stephen. *Not I But Christ*. Wheaton, Ill.: Crossway, 1995.

Owen, John. *Communion with God*. Edited by R. J. K. Law. Edinburgh, Scotland: Banner of Truth, 1991.

Packer, J. I. *Rediscovering Holiness*. Ann Arbor, Mich.: Servant, 1992.

Reisinger, Ernest C. *The Law and the Gospel*. Phillipsburg, N.J.: Presbyterian and Reformed, 1997.

Ridderbos, Herman. *Paul: An Outline of His Theology*. Translated by John Richard de Witt. Grand Rapids, Mich.: Eerdmans, 1975.

Schaeffer, Francis. *True Spirituality*. Wheaton, Ill.: Tyndale, 1971.

—————. *No Little People*. Downers Grove, Ill.: InterVarsity, 1974.

Smallman, Steve. "Understanding the New Birth." World Harvest Mission, 1996.

Sproul, R. C. *Grace Unknown*. Grand Rapids, Mich.: Baker, 1997.

Stott, John. *Life in Christ*. Grand Rapids, Mich.: Baker, 1991.

Warfield, Benjamin Breckenridge. *The Works of Benjamin B. Warfield*. 10 vols. New York: Oxford University Press, 1927–1932. Reprint, Grand Rapids, Mich.: Baker Book House, 1981.

—————. *Biblical and Theological Studies*. Philadelphia, Pa.: Presbyterian and Reformed, 1968.

—————. *The Plan of Salvation*. Grand Rapids, Mich.: Eerdmans, 1975.

The Westminster Standards. Suwanee, Ga.: Great Commission Publications, 1997.

Whitney, Donald. *Spiritual Disciplines Within the Church*. Chicago, Ill.: Moody, 1996.

NOTES

INTRODUCTION: MY SOUL'S DELIGHT

1. The early discussion of this introduction reflects material in the author's article, "From Heaven's Perspective," first presented in *Decision* (May 1995), 32f.

CHAPTER ONE: THE POWER OF JOY

1. Cf. G. C. Berkouwer, *Faith and Sanctification,* trans. John Vriend (Grand Rapids, Mich.: Eerdmans, 1957), 22.

2. Martin Luther, "The Sum of the Christian Life," quoted in Helmut Lehmann, gen. ed. *Luther's Works,* ed. and trans. John Doberstein (Philadelphia: Fortress, 1966), 284-285.

3. *The Westminster Confession of Faith,* XVI.5.

4. Thomas Manton, *A Treatise of the Life of Faith* (Ross-shire, Scotland: Christian Focus, 1997), 96, 101.

5. Augustus M. Toplady, "Rock of Ages," in *The Trinity Hymnal* (Philadelphia: Great Commission Publications, 1998), hymn number 499.

6. John Calvin, *Institutes of the Christian Religion,* ed. John T. McNeil, trans. Ford Lewis Battles (Philadelphia: Westminster, 1960), III. 15.3.

7. Cf. *Westminster Confession of Faith,* XVI. 5, 6:

    "We cannot, by our best works, merit pardon for sin . . . by reason of the great disproportion that is between them and the glory to come; and the infinite distance that is between us and God. . . . by them [i.e., our best works], we can neither profit, nor satisfy for the debt of our former sins; but when we have done all we can, we have done but our duty, and are unprofitable servants; and because, as they are good, they proceed from His Spirit; and as they are wrought by us, they are defiled, and mixed with so much weakness and imperfection, that they cannot endure the severity of God's judgment.

    " . . . [B]elievers being accepted through Christ, their good works also are accepted in Him; not as though they were in this life wholly unblameable and unreprovable in God's sight; but that He, looking upon them in His Son, is pleased to accept and reward that which is sincere, although accompanied with many weaknesses and imperfections."

8. Samuel Bolton's wonderful study of the motives for obedience in *The True Bounds of Christian Freedom* (1645; reprint, Carlisle, Pa., Banner of Truth, 1978) concludes with these thoughtful words regarding temporal rewards: "I conceive that it is safer to find arguments to quicken us in our obedience from the mercies of God bestowed upon us, or made ours in the promise to faith, than to find arguments to obey from the expectation of mercies to be bestowed as the reward of our obedience. It seems better to say that we are not to obey in order that God may bestow blessings upon us, but rather that we obey from the knowledge, the faith, and the persuasion, that God will bless us here and forever. It is this latter that quickens us to obey God. . . . And though God rewards obedience and punishes sin, yet, just as we do not avoid sin because of temporal punishment, so we do not perform duty for the sake of reward. I say 'reward', in the sense of temporal enjoyments. I am unwilling for anything to be introduced as a motive for the obedience of a godly man which is either unsuitable, too low, or uncertain, and temporal rewards seems [sic] to be such. They are unsuited to the spirit which underlies the godly man's service, and they have the nature of uncertainty, for we have no absolute promise of them" (166-176). While not questioning their certainty or our proper enjoyment of them, Bolton also discusses the impropriety of heavenly rewards as a *primary* motivation for obedience (192).

9. Cf. Sinclair Ferguson, "The Reformed View," in Donald Alexander, ed., *Christian Spirituality: Five Views of Sanctification* (Downers Grove, Ill.: InterVarsity, 1988), 66-67.

10. *The Heidelberg Catechism*, Question #86. Cf. Answer #64: "It is impossible for those grafted into Christ by true faith not to produce fruits of gratitude."

11. Anthony A. Hoekema, "The Reformed Perspective," in Melvin E. Dieter, et al., *Five Views on Sanctification* (Grand Rapids, Mich.: Zondervan, 1987), 86, 88.

12. Bolton, *True Bounds of Christian Freedom*, 44.

13. While a full discussion is not possible here, it is important to realize that the subject of sanctification cannot be cast entirely in personal terms. A rightly motivated gospel holiness is only possible in the context of ministry to others for the glory of the God we love. Mission to those yet to acknowledge the goodness of God and ministry to those in need of its expression are as vital to holiness as personal obedience in ethical/moral areas. I am indebted to Steve Smallman of World Harvest Mission and the legacy of Jack Miller for this emphasis (personal letter from Steve Smallman, September 15, 2000; and Jack Miller, *Outgrowing the Ingrown Church* [Grand Rapids, Mich.: Ministry Resources Library, 1986]).

14. B. B. Warfield, "Miserable Sinner Christianity," in *The Works of Benjamin B. Warfield*, vol. 7 (reprint, Grand Rapids, Mich.: Baker, 1981), 113ff.

15. The account is credited to the wonderful Detroit-area pastor Stephen Andrews, who grew up in the same Memphis church as I.

16. *Westminster Confession of Faith*, XX. 1.

17. An important insight comes when we understand that Jesus has used a very specific word change to indicate the renewed state of the former leper. The man is not merely "cleansed" (Greek *ekatheristhesan*, referring to the removal of his disease),

but he is "well" (Greek *sesoken,* a word often used in Scripture to refer to spiritual as well as physical well-being). The nine lepers who walked away from Jesus were cleansed, but only the one who came back to thank Jesus for the healing was really "well." The faith that recognizes Jesus alone as the only source of our healing is the true source of spiritual health.

CHAPTER TWO: UNITED FOR LIFE

1. Walter Marshall, *The Gospel Mystery of Sanctification* (1692; reprint, Grand Rapids, Mich.: Reformation Heritage, 1999), 9.

2. "Sanctification is the work of God's free grace, whereby we are renewed in the whole man after the image of God, and are enabled more and more to die unto sin, and live unto righteousness" (*The Westminster Shorter Catechism,* #35).

3. Cf. Louis Berkhof, *Systematic Theology* (Grand Rapids, Mich.: Eerdmans, 1941), 451: "By this union believers are changed into the image of Christ according to his human nature. What Christ effects in his people is in a sense a replica or reproduction of what took place in him. Not only objectively, but in a subjective sense also they bear the cross, are crucified, die and are raised to newness of life with Christ. They share in a measure in the experiences of their Lord." Similar thoughts are expressed by John Murray, *Principles of Conduct* (Grand Rapids, Mich.: Eerdmans, 1957), 109-110.

4. Samuel Bolton, *The True Bounds of Christian Freedom* (1645; reprint, Carlisle, Pa., Banner of Truth, 1978), 31.

5. Horatio Spafford, "It Is Well with My Soul," in *The Trinity Hymnal* (Philadelphia: Great Commission Publications, 1998), hymn number 691.

6. Cf. Ernest C. Reisinger, *The Law and the Gospel* (Phillipsburg, N.J.: Presbyterian and Reformed, 1997), 184.

7. Anthony A. Hoekema, "The Reformed Perspective," in Melvin E. Dieter, et al., *Five Views on Sanctification* (Grand Rapids, Mich.: Zondervan, 1987), 63-64.

8. Cf. John Calvin, *Institutes of the Christian Religion,* ed. John T. McNeil, trans. Ford Lewis Battles (Philadelphia: Westminster, 1960), II. 16.19: "We see that our whole salvation and all its parts are comprehended in Christ (Acts 4:12). We should therefore take care not to derive the least portion of it from anywhere else. If we seek salvation, we are taught by the very name of Jesus that it is 'of him' (1 Cor. 1:30). If we seek any other gifts of the Spirit, they will be found in his anointing. If we seek strength, it lies in his dominion; if purity, in his conception; if gentleness, it appears in his birth. . . . If we seek redemption, it lies in his passion; if acquittal, in his condemnation; if remission of the curse, in his cross (Gal. 3:13); if satisfaction, in his sacrifice; if purification, in his blood; if reconciliation, in his descent into hell; if mortification of the flesh, in his tomb; if newness of life, in his resurrection. . . . In short, since rich store of every kind of good abounds in him, let us drink our fill from this fountain, and no other."

9. Cf. *Heidelberg Catechism,* Question #60: "How are you righteous before God? Only by a true faith in Jesus Christ; that is, though my conscience accuse me that I have grievously sinned against all the commandments of God and kept none of them, and am still inclined to all evil, yet God, without any merit of mine, of mere grace, grants

and imputes to me the perfect satisfaction, righteousness, and holiness of Christ, as if I had never had nor committed any sin, and myself had accomplished all the obedience which Christ has rendered for me; if only I accept such benefit with a believing heart."

10. Hoekema, "Reformed Perspective," 77.

11. Cf. David Jones, *Biblical Christian Ethics* (Grand Rapids, Mich.: Baker, 1994), 51-57.

12. The original Greek text makes the "now" more emphatic than appears in some English translations. Paul's point is that the past work of Christ's atonement has very present implications for the Christian life. Faith in the Son of God is in fact the means by which Paul says he now lives.

13. The classic discussion of these dynamics is in G. C. Berkouwer's *Faith and Sanctification,* trans. John Vriend (Grand Rapids, Mich.: Eerdmans, 1957), e.g., 21-22, 40-42; however, a wonderful summary of the role of faith in sanctification is in Hoekema, "Reformed Perspective," 65-66. See also *The Belgic Confession,* Article XXIV.

14. Richard Lovelace, *Dynamics of Spiritual Life* (Downers Grove, Ill.: InterVarsity, 1979), 101.

15. See more discussion of God's "fixed regard" in the author's *In the Grip of Grace* (Grand Rapids, Mich.: Baker, 1992), 82-84 (republished 2001 as *The Promise of Grace*).

16. Cf. *The Heidelberg Catechism,* Question # 60: "How are you righteous before God?" to which the following answer is given:

"Only by true faith in Jesus Christ; that is though my conscience accuse me that I have grievously sinned against all the commandments of God and kept none of them, and am still inclined to all evil, yet God, without any merit of mine, of mere grace, grants and imputes to me the perfect satisfaction, righteousness, and holiness of Christ, as if I had never had nor committed any sin, and myself accomplished all the obedience which Christ has rendered for me; if only I accept such benefit with a believing heart."

17. The "instrumental means of grace" historically referred to the preaching of the Word, prayer, and sacraments offered by, and exercised in, the church [cf. Sinclair Ferguson, "The Reformed View," in *Christian Spirituality: Five Views of Sanctification* (Downers Grove, Ill.: InterVarsity, 1988), 67-74.]. Today common usage of the phrase "means of grace" also has an individual association and often refers to the personal disciplines of Bible reading, personal prayer, and regular participation in the communion of believers through worship and fellowship in the local church. Such personal disciplines can also be identified as the "formal means of grace" [cf. Richard J. Foster, "The Daring Goal: What to Expect When We Accept Christ as Our Life," in "1997 Seminary and Graduate School Handbook" (*Christianity Today*)].

18. Edith Schaeffer, symposium at Covenant Theological Seminary, St. Louis, October 13, 1994.

19. John Murray in *Principles of Conduct* (Grand Rapids, Mich.: Eerdmans, 1957) emphasizes that we are not part old man and part new man. The old man is dead.

Only the new man is alive as he is being transformed more into the likeness of Christ. This new identity is fundamentally different than the old (see 219).

20. The classic theological label for our new nature as redeemed creatures who have Christ's power but are still susceptible to the wrongs of our old nature is "posse non pecarre" (i.e., able not to sin). In our glorified state with the Lord in heaven we will be transformed once more to become "non posse pecarre" (i.e., not able to sin). For more formal discussion of the powers and limitations of our present ability, see Hoekema, "Reformed Perspective," 78-82.

21. Ibid., 81.

22. Lovelace, *Dynamics of Spiritual Life,* 114-115.

23. Augustus M. Toplady, "Rock of Ages," in *The Trinity Hymnal* (Philadelphia: Great Commission Publications, 1998), hymn number 499.

24. Jerry Bridges, *The Discipline of Grace* (Colorado Springs: NavPress, 1994), 103; see also Sinclair Ferguson, *The Holy Spirit* (Downers Grove, Ill.: InterVarsity, 1996), 112, 148-150.

25. James Buchanan, *The Office and Work of the Holy Spirit* (1843; reprint, Carlisle, Pa., Banner of Truth, 1966), 244.

26. Hoekema, "Reformed Perspective," 82.

27. Ibid., 65.

28. Marshall, *Gospel Mystery of Sanctification,* 31.

29. Marshall and Spurgeon, quoted by Joel Beeke, in his introduction to ibid., xx.

30. Marshall, *Gospel Mystery of Sanctification,* 175.

CHAPTER THREE: REPENTANCE THAT SINGS

1. Samuel Bolton, *The True Bounds of Christian Freedom* (1645; reprint, Carlisle, Pa., Banner of Truth, 1978), 107-108.

2. Steve Brown, commencement address at Covenant Theological Seminary, St. Louis, May 1989.

3. Paul's self-assessment as he progressed through life was first that he was the "least of the apostles" (1 Cor. 15:9), then that he was "less than the least of all God's people" (Eph. 3:8), and finally that he was the "worst of sinners" (1 Tim. 1:16).

4. Cf. B. B. Warfield, "Miserable Sinners Christianity," *The Works of Benjamin B. Warfield,* vol. 7 (Grand Rapids, Mich.: Baker, 1931), 126-132.

5. Cf. John Calvin, *Institutes of the Christian Religion,* ed. John T. McNeil, trans. Ford Lewis Battles (Philadelphia: Westminster, 1960), III. 15.3.

6. *The Westminster Confession of Faith,* XVI.5-6.

7. John Colquhoun, *Repentance* (1826; reprint, Carlisle, Pa., Banner of Truth, 1965), 17.

8. Rick Gray, World Harvest Mission and Mission to the World prayer letter, summer 1999.

9. Cf. G. C. Berkouwer, *Faith and Sanctification,* trans. John Vriend (Grand Rapids, Mich.: Eerdmans, 1957), 117.

10. Even the faith through which God saves us is itself not a work. Rather it is also a

resting in Christ. *The Westminster Shorter Catechism* describes it thus: "Faith in Jesus Christ is a saving grace, whereby we receive and rest upon him alone for salvation, as he is offered to us in the gospel" (Question #86).

11. The New Testament term is *metanoia,* which means to change one's mind. However, the biblical context for the term implies more than simply thinking new and right thoughts that God will honor because we are now doing (or even thinking) good stuff to make up for the previous bad stuff. *Metanoia* is a total change of personal orientation, a grieving for what formerly brought us gratification and a looking away from anything in us to merit God's forgiveness as we depend instead on his mercy alone.

12. Horatius Bonar, "Not What My Hands Have Done," in *The Trinity Hymnal* (Philadelphia: Great Commission Publications, 1998), hymn number 461.

13. *The Westminster Shorter Catechism,* #87.

14. *Westminster Confession of Faith,* XVI.6.

15. Lynn DeShazo, "More Precious than Silver" (Mobile, Ala.: Integrity Music, 1979).

16. Thomas Ken, "Doxology," in *The Trinity Hymnal* (Philadelphia: Great Commission Publications, 1998), hymn number 731.

CHAPTER FOUR: ESCAPE FROM TEMPTATION

1. This story, with different names, was presented as true by an attorney discussing legal standards for institutions at the national meeting of the Fellowship of Evangelical Seminary Presidents, in 1996.

2. As quoted by Jerry Bridges in *The Discipline of Grace* (Colorado Springs: NavPress, 1994), 41.

3. Private conversation with Robert Yarbrough at Covenant Theological Seminary, April 13, 1995.

4. David Blankenhorn, *Fatherless America* (New York.: Harper, 1996), 1.

5. Thomas Kelly, "Stricken, Smitten and Afflicted," in *The Trinity Hymnal* (Philadelphia: Great Commission Publications, 1998), hymn number 257.

6. John Owen, as quoted in Jerry Bridges, *Discipline of Grace,* 133.

7. Louis Berkhof, *Systematic Theology* (Grand Rapids, Mich.: Eerdmans, 1996), 535.

8. Cf. John Murray, *The Covenant of Grace* (1953; reprint, Phillipsburg, N.J.: Presbyterian and Reformed, 1988), 19.

9. Archibald Alexander, *Thoughts on Religious Experience* (1845; reprint, Carlisle, Pa., Banner of Truth, 1967), 165-166.

10. Cf. *The Westminster Confession of Faith,* XVI.3: "Their [i.e., Believers'] ability to do good works is not at all of themselves, but wholly from the Spirit of Christ. And that they may be enabled thereunto, beside the graces they have already received, there is required an actual influence of the same Holy Spirit, to work in them to will and to do of His good pleasure: yet are they not hereupon to grow negligent, as if they were not bound to perform any duty unless upon a special motion of the Spirit; but they ought to be diligent in stirring up the grace of God that is in them." Cf. also the Lutheran Collect for Peace: "O, God, from who all these proceed, all holy desires, all just councils and all good works."

11. Charles Haddon Spurgeon, "Repentance After Conversion," in *The Metropolitan Tabernacle Pulpit,* vol. 41 (London: Banner of Truth, 1895), sermon #2419.

12. Bridges, *Discipline of Grace,* 108.

CHAPTER FIVE: CONSTRAINED BY THE LAW OF FREEDOM

1. Ernest C. Reisinger, *The Law and the Gospel* (Phillipsburg, N.J.: Presbyterian and Reformed, 1997), 67.

2. Mark D. Baker, *Religious No More: Building Communities of Grace and Freedom* (Downers Grove, Ill.: InterVarsity, 1999), 37.

3. I am borrowing the term "neo-nomianism" to convey the idea of "new law" (rules without scriptural authority) although historically it has been used differently by theologians.

4. Samuel Bolton, *The True Bounds of Christian Freedom* (1645; reprint, Carlisle, Pa., Banner of Truth, 1978), 41.

5. B. B. Warfield, "Miserable Sinners Christianity," *The Works of Benjamin B. Warfield,* vol. 7 (Grand Rapids, Mich.: Baker, 1931), 113ff.

6. We traditionally divide Old Testament laws into three categories: civil (or judicial), ceremonial, and moral. The civil laws applied to the theocratic nation of Israel and, beyond exemplifying principles of equity and ethics, ceased to have direct application when God extended his covenant to all nations. The judicial and ceremonial laws passed away when Christ fulfilled the truths they foreshadowed and nullified the temple system (Heb. 7:11-20; 8:8-13; 9:1-4). The moral law—summarized in the Ten Commandments—never ceases to apply, as the New Testament writers indicate in their reiteration of its standards here and elsewhere (e.g., Rom. 12–13; Eph. 4:17–5:7; Heb. 13:15-16; 1 Pet. 2 and 4; 1 John 3; Jude 4). The borders between these three divisions of the law can be quite challenging to determine, and particulars have vexed theologians for centuries, but the disputable matters should not distract anyone from the clarity with which God speaks of the enduring character of the moral standards that reflect his own nature. See David Jones, *Biblical Christian Ethics* (Grand Rapids, Mich.: Baker, 1994), 103-124; *The Westminster Confession of Faith,* XIX, 3-5; John Calvin, *Institutes of the Christian Religion,* ed. John T. McNeil, trans. Ford Lewis Battles (Philadelphia: Westminster, 1960), II. vii. 14-17; Bolton, *True Bounds of Christian Freedom,* 54-76; and Reisinger, *Law and the Gospel,* 49-57.

7. Cf. Bolton, *True Bounds of Christian Freedom,* 44-45.

8. Thanks to my friend A. Gordon Wetmore, recently retired president of the Nazarene Seminary in Kansas City, for this anecdote.

9. Baker, *Religious No More,* 19-20.

10. Ibid., 35.

11. Jones, *Biblical Christian Ethics,* 97-98.

12. Cf. John Murray, *Principles of Conduct* (Grand Rapids, Mich.: Eerdmans, 1957), 183, 201.

13. Reisinger, *Law and the Gospel,* 67.

14. Cf. Bolton, *True Bounds of Christian Freedom,* 147-148.

15. Only reference to the fourth and fifth commandments seems lacking—probably

because the Sabbath will be dealt with in other ways (cf. 2:16-17; 3:16-17), and the child-parent relationship will be dealt with later as well (3:20).

16. Reisinger, *Law and the Gospel,* 96; see also Murray, *Principles of Conduct,* 183.

17. These ideas in part are attributed to Max Belz, pioneer Christian educator, who reminded us that the law prior to the cross is a condemnation code, but after the cross it is a "flight manual." The reason we need it now is that no good pilot who flies will fly in the clouds any longer than he must, but will rise above them as soon as possible.

18. The fact that the law holds no more curse for Christians does not mean that it holds no more purpose for us. We traditionally think of the law as having three positive purposes: 1) it acts as a mirror reflecting God's holiness so that we will see our sin and need of Christ's grace; 2) it acts as a bridle guiding even the unregenerate from evil and toward godliness through the disciplines and blessings that accompany God's expression of his standards; and, 3) it acts as a prod (whip) pricking the conscience of those who love the Lord (i.e., "those whom he inwardly instills with a readiness to obey"—Calvin) for closer self-examination and continual expression of thankful obedience to God (see Calvin, *Institutes,* II. vii. 6-14; *Westminster Confession of Faith,* XIX. 6; and an additional helpful formulation by Bolton, *True Bounds of Christian Freedom,* 78-83). These traditional distinctions may still prove problematic without the wise words of Bolton: "We now (as new creatures in Christ) obey, but it is from other principles, by other strength, unto other ends than we did before. Previously, the principles of obedience were legal and servile, now they are filial and evangelical . . . principles of faith, love, and delight which causes the soul to obey. . . . The grounds of obedience differ: heretofore, fear, now love. Previously the strength was our own; now we have fellowship with the strength of Christ. . . . The ends before were for justification and life; now they are for other ends—to glorify God, to dignify the Gospel, to declare our sincerity, to express our thankfulness. Before, we obeyed but out of compulsion of conscience; now we obey out of the promptings of [our new] nature, which, so far as it works, works to God, as naturally as stones move downward and sparks fly upward" (72-73). See also Anthony A. Hoekema, "The Reformed Perspective," in Melvin E. Dieter, et al., *Five Views on Sanctification* (Grand Rapids, Mich.: Zondervan, 1987), 85-86.

19. Adapted from personal e-mail from Cliff Morton, July 1, 1998.

20. Cf. Murray, *Principles of Conduct,* 193.

21. James Buchanan, *The Office and Work of the Holy Spirit* (1843; reprint, Carlisle, Pa., Banner of Truth, 1966), 245.

22. John Murray, *Collected Writings of John Murray* (Carlisle, Pa.: Banner of Truth, 1976), vol. 4, offers helpful discussion of how the unconditional nature of our salvation intersects with the conditional nature of experiencing the blessings of obedience: "Frances Turretin resolves the question by his characteristic method of distinguishing the different respects in which the term condition may be understood. If condition is understood as meritorious cause, then the Covenant of Grace is not conditioned: it is wholly gratuitous and depends solely upon God's good pleasure. But if understood as instrumental cause, receptive of the promises of the covenant, then it cannot be denied that the Covenant of Grace is conditioned" (233). See also Thomas Manton, *A Treatise of the Life of Faith* (Ross-shire, Scotland:

Christian Focus, 1997), 65; and, Jerry Bridges, *The Discipline of Grace* (Colorado Springs: NavPress, 1994), 179.

23. See the author's *Christ-centered Preaching* (Grand Rapids, Mich.: Baker, 1994), 280-286, for a discussion of the dangers of preaching "Deadly Be" messages that only instruct "Be Like . . . , Be Good, and/or Be Disciplined."

24. Herman Ridderbos, *Paul: An Outline of His Theology*, trans. John Richard de Witt (Grand Rapids, Mich.: Eerdmans, 1975), 253.

25. Baker, *Religious No More*, 152. A helpful corrective to Baker's community faith perspectives is David Jones's articulation of how a properly configured personal faith radiates into community ethics, in *Biblical Christian Ethics*, 155. Still, Baker's insights into the bondage of individualism are extremely valuable.

26. Cf. G. C. Berkouwer, *Faith and Sanctification*, trans. John Vriend (Grand Rapids, Mich.: Eerdmans, 1957), 144; and Hoekema, "Reformed Perspective," 87.

27. Hoekema, "Reformed Perspective," 88.

28. Cf. Berkouwer, *Faith and Sanctification*, 145, 157; and, Hoekema, "Reformed Perspective," 89.

29. A danger in any grace-based discussion of personal sanctification is a solitary focus on the person that eclipses the important role of the individual in creating a Christlike community, and the importance of the community in forming the character of the individual. North American evangelicalism has been rightly faulted for fostering a privatized and individualistic view of faith that does not necessarily consider our responsibilities to and for others. For a biblical perspective on these issues, see the author's larger discussion of the responsibilities of grace in community relationships as presented in Paul's letter to Titus: *1 and 2 Timothy and Titus: To Guard the Deposit*, Preaching the Word, ed. Kent Hughes (Wheaton, Ill.: Crossway, 1999), esp. 323-351.

CHAPTER SIX: FIGHTING WITH ALL HIS MIGHT

1. In traditional terms, the process of removing the deadness of our old nature is called "mortification," and the cultivation of our new life in Christ through obedience is called "vivification." The terms remind us that despite the entirely new reality of our union with Christ, we are not simply to sit back and let sanctification happen. Faithful believers engage in a lifelong and constant battle to overcome evil with good, "killing" the sinful actions of our present humanity while "being renewed" (Col. 3:9-10) and "transformed" (2 Cor. 3:18) by the presence of the Spirit so that we might "work out" the new life that God has already "worked in" us (Phil. 2:12-13). Our working does not make us new, but rather enables us to experience the full joys and blessing of the new life that God alone has granted for the believer (see Anthony A. Hoekema, "The Reformed Perspective," in Melvin E. Dieter, et al., *Five Views on Sanctification* [Grand Rapids, Mich.: Zondervan, 1987], 75-77, 84; and Jerry Bridges, *The Discipline of Grace* [Colorado Springs: NavPress, 1994], 188-198).

2. Cf. Richard J. Foster, "The Daring Goal: What to Expect When We Accept Christ as Our Life," in "1997 Seminary and Graduate School Handbook" (*Christianity Today*).

3. John Stott, *Life in Christ* (Grand Rapids, Mich.: Baker, 1991), 38.

4. The powers of resurrection and rule have special significance in this passage where Paul indicates that believers war not against flesh and blood but against authorities and powers of this dark world (6:12). Since Paul has earlier said that the risen Christ is above all authorities and powers (1:21), then we who are in union with Christ are spiritually seated with him in heaven and, thus, have rule with him over the authorities and powers of Satan.

5. Cf. John Murray, *Principles of Conduct* (Grand Rapids, Mich.: Eerdmans, 1957), 207-221.

6. Sinclair Ferguson, *The Holy Spirit* (Downers Grove, Ill.: InterVarsity, 1996), 112.

7. Isaac Watts, "Stand Up, My Soul; Shake Off Your Fears," in *The Trinity Hymnal* (Philadelphia: Great Commission Publications, 1998), hymn number 577.

8. Walter Marshall, *The Gospel Mystery of Sanctification* (1692; reprint, Grand Rapids, Mich.: Reformation Heritage, 1999), 102.

9. Richard Lovelace well describes the strategies of Satan in *Dynamics of Spiritual Life* (Downers Grove, Ill.: InterVarsity, 1979), 137-141.

10. See Ferguson, *Holy Spirit,* 167: "This work of the Spirit in uniting us to Christ brings the Christian life into an eschatological atmosphere. It is lived out in the heavenly realms (Eph. 1:3; 2:6). But these are also the realms of eschatological conflict where the evil day is faced (Eph. 6:12-13)."

11. Kent Hughes, *Ephesians,* Preaching the Word, ed. Kent Hughes (Wheaton, Ill.: Crossway, 1990), 217.

12. Rose Marie Miller, *From Fear to Freedom* (Wheaton, Ill.: Harold Shaw, 1994), 116.

13. Following the initial imperative, "Stand firm," is this series of aorist (i.e., completed action) participles.

14. Cf. Lovelace, *Dynamics of Spiritual Life,* 86: "Apart from grace our best actions are still built upon the foundation of unbelief, and even our virtues are organized as weapons against the rule of God."

15. Note that in the armor imagery, it is the belt of truth that holds all the other pieces of armor in place. Trust in the ultimate truth of Scripture enables us to keep the rest of our spiritual defenses ready.

16. See Paul earlier in Ephesians (2:8-9), and also Acts 13:48; Phil. 1:29; 2 Pet. 1:1; *The Westminster Shorter Catechism,* #30: "The Spirit applieth to us the redemption purchased by Christ, by working faith in us, and thereby uniting us to Christ in our effectual calling."

17. For a helpful and humble response to a merely passive approach to sanctification, see Bridges, *Discipline of Grace,* 132-134. See also the excellent discussion of the imperatives of grace in Ferguson's *The Holy Spirit,* 151.

18. Foster, "The Daring Goal," 47.

19. Archibald Alexander, *Thoughts on Religious Experience* (Carlisle, Pa.: Banner of Truth Trust, 1989), 165-168.

20. Miller, *From Fear to Freedom,* 120.

21. Don Matzat, *Truly Transformed* (Eugene, Ore.: Harvest House, 1992), 186.

22. Ferguson, *Holy Spirit,* 188.

23. See the author's *In the Grip of Grace* (Grand Rapids, Mich.: Baker, 1992), 58-64 (republished 2001 as *The Promise of Grace*).

24. Charles Wesley, "Love Divine, All Loves Excelling," in *The Trinity Hymnal* (Philadelphia: Great Commission Publications, 1998), hymn number 529.

25. Thomas Chalmers, *Sermons and Discourses*, vol. 2 (New York: Carter, 1846), 271.

26. Ferguson, *Holy Spirit*, 122.

27. Samuel Bolton, *The True Bounds of Christian Freedom* (1645; reprint, Carlisle, Pa., Banner of Truth, 1978), 145-146.

28. Miller, *From Fear to Freedom*, 86.

29. Sinclair Ferguson, "The Reformed View," in *Christian Spirituality: Five Views of Sanctification* (Downers Grove, Ill.: InterVarsity, 1988), 69, 71.

30. John Calvin, *Institutes of the Christian Religion*, ed. John T. McNeil, trans. Ford Lewis Battles (Philadelphia: Westminster, 1960), II.7.12.

31. I trust my readers will appreciate this modern rewrite of a very old but (to me, at least) very useful illustration.

32. Cf. Adolf Köberle, *The Quest for Holiness*, trans. from the third German edition by John C. Mattes (Minneapolis: Augsburg, 1936), 2-3.

33. Steve Smallman, "Understanding the New Birth" (essay distributed by World Harvest Mission, 1995; rev. 1996), 8.

34. The phrase is Jack Miller's paraphrase of Luther's oft-repeated urging to return to the essential message of Christ's justifying work as the basis and strength for daily Christian living. Cf. Miller's phrasing as found in Jerry Bridges, *Discipline of Grace*, 8; and Luther's "Introduction" to his *Commentary on Galatians*: "[I]t is necessary that this doctrine [of grace] be kept in continual practice and public exercise, both of hearing and reading . . . . [T]he most excellent righteousness of faith, which God through Christ, without any works, imputes to us, is neither political, nor ceremonial, nor the righteousness of God's law, nor consists of works, but is clean contrary to these; that is to say, it is a mere passive righteousness, as the others are active. . . . This 'passive righteousness' is a mystery that someone who does not know Jesus cannot understand. As a matter of fact, Christians do not completely understand it and do not take advantage of it when they are tempted. So we have to constantly teach it over and over again to others and repeat it to ourselves, because if we do not understand it and have it in our hearts, we will be defeated by the enemy, and we will be totally confused. There is nothing that gives us peace like this 'passive righteousness'" [for clarity I have included a portion of the translation of Erasmus Middleton, edited by John Prince Fallowes (Grand Rapids, Mich.: Kregel, 1979), and the paraphrase of World Harvest Mission in the workbook *Discipling by Grace* (1996), lesson 2:1].

35. Murray, *Principles of Conduct*, 221-226.

36. Ibid., 226.

37. See the author's *Christ-centered Preaching* (Grand Rapids, Mich.: Baker, 1994), 269-270.

38. Cf. Lovelace, *Dynamics of Spiritual Life*, 142.

39. Cf. Thomas Manton, *A Treatise of the Life of Faith* (Ross-shire, Scotland: Christian Focus, 1997), 134-135.

CHAPTER SEVEN: WHAT'S DISCIPLINE GOT TO DO WITH IT?

1. Samuel Bolton, *The True Bounds of Christian Freedom* (1645; reprint, Carlisle, Pa., Banner of Truth, 1978), 122-123.

2. Cf. ibid., 123-125.

3. Commentators are divided over whether the sin being described in verse 4 is internal moral evil or external persecution of the Hebrew Christians. Both are probably in view to some degree, since in its wider context the book is preparing the Hebrews for persecution but in the immediate context they are told to "throw off everything that hinders and the sin that so easily entangles" (v. 1). Both internal and external pressures are addressed because personal holiness is necessary for faithfulness in persecution.

4. Rippon's *Selection of Hymn's* (1787), in *The Trinity Hymnal* (Philadelphia: Great Commission Publications, 1998), hymn number 94.

5. Quoted in Susan Hunt, *The True Woman* (Wheaton, Ill.: Crossway, 1997), 19-20.

6. Cf. Edmund Clowney, *The Unfolding Mystery* (Colorado Springs: NavPress, 1988), 202. See the author's *Christ-centered Preaching* (Grand Rapids, Mich.: Baker, 1994), 275-280, 292-298.

7. C. S. Lewis, *The Problem of Pain* (New York: Macmillan, 1959), 81.

8. See the author's *In the Grip of Grace* (Grand Rapids, Mich.: Baker, 1992), 75-76 (republished 2001 as *The Promise of Grace*).

9. Cf. Martin Luther, "The Theology of the Cross," in Adolf Köberle, *The Quest for Holiness,* trans. John C. Mattes (Minneapolis: Augsburg, 1936), 159-160.

10. Quoted in Susan Bergman, "In the Shadow of the Martyrs," *Christianity Today* (August 12, 1996), 22.

11. Quoted in ibid., 22.

12. Quoted in ibid., 23.

CHAPTER EIGHT: THE POWER OF MERCY

1. For an excellent discussion of the nature of God's mercy, see David Jones, *Biblical Christian Ethics* (Grand Rapids, Mich.: Baker, 1994), 86-92.

2. Samuel Bolton, *The True Bounds of Christian Freedom* (1645; reprint, Carlisle, Pa., Banner of Truth, 1978), 145.

3. *The Westminster Confession of Faith,* XX. 1; also, Bolton, *True Bounds of Christian Freedom,* 97.

4. Jones, *Biblical Christian Ethics,* 12.

5. Cf. *Westminster Confession of Faith,* XX. 1.

6. See additional discussion of these principles in chapter 1 of this book.

7. Personal conversation, September 1988.

8. See the earlier discussion of the priority of loves that should motivate the believer, in chapters 1 and 5 of this book.

9. J. I. Packer, *Rediscovering Holiness* (Ann Arbor, Mich.: Servant, 1992), 75.

10. For more on this, review chapter 7 in this book, "What's Discipline Got to Do with It?"

11. Bolton, *True Bounds of Christian Freedom,* 43.

12. See the author's fuller discussion of the assurance indicated by our longings and sorrows, in *In the Grip of Grace* (Grand Rapids, Mich.: Baker, 1992), 33-37 (republished 2001 as *The Promise of Grace*).

13. By "fellowship" I mean the day-to-day sense of enjoyment we have in communing with God and knowing his approval of our actions. For a more technical discussion of the term and its conditional nature, see John Murray, *The Covenant of Grace* (1953; reprint, Phillipsburg, N.J.: Presbyterian and Reformed, 1988), 19; also, John Murray, *Principles of Conduct* (Grand Rapids, Mich.: Eerdmans, 1957), 198.

14. God never ceases to bless his people in the sense that he is working all things together for their good (Rom. 8:28). Even his discipline intends to turn them from harm and toward the Savior (Heb. 12:11). However, our experience of his chastening love is quite different from our experience of his approving love.

15. Cf. *Westminster Confession of Faith,* XVIII.4: "True believers may have the assurance of their salvation divers ways shaken, diminished, and intermitted; as, by negligence in preserving of it, by falling into some special sin, which woundeth the conscience and grieveth the Spirit; by some sudden or vehement temptation, by God's withdrawing the light of his countenance, and suffering even such as fear Him to walk in darkness and to have no light: yet are they never utterly destitute of that seed of God, and life of faith, that love of Christ and the brethren, that sincerity of heart, and conscience of duty, out of which, by operation of the Spirit, this assurance may, in due time, be revived; and by the which, in the mean time, they are supported from utter despair."

16. God's unconditional and eternal affection for us does not mean that he approves wrongdoing, nor that he will fail to deal with it for our good (Ps. 118:18; Eph. 4:30).

17. John 10:28; Romans 8:28-30, 35-39. See also the author's *In the Grip of Grace,* 91-116 (republished 2001 as *The Promise of Grace*).

18. Romans 8:1.

19. Horatius Bonar, "Horatius Bonar Talks about Holiness," *Free Grace Broadcaster* 146 (October 1993), 32.

20. Ibid.

21. Cf. Rose Marie Miller, *From Fear to Freedom* (Wheaton, Ill.: Shaw, 1994), 4.

22. Cf. Murray, *Principles of Conduct,* 231-237.

23. Cf. Miller, *From Fear to Freedom,* 51.

CHAPTER NINE: WORKS THAT REALLY MATTER

1. Roy Atwood, "A Father's Legacy," *Credenda Agenda* 8, no. 4 (1996): 33.

2. Cf. Samuel Bolton, *The True Bounds of Christian Freedom* (1645; reprint, Carlisle, Pa., Banner of Truth, 1978), 168-171.

3. Cf. Ibid., 176.

4. David Clelland, Dallas, Tex., personal conversation (March 1996).

5. John Murray, *Principles of Conduct* (Grand Rapids, Mich.: Eerdmans, 1957), 236-237, 242.

6. Jerry Bridges writes, "His [the apostle Paul's] usual 'shorthand' expressions for union with Christ are 'in Christ,' 'in Him,' and 'in the Lord.' British author John Stott

says those three expressions occur no less than 164 times in Paul's letters" (Bridges, *Discipline of Grace* [Colorado Springs: NavPress, 1994], 65).

7. *The Westminster Confession of Faith*, XVI.6.

8. John Owen, *Communion with God*, ed. R. J. K. Law (Edinburgh: Banner of Truth, 1991), 117.

9. Francis Schaeffer, *True Spirituality* (Wheaton, Ill.: Tyndale, 1971), 84, 102.

10. Atwood, "A Father's Legacy," 33.

11. Cf. Francis Schaeffer, *No Little People* (Downers Grove, Ill.: InterVarsity, 1974), 25.

12. Line from Anna Waring's hymn, "Father, I Know That All My Life," in *The Trinity Hymnal* (Philadelphia: Great Commission Publications, 1998), hymn number 559.

13. David Calhoun, quoted in Bryan Chapell, *Using Illustrations to Preach with Power* (Wheaton, Ill.: Crossway, 2001), 120.

CHAPTER TEN: THAT'S NOT FAIR

1. Some translations omit this first reference to idleness, but the description is definitely present in verse 6, and repeated twice there in some translations.

2. Anthony A. Hoekema, "The Reformed Perspective," in Melvin E. Dieter, et al., *Five Views on Sanctification* (Grand Rapids, Mich.: Zondervan, 1987), 68-72; and Sinclair Ferguson, "The Reformed View," in *Christian Spirituality: Five Views of Sanctification* (Downers Grove, Ill.: InterVarsity, 1988), 67.

3. Hoekema, "Reformed Perspective," 72.

4. Adolf Köberle, *The Quest for Holiness*, translated from the third German edition by John C. Mattes (Minneapolis: Augsburg, 1936), 154-155.

5. Cf. the line of Bernard of Clairvaux (1091–1153) in the hymn, "O Sacred Head Now Wounded," as translated by James Waddell Alexander: "Mine, mine was the transgression, but thine the deadly pain" (*The Trinity Hymnal* [Philadelphia: Great Commission Publications, 1998], hymn number 247).

6. While few make the mistake of asserting that we are saved by right works, it is a common error to believe that we are saved by right thoughts. However, the biblical perspective is that nothing that originates in us is the basis of our salvation. Though our commitments are expressed in actions and thoughts, faith and understanding are gifts of God (Eph. 2:8-9; 1 Cor. 2:9-10). The realization that we possess in mind and heart only what God has granted to be there should preclude any prejudice based on the notion that we have formulated our faith commitments better than others. I am not denying the importance of biblical truth nor of its propagation and defense, but I am seeking to declaw those whose method of defense of superior thought is the insensitive mauling of fellow believers with whom they disagree (cf. 2 Tim. 2:24-25). We are allowed no pride for what God enables us to understand through no merit of our own.

7. Cf. D. A. Carson, *How Long, O Lord?* (Grand Rapids, Mich.: Baker, 1990; and, Leicester, England: InterVarsity, 1990), 201-206, 212-220.

8. See *The Westminster Confession of Faith*, IX.4; G. C. Berkouwer, *Faith and Sanctification*, trans. John Vriend (Grand Rapids, Mich.: Eerdmans, 1957), 40; and Ferguson, "The Reformed View," 62-63.

9. Cf. Carson, *How Long, O Lord?* 214-215, 218-219.

10. Cf. Köberle, *Quest for Holiness,* 84, 95, 150-152.

11. Even Calvinistic systems that accurately reflect Scripture's emphasis on God's sovereignty struggle to explain salvation history without referring to the freedom of the human will. Reason demands the absolute sovereignty of an all-powerful Creator who knows the end from the beginning and controls all things. At the same time, the freedom of the human will at some stage of existence cannot be denied without impugning the justice of God. Thus, even *The Westminster Shorter Catechism* says that Adam and Eve were "left to the freedom of their own will," though such a premise cannot be logically reconciled with a theology of absolute divine sovereignty (cf. *Westminster Shorter Catechism,* #13; and *Westminster Confession of Faith,* IX.1-2). The difference between Calvinistic and Arminian systems does not so much lie in the former denying free will and the latter insisting upon it. Rather, Calvinism locates free will in the representative headship of Adam, whereas Arminian systems demand the autonomous free will of each person. Neither system of thought can dispense with all logical tensions. However, Calvinism makes the salvation and sanctification of fallen persons entirely dependent upon the grace of God, whereas Arminianism always requires us in some measure to supply the means of our own rescue. Putting the responsibility on us appeals to our democratic values and our sense of justice, but it also troubles the conscience of one fully aware of the Bible's assessment of the earthly limitations and divine dependence of fallen creatures.

12. B. B. Warfield, *Biblical and Theological Studies* (Philadelphia, Pa.: Presbyterian and Reformed, 1968); see also Warfield's *The Plan of Salvation* (Grand Rapids, Mich.: Eerdmans, 1978), 98, 100. In the ancient Greco-Roman and Jewish cultures, status with God was supposedly determined by superior knowledge, achievement, experience, and/or heritage. The countercultural message of Christianity was that God loved and chose a people for himself before the foundations of the earth were laid. The motive behind this message of sovereign predestination was not to encourage exclusivism, promote fatalism, nor foster pride, but rather to make it clear that our salvation was based solely on God's mercy and not on the merit of our reasoning, achieving, birth, or choosing. None may boast of personal merit, because God has made Christ Jesus our "wisdom from God—that is our righteousness, holiness and redemption" (cf. 1 Cor. 1:29-31). Emphasizing salvation based on mercy alone rather than on personal merit offends ancient and modern notions of autonomy and choice, but Christianity risks offending these sensibilities for the greater good of assuring those who have faced their spiritual desperation that God's rescue does not depend on any human contribution, and is not thwarted by anything we have done or will fail to do. Sadly, this unifying message of eternal, unconditional mercy too often becomes a sword of division in the hands of those who make its possession and right articulation the nexus of personal and denominational pride rather than an expression of the loving grace of God that Scripure intends to highlight.

13. Cf. Carson, *How Long, O Lord?* 214-215.

14. Robert Peterson, personal letter.

GENERAL INDEX

SCRIPTURE INDEX